Mighty Mississippi

DISCOVER
HISTORIC
AMERICA
SERIES

THE MIGHTY Mississippi

A TRAVELER'S GUIDE

by

Lori Erickson

A VOYAGER BOOK

The
Globe
Pequot
Press

OLD SAYBROOK, CONNECTICUT

Photo credits: Pp. 4, 103, 107: courtesy Hannibal Visitors Bureau; pp. 7, 32, 36: courtesy La Crosse Area Convention & Visitors Bureau; pp. 12, 20: courtesy Minnesota Historical Society; p. 47: photo by Lori Erickson; p. 56: courtesy Quad Cities Convention & Visitors Bureau; pp. 69, 111: courtesy St. Louis Convention & Visitors Commission; pp. 73, 76: courtesy Galena/Jo Daviess County Convention & Visitors Bureau; pp. 125, 189, 196: courtesy Louisiana Office of Tourism; p. 129: courtesy Kentucky Department of Travel Development; p. 134: courtesy Tennessee Tourist Development; p. 138: courtesy Memphis Convention & Visitors Bureau; p. 146: courtesy Arkansas Department of Parks and Tourism; pp. 156, 169: courtesy Mississippi Division of Tourism; p. 201: courtesy Greater Cincinnati Convention & Visitors Bureau; p. 219: courtesy City of Independence Tourism; p. 223: permission granted by the Missouri Division of Tourism; pp. 235, 242: courtesy Kentucky Department of Travel Development; p. 249: courtesy Indiana Department of Tourism; p. 255: photo by Jeff Friedman.

Cover and text design by Nancy Freeborn

Library of Congress Cataloging-in-Publication Data

Erickson, Lori.
    The mighty Mississippi : a traveler's guide / by Lori Erickson. — 1st ed.
        p.   cm. — (Discover Historic America series)
    "A voyager book."
    ISBN 1-56440-649-0
    1. Mississippi River—Guidebooks.   2. Mississippi River Valley—Guidebooks.
    I. Title.   II. Series.
        F355.E67   1995
        917.704'33—dc20   95-7542
                                                                CIP

Manufactured in the United States of America
First Edition/First Printing

For the young voyageurs,
Owen and Carl

The Mississippi River

Contents

ACKNOWLEDGMENTS

I am indebted to many people for their assistance with the research for this book, particularly to the many visitors bureaus, museums, and historical societies that provided information and offered suggestions. I am especially grateful to my research assistant, Mark Palmberg, whose unflagging enthusiasm and hard work made this a much more manageable and enjoyable project than it would otherwise have been. My husband, Bob Sessions, also deserves special thanks for his willingness to play chauffeur, read road maps, watch the kids, and provide encouragement.

Finally, I'd like to dedicate this book to my sons, Owen and Carl, who are at the very beginning of their own journeys. My fervent hope is that their generation, and the generations after theirs, will treasure and protect the mighty Mississippi.

Introduction

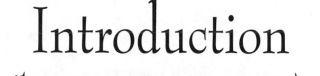

I grew up landlocked on an Iowa farm, but the Mississippi River beckoned with its irresistible siren song just forty miles to the east. My head full of Mark Twain's words, I can remember tracing on maps the snake coils of the river's bends, reading the evocative names of the towns and cities that lined its banks: Lansing, Dubuque, Savanna, Davenport, Keokuk, Quincy, Hannibal, Cairo.

"River towns," farmers called them, hinting that something in the air of these places made people stray from the steady and responsible path. My friends and I noticed the difference, too. We felt it whenever we visited them, sensing a certain laziness, especially on hot summer days when the river seemed to be the only thing that moved. People in the river towns owned boats just for the fun of it, we knew, and sometimes spent the entire day fishing. Taverns would be full of strangers instead of just locals, and people would lounge around the docks as if their sole occupation were watching the river flow by. We also knew that it was the Mississippi that caused all of this, that the river was the catalyst that turned ordinary towns into places of adventure.

It was only after I grew older that I came to appreciate the mythic status that the Mississippi has had not just in my own life, but also in the consciousness of America. While the Ojibwe Indians called it *Missi Sipi,* or "great river," I think the poet T. S. Eliot's description of the river is even better: In his words it was "the strong brown god." The Mississippi is the wellspring of life for this continent, a restless, elemental force that runs like a shining ribbon through our history.

1

It was Mark Twain, of course, who fixed the Mississippi forever in our national psyche. The Mississippi played muse to Twain in countless ways: It was a refuge from civilization for Huck and Jim, a playground for Tom Sawyer, a nemesis for the young cub-pilot in *Life on the Mississippi*. In Twain's world the river was "the great Mississippi, the majestic, the magnificent Mississippi, rolling its mile-wide tide along, shining in the sun."

More than a century later, the Mississippi continues to be a national treasure. It is one of the globe's most complex and important ecosystems, the ecological lifeline of North America. Its watershed drains three-fifths of the continent, and it is home to an incredible array of fish and wildlife. The river provides nesting and feeding grounds for hundreds of species of waterfowl, and each fall and spring it serves as a vital migration corridor for millions of birds. It is also essential for the flow of our economy: As the Mississippi passes through the nation's most productive agricultural and industrial areas, it transports millions of tons of goods and produce each year.

More than any other event in recent memory, the great flood of 1993 brought home to the nation the river's importance. For those of us living near its banks, the experience was both horrific and awe inspiring. We had grown accustomed to thinking of the Mississippi as a playground and a picturesque escape away from the everyday world. But as it rained and rained and rained, as the water crept inexorably higher and levees burst and bridges were submerged, as buildings, streets, and even entire towns were threatened by the muddy waters, the Mississippi showed us that it can still be a tyrannical force of nature. Levees, flood walls, and locks and dams may appear to tame it, but with the right conditions, it can still shrug off its chains and go where it wishes.

As usual, Twain said it best: "Ten thousand River Commissions, with the mines of the world at their back, cannot tame that lawless stream, cannot curb it or confine it, cannot say to it, Go here, or Go there, and make it obey; cannot save a shore which it has sentenced; cannot bar its path with an obstruction which it will not tear down, dance over, and laugh at."

The Mississippi's power should not obscure the fact that it is a threatened ecosystem. Wetland drainage, runoff from cities and farms, increasing sedimentation, floodplain encroachment, and habitat destruction threaten not only wildlife and plants, but also we humans who live in its watershed. Ironically, one of the benefits of the great flood is an increasing awareness of the fragility of the Mississippi.

This book is meant as a guide for those who wish to explore the nation's most famous waterway and its two main tributaries, the Missouri and Ohio rivers. In particular it focuses on attractions and events that evoke the golden age of the Mississippi, the time period between 1811 and 1900, which is often called the steamboat era.

The steamboat era began when an odd craft named the *New Orleans* ventured onto the Ohio River at Pittsburgh. It was a smoking, noisy contraption far different from the flatboats and keelboats that had dominated river transportation up to that time. This vessel was propelled by steam and was able to move at far faster speeds both up and down the river. Over the course of four months, the *New Orleans* followed the path of the Ohio and Mississippi to the city that was its namesake, enduring earthquakes, floods, fires, and hostile Indians as it ignited interest in a radically new form of transportation.

Within a few years, the steamboat had changed the face of America. Its design was further refined to better fit the shallow inland rivers: The hull could glide over snags, a lower deck housed the steamboat's boiler and engines, a second deck provided additional space, a little house perched on top for its pilot, and a paddlewheel propelled it through the water. The steamboat made possible large-scale transportation of cargo and passengers and turned the nation's rivers into a vast highway system. Huge fortunes were made as a result of the river trade, and river villages grew into busy ports lined with steamboats.

People from all walks of life and all economic levels traveled by steamboat. The wealthy bought cabin passage and slept and dined in comparative luxury while the less fortunate slept in whatever space they could find on the lower deck, amid the livestock and cargo. On board were merchants, farmers, preachers, slaves, immigrants, rogues, gamblers, and ladies—a cross-section of American society.

The rapid growth of the steamboat trade came to a virtual halt during the Civil War, and many predicted that the industry would never recover. After the war's end, however, steamboating confounded the doomsayers and more elaborate boats were launched than ever before. Boats like the *J. M. White* were truly floating palaces, with extravagant filigree work around their decks and stained-glass windows, hand-carved moldings, rich draperies, gilded mirrors, gold-plated chandeliers, furniture of rosewood and walnut burl, and parquet floors.

Though the steamboat trade had survived the war, the rise of the railroad proved to be a far greater threat. By the closing decades of the nineteenth century, trains offered more convenient and more reliable transportation to far more places, and steamboats were a dying species. In the early twentieth century, diesel-powered boats took over river transportation, and gradually the glory days of steamboats became a distant memory.

The past fifty years, however, have seen a rebirth of interest in the Mississippi, as new generations have discovered its timeless allure. Today hundreds of excursion boats—many of them modeled after nineteenth-century paddlewheelers—cruise the Mississippi and its tributaries, offering passengers the chance to relive the days when the blast of a steamboat whistle meant that adventure was on its way. There are even a half-dozen boats still powered by steam—the *Delta Queen, Mississippi Queen* and *American Queen,* the *Julia Belle Swain,* the *Belle of Louisville,* and the *Natchez.*

This book lists those cruises as well as the many other historic attractions to be found in the cities and towns that line the Mississippi and its two main tributaries, the Ohio and Missouri rivers. The journey begins at the headwaters of the Mississippi, in northern Minnesota, and follows the river for 2,350 miles to New Orleans. Most of the attractions are found along the

Hannibal's Mark Twain Riverboat *helps passengers relive the glory days of the Mississippi.*

Great River Road, the network of federal, state, and local roads that lines both sides of the Mississippi. The road is marked by signs sporting a green-and-white steamboat pilot's wheel, and most maps also detail its route.

Following each chapter in this book, you'll find a listing of the phone numbers for visitors bureaus, chambers of commerce, and other sources of additional information for each state.

Whether your journey along the Mississippi is by car, bicycle, paddle-wheeler, or raft, the river is likely to weave its way into your soul. I hope this book will increase the pleasure of your trip.

Please note that admission fees for most attractions are not listed unless they exceed $5. Restaurants are rated as follows (prices refer to average cost of a meal):

Inexpensive: under $5

Moderate: $5 to $15

Expensive: over $15

> *The prices and hours listed in this guidebook were confirmed at press time. We recommend, however, that you call establishments before traveling to obtain current information.*

The face of the water, in time, became a wonderful book—a book that was a dead language to the uneducated passenger, but which told its mind to me without reserve, delivering its most cherished secrets as clearly as if it uttered them with a voice. And it was not a book to be read once and thrown aside, for it had a new story to tell every day. Throughout the long twelve hundred miles there was never a page that was void of interest, never one that you could leave unread without loss, never one that you would want to skip, thinking you could find higher enjoyment in some other thing. There never was so wonderful a book written by man; never one whose interest was so absorbing, so unflagging, so sparklingly renewed with every reperusal.

Mark Twain
Life on the Mississippi

BLUFF
COUNTRY

Minnesota, Wisconsin, and Iowa

Minnesota

he Mississippi begins its long journey to the Gulf of Mexico in northern Minnesota, a land of deep woods and
pristine lakes. This portion of the Great River Road offers
glimpses of a land largely unchanged from that encountered
by the first white settlers to the region. The road follows the Mississippi's
lazy, meandering path, passing through shadowy stands of great pines and
circling shallow lakes where wild rice is still harvested by Ojibwe Indians.
The loon's call can be heard on the quiet lakes, and bear and deer wander
through the forests.

In Minnesota the river is closely linked with two industries that were
largely responsible for opening up the northern wilderness to European settlement. From the 1750s to the 1850s, French-Canadian voyageurs operated
a fur trade that supplied beaver and other pelts for the fashionable clothing
of the day. Traveling mainly by canoe, the voyageurs used the Mississippi and
other inland arteries to establish a vast trade network that stretched into
Canada and throughout the Upper Mississippi Valley. Next came the logging
industry of the 1800s, when the region's great pine forests were cut and
floated downriver to sawmills farther south. Lumber money built immense
fortunes and nourished the growth of many towns and cities that lined the
river. On your journey through Minnesota you'll see many sites that relate
to the history of these enterprises, which helped transform uncharted
wilderness into a booming new territory.

One point to note: In Minnesota the Great River Road has two com-
ponents, a federally designated, 430-mile national route and a 755-mile,
state–designated alternate route. Together they provide 1,185 miles of scenic,

9

historic, and recreational opportunities. For brochures describing the two routes, call the Minnesota Office of Tourism at (800) 657–3700.

LAKE ITASCA TO THE TWIN CITIES

Each year thousands of visitors wade across the headwaters of the great river in **Lake Itasca State Park.** Though the explorer Hernando de Soto first saw the Mississippi in 1541, finding the river's source proved a formidable challenge. Over the next three centuries, various expeditions to find its headwaters were all unsuccessful. Finally, in 1832, an explorer and ethnologist named Henry Schoolcraft, assisted by an Ojibwe village chief named Ozawindib, was able to locate the river's source amid the region's many streams and lakes. He dubbed the spot Lake Itasca, a blending of the middle syllables of the Latin words *veritas caput,* meaning "true head." (Schoolcraft's travels among the Ojibwe later became the basis for Longfellow's poem "The Song of Hiawatha.")

Lake Itasca State Park was established in 1891, making it the oldest state park in Minnesota. Its 32,000 acres are listed on the National Register of Historic Places and include over 150 lakes. Follow the park's scenic Wilderness Drive, and you will see stands of majestic red and white pine, archeological sites, and many historic log buildings. There's also a visitors center with information on the river and the discovery of its source. Phone (218) 266–3654 for information.

From Lake Itasca take Highways 3 and 7 north for 25 miles to **Bemidji,** a resort community that began as a trading post in 1888. Bemidji served as a bustling lumber center following the coming of the railroad, and its colorful logging heritage is commemorated by the imposing statues of **Paul Bunyan** and **Babe the Blue Ox,** which stand on the lakefront. The 18-foot statues of the famous folklore heroes were erected in 1937 and are among Minnesota's most photographed attractions. Legend has it that the Mississippi River was formed one day when a huge tank wagon that Babe was hauling sprang a leak. The rushing water created Lakes Bemidji and Itasca, and the overflow trickled down to New Orleans to form the Mississippi River.

Native Americans have played a prominent role in the history and settlement of Bemidji. A statue of **Chief Bemidji** stands in Library Park, and traditional Indian culture thrives in the region. Many area stores sell beadwork and basketry made by local Ojibwe artisans.

When you're in the area, don't miss a visit to **Lake Bemidji State Park,** whose rolling terrain was created by glacial meltwater centuries ago. The park offers a wide variety of recreational opportunities, including a board-walk trail through a tamarack bog containing fragile mosses, orchids, and insect-eating pitcher plants.

Shifting Allegiances

T he history of European settlement along the Mississippi is one of shifting allegiances and diverse claims. The first European to see the river was Hernando de Soto, who crossed the Mississippi in 1541 near what is now Memphis. In 1682 the explorer Robert Cavelier, Sieur de La Salle, claimed the entire Mississippi Valley for his native France, but the country lost its North American territories during the French and Indian War of 1754 to 1763.

The land east of the Mississippi then came under British control, while Spain claimed the land west of the river. The Revolutionary War made the eastern part of the continent part of the United States, and in 1800 France regained control of the west. Finally, in 1803 the Louisiana Purchase brought the entire valley into American hands.

The varied history of the Upper Mississippi Valley is illustrated by the fact that at various times Minnesota has been under the flags of England, France, Spain, the Northwest Territory, the colony of Virginia, and the territories of Illinois, Indiana, Iowa, Louisiana, Michigan, Missouri, and Wisconsin. In 1858 the region at last became the state of Minnesota.

From Bemidji follow Highway 2 east for 45 miles through the **Leech Lake Indian Reservation** and the small towns of Cass Lake, Bena, and Ball Club. The Ojibwe tribe was forced onto the reservation in the mid-1800s to make more land available for logging and continues to exist as a separate nation.

From Ball Club continue east for 20 miles to **Grand Rapids,** which once thrived as a lumbering center and a landing point for steamboats coming up the Mississippi. A 3½-mile series of cataracts here on the Mississippi River provided the name for the city and made Grand Rapids the northern termination point for river navigation. Logging in the area declined around the turn of the century, but paper manufacturing continues to be an important industry. The city is also a popular resort community and boasts that within a 50-mile radius there are some 1,200 lakes teeming with fish.

Grand Rapids' logging past lives again at the **Forest History Center,** an authentically reconstructed logging camp and interpretive center designed to portray the life of a lumberjack at the turn of the century. Costumed staff explain camp operations as they go about their work, and they often try to sign up visitors for a stint. The center includes a forest ranger's cabin and a *wanigan,* a floating cook shack, moored on the Mississippi River. The center (218–327–4482) is located near the junction of Highways 169 and 2, and is open daily year-round.

A wanigan—*a floating cook shack—gives visitors a taste of lumberjack life at the Forest History Center.*

Another part of Grand Rapids history is celebrated during weekends in July, when the *Mississippi Melodie Showboat* steams into town. This paddlewheeler-turned-floating-theater presents nineteenth-century songs, dances, and comedy routines in performances that recall the glory days of the showboats that once traveled the length of the river. The *Mississippi Melodie* has been a fixture of Grand Rapids summers for over forty years. For information, call (800) 722-7814.

Finally, Grand Rapids also takes pride in a more recent bit of history: its status as the birthplace of the actress Judy Garland. For more information you can follow the yellow brick road that leads to the **Central School Heritage and Arts Center,** which is housed in a Romanesque-Revival structure at 10 NW Fifth Street. The center (800–472–6366) is open year-round and also houses displays on local history.

The Voyageurs

Anyone who has ever tried to travel on foot through the dense forests of northern Minnesota and Wisconsin can see why the French-Canadian voyageurs traveled by canoe whenever possible. The hardy traders found that the birch-bark canoes built by the region's Native American tribes suited their needs admirably: Sturdy and swift, the canoes were easy to build and could accommodate large cargoes.

Traveling on a far-reaching network of rivers, lakes, and streams, the voyageurs traded with the Indians, exchanging clothing, implements, guns, and other goods for fur pelts. The voyageurs often adopted elements of Native American dress and used Indian tools, and many of them married Indian women.

The voyageurs became legendary both for their endurance (often they paddled their heavily loaded canoes for fifteen to eighteen hours a day) and for their love of life. "I could carry, paddle, walk, and sing with any man I ever saw," a seventy-year-old voyageur said near the end of his life. "I have saved the lives of ten voyageurs, have had twelve wives and six running dogs. I spent all my money on pleasure. Were I young again, I should spend my life the same way over. There is no life so happy as a voyageur's life."

From Grand Rapids follow the Mississippi's winding path for 75 miles, heading south on Highway 3 to Jacobson, then south on Highway 65 to McGregor, then west on Highway 210 to **Aitkin.** The town was once the site of an Ojibwe village, and later became a white settlement named Mud River. Aitkin served as a headquarters for the Northern Pacific Railroad and a supply base for hundreds of northern logging camps, and between Grand Rapids and Aitkin you can still see many former steamboat landings, now converted into water access and camping sites. Sometimes you can even spot the remains of sunken boats that were lost to the challenging river.

In Aitkin itself, visit the **Aitkin County Historical Museum** (218–927–3348) at 20 Pacific Street for information on local history. It's open from June through August, 10:00 A.M. to 5:00 P.M., on Tuesday, Wednesday, Friday, and Saturday.

Along the Mississippi between Aitkin and Brainerd stretches the **Cayuna Iron Range.** Beginning in the early 1900s, this range produced over one hundred million tons of iron ore, known for its high manganese content. The range was named after Cuyler Adams, the surveyor who discovered the ore in the 1890s, and his dog, Una. Some of the area lakes are actually old strip-mining pits that today offer good fishing opportunities plus fine scuba diving because of their depth.

Before you get to Brainerd, however, stop in the town of **Crosby** for a visit to the **Croft Mine Historical Park.** The mine operated between 1916 and 1934, producing some of the richest ore in the entire Cayuna Range. The park at Eighth Street in Crosby offers self-guided tours of an old underground mining shaft and other restored mine structures and buildings as well as displays of mining history. The park is open from 10:00 A.M. to 6:00 P.M. daily from Memorial Day to Labor Day. Phone (218) 546–5466 for information.

From Crosby continue on Highway 210 for 15 miles to **Brainerd,** a city founded in the 1860s at the point where the railroad crossed the Mississippi River. Brainerd quickly grew from a small woodland trading post into a railroad and logging boom town, and timber cut from far up the Mississippi's tributaries filled the river. Later, when the logging era ended, Brainerd became a tourism and resort center. Many farmers, railroad employees, and former loggers owned lakeshore property, and they began providing visitors with camping sites, home-cooked meals, and access to excellent hunting and fishing. As the resorts grew, the amenities improved, and today northern

Minnesota contains thousands of resorts ranging from primitive cabins to luxurious retreats.

The **Crow Wing County Historical Museum** is housed in the old county jail and sheriff's quarters and has exhibits on county history, the railroad and lumbering industries, and Native Americans living in the area. The museum (218–829–3268) is at 320 Laurel Street and is open September through May.

Fifteen miles south of Brainerd on Highway 371 is **Camp Ripley,** a 53,000-acre center for the National Guard and U.S. Army Reserves. The camp is named after the original Camp Ripley, which was built on the banks of the Mississippi near here in 1849 to bring peace to warring Dakota and Ojibwe Indians. The **Camp Ripley Military Museum** has detailed replicas of frontier forts as well as weapons, medals, uniforms, and other memorabilia that tell the story of Minnesota units in the nation's wars. The museum (612–632–6631) is open from May through September.

Next continue south on Highway 371 for 15 miles to **Little Falls,** which is named for the rapids that supplied power to the town's lumber, flour, and paper mills. Charles Lindbergh, who made the first solo flight across the Atlantic Ocean in 1927, spent his boyhood summers on his family's farm here beside the Mississippi and relished playing in the river and woods that lined its banks. The Mississippi, he once wrote, "has wound its way in and out of my life like the seasons." The family farm is now **Lindbergh State Park,** and the 1906 farmhouse is restored with original furnishings. The neighboring **Lindbergh Interpretive Center** (612–632–3154) has exhibits on three generations of the remarkable Lindbergh family. The Lindbergh site is located 2 miles south of Little Falls on Lindbergh Drive and is open daily from May 1 through Labor Day.

Also on Lindbergh Drive is the **Charles A. Weyerhaeuser Museum** (612–632–4007), which features exhibits on the lumber industry, the region's diverse ethnic settlements, and the impact of the Mississippi River on this part of the state. The museum is open Tuesday through Saturday, from 10:00 A.M. to 5:00 P.M., and 1:00 to 5:00 P.M. Sunday (closed Sundays during the winter).

At 1200 West Broadway you'll find another Little Falls landmark, the **Dewey–Radke House,** an 1890 home with period furnishings. The house is open from Memorial Day through Labor Day; phone (612) 632–2341 for information.

The Lumber Trade

From the early 1800s to about 1900, the huge pine forests of northern Minnesota and Wisconsin were harvested to help build a growing nation. Lumberjacks typically cut the logs during the summer and in winter loaded them onto sleds and hauled them across icy roads to rivers and streams. After the ice melted the logs were floated downriver and were later sorted according to the lumber company brand on each one. From the 1830s to the 1860s, hardy steersmen were responsible for guiding the massive log rafts down the Mississippi. After 1870, most of the logs were pushed downriver by steamboats, though the expert guidance of skilled woodsmen was still needed.

Riding the logs down the mighty Mississippi was dangerous, grueling work. Accidents were common, and many men lost their lives when they became pinned between logs and were pulled underwater by the swift current.

From Little Falls travel south for 30 miles on Highway 10 to **St. Cloud,** the hub of central Minnesota and one of the state's fastest growing communities. The city began as an outfitting center for the fur trade, with steamboats traveling in and out of its harbor laden with furs and provisions. Today St. Cloud is known for its thriving granite industry, which is commemorated in a downtown sculpture called *The Granite Trio.* Half a million pounds of area granite were used in the recent restoration of the Statue of Liberty, and colored granite from local quarries has been used in some of the country's finest buildings.

The one-hundred-acre **Heritage Center** in St. Cloud features a replica of a granite quarry and displays of river lore and history plus a log cabin and exhibits on central Minnesota history. The center (612–253–8424) is located at 235 Thirty-third Avenue South, and is open daily from June through August.

A good place to view the river is from the beautiful **Munsinger Gardens,** which are located in Riverside Park along the Mississippi. The gardens feature a lovely display of color from spring through fall, with rock gardens, a gazebo, and a lily pond. You can explore the river itself on board vessels operated by **Pirates Cove Paddle Boat Tours** (612–252–8400), which offers Mississippi cruises from May through October.

From St. Cloud continue south on Highway 10 for 36 miles to **Elk River,** which was named for the herds of elk once sighted here by the explorer Zebulon Pike. A major attraction today is the **Oliver H. Kelley Farm,** a state historic site that was first homesteaded in 1849 by Oliver Kelley, who later founded the National Grange, the first nationwide farm organization. The farm has been restored as an interpretive center, bringing to life the rural history of the 1860s, as well as Kelley's life and the history of the National Grange. At this working farm you can visit with costumed interpreters as they attend to the myriad tasks of nineteenth-century farm life, from churning butter to tilling the fields with oxen and horses.

The Oliver H. Kelley Farm (612–441–6896) is located on Highway 10, 2.5 miles southeast of Elk River. It's open May 1 to October 31, 10:00 A.M. to 5:00 P.M., Monday through Saturday, and from noon to 5:00 P.M. Sunday.

MINNEAPOLIS AND ST. PAUL

From Elk River continue south on Highway 10 for 20 miles to the **Twin Cities** metropolitan area. The Mississippi and Minnesota rivers converge here, creating a land that the Dakota Indians considered the center of heaven and earth. Father Louis Hennepin first saw the region in 1680, encountering what he called the "astonishing" Mississippi River falls, the only true waterfalls along the length of the river. That 16-foot tumble of water, which Hennepin christened St. Anthony Falls, would later spawn sawmills and flour mills, and from them developed the city of **Minneapolis.** By the 1880s nearly one hundred waterwheels were producing six million barrels of flour a year, making Minneapolis the flour milling capital of the world at the turn of the century. The city itself was named from a blend of the Dakota and Greek words meaning "city of waters."

Neighboring **St. Paul** was fortuitously positioned on the last navigable stretch of the Mississippi before the falls, and it soon reigned as a steamboating hub and later as a railroad center. You can learn more about both cities' beginnings at **Fort Snelling,** which overlooks the confluence of the Mississippi and Minnesota rivers. It was constructed in the 1820s as one of a series of forts built to protect the rich fur trade and begin the taming of the Minnesota frontier. Fort Snelling soon became a haven for explorers, settlers, traders, and missionaries.

The fort has been restored to its original appearance and recreates the colorful community that lived here in 1827. You can tour the buildings and visit with soldiers, cooks, laundresses, storekeepers, and craftspeople. Tours, skits, demonstrations, and special events invite visitors to participate in a fascinating era. Fort Snelling is at the junction of Highways 5 and 55 in St. Paul, near the Twin Cities International Airport. From May through October it's open from 10:00 A.M. to 5:00 P.M., Monday through Saturday, and from noon to 5:00 P.M. Sunday. Phone (612) 726–1171 for information.

The Twin Cities preserve their rich history in a variety of attractions. **The Minnesota State Capitol** is one of the most beautiful capitols in the country, a structure of soaring domes and arches filled with carved marble and stone, stenciled ceilings, hand-painted murals, and impressive sculpture.

Pig's Eye Landing

A lthough the city of St. Paul owes its birth to the Mississippi River, its midwife was an unsavory, eye-patch-sporting saloon owner who did a brisk business selling bootleg rum to soldiers. During its earliest years, in the 1840s, the city was a French village known as "Pig's Eye Landing" in honor of Pierre "Pig's Eye" Parrant, a retired fur trader who owned a saloon near the river. Squatters evicted from Fort Snelling settled near his tavern, creating a village infamous for its rowdiness.

St. Paul missed its chance to become Pig's Eye, Minnesota, however, when Father Lucien Galtier arrived in 1841 and built a chapel dedicated to St. Paul. He asked local citizens to change their settlement's name to a more dignified moniker, and so the name Pig's Eye Landing faded into obscurity.

Mark Twain tells the story of Pig's Eye Parrant in *Life on the Mississippi*, then comments, "How solemn and beautiful is the thought that the earliest pioneer of civilization, the van-leader of civilization, is never the steamboat, never the railroad, never the newspaper, never the Sabbath School, never the missionary—but always whiskey!"

The building was designed by Cass Gilbert, architect of the U.S. Supreme Court building, and has one of the largest self-supporting marble domes in the world. Special tours on art and architecture, women in government, and many other topics complement year-round guided tours. The capitol is located at 75 Constitution Avenue, north of downtown St. Paul (watch for exits off Interstates 94 and 35 East). Phone (612) 296–2881 for tour information.

Near the capitol is the **Minnesota History Center,** an architectural masterpiece blending classic and modern elements that has been hailed as one of the most outstanding public buildings constructed in Minnesota since the capitol was built at the turn of the century. The innovative museum houses a state-of-the-art research center and is a great place to learn more about the early years of the state and the Mississippi River, which shaped so much of its history. The History Center (800–657–3773) is located at the junction of I–35E and I–94, on the western edge of downtown St. Paul.

Nearby is the Cathedral of St. Paul, whose design is based upon St. Peter's in Rome. The cathedral marks the beginning of 5-mile Summit Avenue, a boulevard lined with many stately homes constructed during the steamboat era. One of its gems is the **James J. Hill House,** a massive, imposing Richardsonian Romanesque structure built in 1891 by James J. Hill, builder of the Great Northern Railway. Its craggy stone, massive scale, and ingenious mechanical systems all recall the powerful presence of Hill, who amassed an enormous railroad empire between 1862 and 1892. Thanks to Hill over a dozen rail lines converged in St. Paul, changing the city from a river town into a major railroad hub. The Hill House (612–297–2555) is located at 240 Summit Avenue, in St. Paul, and is open year-round Wednesday through Saturday, from 10:00 A.M. to 3:30 P.M.

The 1872 **Alexander Ramsey House** at 265 South Exchange Street, in St. Paul, is another of the Twin Cities' best-preserved mansions. The residence of Minnesota's first territorial governor features carved walnut woodwork, marble fireplaces, crystal chandeliers, and many original furnishings. The museum store, located in the reconstructed carriage house, offers quality Victorian reproductions. The house is open daily April through December; call (612) 296–8760 for more information.

To see the area that gave birth to the Twin Cities, head to the **Mississippi Mile** in Minneapolis, a thriving complex of shops, restaurants, bars, parks, historic buildings, and lodging places. Among its highlights are the Father Hennepin Park, with views of the river gorge and a stone arch bridge,

The life and times of Minnesota's first territorial governor are remembered at the Alexander Ramsey House.

and the Upper St. Anthony Falls Lock and Dam, the first in a series of twenty-nine locks on the river. Elegant accommodations can be found at the **Whitney Hotel** (612–339–9300), an establishment built on the river in the grand European tradition, and the **Nicollet Island Inn** (612–331–1800), a charming 1893 structure that now houses a lovely inn. The area also sponsors many festivals and concerts throughout the warm months, including the **Minnesota Heritage Festival** in July and the **Riverfront International Food Fair** in August. For more information, call the Mississippi Mile Hotline at (612) 348–9300.

St. Paul's riverfront area is called **Lowertown.** Once a major railroad, warehouse, and manufacturing center, Lowertown has been given new life as a residential neighborhood that preserves its distinctive nineteenth-century character. The area has a wide selection of shops, restaurants, and other attractions, and it has become an international model for urban design because of its innovative blend of residential and commercial establishments, many housed in vintage buildings. For information and a walking tour brochure of the area, call (612) 228–3399.

A Twin Cities restaurant with a Victorian theme is **Forepaugh's,** housed in the former residence of St. Paul pioneer merchant Joseph Lybrandt Forepaugh. The 1870 mansion was built as a lavish showplace, surrounded by landscaped gardens and filled with imported furnishings. In the years that followed, however, the house and surrounding Irvine Park neighborhood slipped into decline. Today both have experienced a renaissance, and

Fraternal Twins

The river towns of Minneapolis and St. Paul were first settled by New Englanders, but beginning in the 1850s they began to attract increasing numbers of European immigrants fleeing political upheaval and famine. In St. Paul they helped create what's been called the "last city of the East." St. Paul buildings often have a European feel about them, with lofty arches, Baroque domes, and elaborate embellishments. Irish and German immigrants gave St. Paul a Catholic heritage and created tightly knit neighborhoods in the angled, hilly streets that line the river.

Minneapolis, in contrast, became known as the "first city of the West." Expansive and sprawling, it was settled mainly by Scandinavian and North German Lutherans, and as it grew, it became a gleaming metropolis of glass and steel, a center for business, finance, and high technology.

During the past fifty years, new waves of immigrants, including many from Southeast Asia, have further enriched the diversity of the Twin Cities. The two metropolitan areas maintain a friendly rivalry, which enhances life in both cities, and they are routinely rated as two of the best places in the country to live and work.

Forepaugh's is now one of the city's finest restaurants, serving French cuisine in elegant dining rooms. The restaurant is open for lunch and dinner; call (612) 224–5606 for information.

Finally, enjoy the slow charms of the river itself on board riverboats operated by the **Padelford Packet Boat Company.** Two boats dock at Harriet Island Park in downtown St. Paul; two others dock at Boom Island Park in downtown Minneapolis. Phone (612) 227–1100 for information.

HASTINGS TO LA CRESCENT

South of St. Paul the Mississippi is bordered by the beautiful bluffs that line the river's course through southern Minnesota, Wisconsin, and Iowa. John Madson, writing in his chronicle of the Upper Mississippi entitled *Up On the River,* says that this is "country that stands on its hind legs and shows its limestone muscles, rising sublimely over a river that flows in broad running lakes."

A natural harbor in the river 10 miles south of St. Paul led to the founding of the town of **Hastings,** where many historic homes and buildings reflect its days as a booming steamboat port. The town's chamber of commerce (612–437–6775) publishes a helpful guide to the town's vintage buildings, including the **LeDuc–Simmons Mansion,** an 1865 showplace, at 1629 Vermillion Street, that is one of the country's few remaining examples of Hudson River Valley architecture. Each May, Hastings hosts the **Front Porch Festival,** which celebrates both the town's civic pride and the many beautiful porches on its Victorian homes.

From Hastings head south on Highway 61 for 25 miles to the historic river town of **Red Wing,** which was founded in 1837 by white missionaries near a Dakota village led by Chief Red Wing. The city soon grew to be a booming center for the river trade, and the area's clay deposits spawned pottery and pipe manufacturing industries. Red Wing has worked hard to preserve the architectural treasures that date back to those nineteenth-century glory days. With its downtown lined with brick storefronts and its bright, blooming flowers, Red Wing is one of the most picturesque towns along the Mississippi.

Begin your tour at the town's visitors center, which is housed in a restored brick train depot on the banks of the river. Then stroll up the hill to the **St. James Hotel** (800–252–1875), an Italianate structure at 406 Main Street that was one of the most ornate buildings on the Upper Mississippi when it was built in 1875. It now houses sixty elegantly furnished rooms, a variety of specialty shops, and the **Port of Red Wing Restaurant,** which offers fine dining in a riverboat-era atmosphere (prices are moderate to expensive).

The **Red Wing Trolley,** a motorized San Francisco cable car, offers thirty-minute narrated tours of the city from Thursday through Sunday during the summer months. The trolley leaves from the St. James Hotel on the hour.

You can get another introduction to the city and its history at the **T.B. Sheldon Auditorium Theatre,** a restored 1904 theater at 443 West Third Street. The structure was built in the Renaissance Revival style with a "jewel box" interior of ornate plasterwork in ivory and gold. The theater (800–899–5759) offers a multimedia presentation at 1:00 P.M. on Thursday, Friday, and Saturday, from June through October.

More local history can be found at the **Goodhue County Historical Museum,** at 1166 Oak Street. The museum complex is one of the largest and most comprehensive museums in Minnesota, offering exhibits on thousands of years of local and regional history. Included are exhibits on steamboats that brought wealth and goods to the city, as well as a diorama of Chief Red Wing's Dakota village and a pioneer log cabin. The museum (612–388–6024) is open 10:00 A.M. to 5:00 P.M., Tuesday through Friday, and 1:00 to 5:00 P.M., Saturday and Sunday.

To view Red Wing from the river, step on board the **Schatze Excursion Boat,** which offers luncheon and dinner cruises that leave from the waterfront near the visitors center. Call (612) 388–0800 or 430–1234 for information.

If you're feeling energetic, hike up to the top of **Barn Bluff,** a striking landmark on the river, which you can reach off East Fifth Street. The dramatic bluff was climbed by many of Minnesota's early explorers and visitors, including Henry David Thoreau. Markers along the trail give information about the history and ecology of the Red Wing area.

Red Wing's long tradition of pottery making is recalled at the **Pottery Place Outlet Center.** The building housed the original Red Wing Pottery factory and is listed on the National Register of Historic Places. It now houses a complex of shops and restaurants as well as information about the early years of the pottery industry. You'll find the center at the west end of town, off Highway 61.

For accommodations with a Victorian ambiance, stay at the **Pratt–Taber Inn** (612–388–5945) at 706 West Fourth Street. The thirteen-room Italianate mansion was built in 1876 by one of Red Wing's first bankers and offers six bedrooms furnished with period antiques. The **Candle Light Inn** (612–388–8034), at 818 West Third Street, also offers Victorian-era lodging in four guest rooms.

From Red Wing continue south on Highway 61 for 11 miles to the twin communities of Frontenac and **Old Frontenac.** Frontenac grew up along the railroad, while Old Frontenac had its beginnings as a river port. In the 1870s and 1880s, Old Frontenac was one of the most fashionable summer resorts in the country. Visitors traveled by steamboat from as far away as New Orleans and St. Louis to stay in the area for weeks at a time. Today there are no commercial establishments in the village, but many of its grand homes remain. Also in the area are Frontenac State Park and the Villa Maria, a former convent built in 1891 that now houses a nondenominational retreat center.

Old Frontenac is located at the widest expanse of **Lake Pepin,** a naturally formed, 3-mile-wide section of the river, which stretches for 21 miles. The river valley here is particularly scenic on both the Minnesota and Wisconsin sides. Some travelers have compared its beauty to that of the Rhine Valley of Germany and Switzerland—every turn of the road brings another dramatic vista of high bluffs and thickly wooded valleys. "The Lake Pepin area ought to be visited in the summer by every poet and painter in the land," the nineteenth-century poet William Cullen Bryant once said.

From Old Frontenac travel south on Highway 61 for 6 miles to **Lake City,** which lays claim to being the birthplace of waterskiing. Its chamber of commerce (800–369–4123) can direct you on a walking tour of the town's historic buildings, which include several bed-and-breakfasts. The **Red Gables Inn** is an intimate B & B built by a wealthy wheat merchant in 1865 in a mixture of Italianate and Greek Revival styles. You'll find it at 403 North High Street; call (612) 345–2606 for information. The 1896 **Victorian Bed and Breakfast** (612–345–2167) and 1905 **Pepin House** (612–345–4454) also offer Victorian-era hospitality.

From Lake City head south on Highway 61 for 11 miles to the small village of **Reads Landing,** which was once a thriving steamboat and logging center. You can learn more about those industries and about the town's pioneer heritage at the **Wabasha County Museum,** housed in an 1870 schoolhouse overlooking the Mississippi. The museum (612–345–3987) is open from mid-May until October.

A Foolhardy Daredevil

Water-skiers are such a common sight on the Mississippi today that it's easy to forget what a marvel the sport first appeared to be. Ralph W. Samuelson, the father of waterskiing, grew up along the Mississippi in the town of Lake City. In 1922 the eighteen-year-old daredevil came up with an incredibly foolish idea: He figured that if people could ski on snow, they should also be able to ski on water. First he tried snow skis and then barrel staves, both of which promptly sank. Then he went to a lumber yard and fashioned two 8-foot lengths of wood with leather foot straps near the middle. Strapping them on his feet, he gave the signal to a waiting towboat, and the next moment he was skiing on top of the water—a veritable miracle to those watching.

Not content to rest on his laurels, Samuelson soon learned to ride on one ski, jump from a ramp with his skis on, ski behind an airplane, and perform a variety of other tricks. For the next decade he put on skiing exhibitions all over the country, drawing large crowds wherever he performed and spreading the popularity of the new sport. Today you can see a replica of his first pair of skis at the Lake City Chamber of Commerce—and marvel at the young man's daring.

Continue south on Highway 61 for 3 miles to **Wabasha,** which was named after a lineage of Dakota chiefs named Wapasha who were powerful leaders in the southeastern Minnesota region. Settled in the 1830s, the town lays claim to being Minnesota's oldest community. Its commercial district is listed on the National Register of Historic Places, and many of its buildings are newly renovated.

Don't leave Wabasha without paying a visit to the **Anderson House,** the oldest operating hotel in Minnesota. Built in 1856, the hotel, at 333 West Main Street, has been featured frequently in national publications and broadcasts for both its quaint accommodations and its resident cats. When you book your room, you can request the company of one of the hotel's fifteen felines at no extra charge. This is a hotel that takes pampering seriously! The hotel is also known for its excellent restaurant, whose recipes have been collected in several cookbooks (prices are moderate). To reserve your room and cat, call (800) 535–5467.

Each July Wabasha celebrates its Mississippi heritage with **Riverboat Days.** Street dances, a water-ski show, a parade, arts and crafts, and a water fight are part of the festivities. Call (612) 565–4158 for information.

About 30 miles south of Wabasha on Highway 61 is **Winona,** a beautiful town nestled between steep sandstone bluffs and the Mississippi. Founded by a steamboat captain in 1851, Winona was one of Minnesota's busiest steamboat landings during the nineteenth century and by 1900 was among the world's wealthiest cities. Winona's millionaires spent freely on the construction of homes and businesses, leaving an architectural legacy unequaled among midsized Minnesota cities. For a walking tour brochure, stop at the town's visitor center off Highway 6. (On your way into town, take note of **Sugar Loaf Mountain,** which towers 500 feet above Lake Winona and was a landmark for early river pilots.)

Then visit the **Julius C. Wilkie Steamboat Museum,** on Main Street next to the river. The paddlewheeler is a full-size replica of a steamboat that burned in 1981 and houses on its first deck a fine museum of river lore. Included are numerous early photographs, lithographs, and models of steamboats, plus a collection of letters and documents written by Robert Fulton, who invented the first functioning steamboat in 1807. On the second deck is a grand salon furnished in magnificent Victorian style, with flowered carpets, flowing draperies, and imported brass and crystal chandeliers. The museum (507–454–1254) is open noon to 5:00 P.M., Thursday through Sunday, from June through August.

The **Winona Armory Museum** is one of the largest historical society museums in Minnesota and presents information on the city's close ties to the river as well as other aspects of its history. The museum (507–454–2723), at 160 Johnson Street, is open daily. Two other museums give more insights into the heritage of Winona: The **Polish Cultural Institute of Winona** (507–454–3431), at 102 Liberty Street, gives information on the town's substantial Polish community, and the **J. R. Watkins Heritage Museum** (507–457–6095), on East Third Street, tells the story of the Winona-based Watkins Company, which pioneered direct-sales techniques in the 1860s.

Victorian-era accommodations in Winona can be found at the **Carriage House,** which was built by lumber baron Conrad Bohn in 1870 next to his elegant home. The structure was designed to accommodate six carriages and several horses, and it had a second-floor hayloft and rooms for stable boys. Today humans rather than horses stay here in four elegantly appointed rooms. You'll find the Carriage House (507–452–8256) at 420 Main Street.

Winona celebrates **Steamboat Days** each year during the week of July 4 with a carnival, parade, beer garden, art show, food fair, fireworks, and many other activities. During the **Victorian Fair** in early October, the town's nineteenth-century heritage comes alive with old-time music, food, and festivities, including horse-drawn buggy rides, high-wheel bicycle riding, candle-dipping, and other nineteenth-century crafts and amusements.

At any time of year, stop for a bite to eat at the **Jefferson Pub and Grill,** an old railroad freight house and National Historic Landmark that has been renovated into a cozy restaurant. Exposed beams and brick walls recall its history, and old movie posters line the walls. It's located next to the river at 58 Center Street, one block east of the Wilkie Steamboat Museum. Prices are moderate.

From Winona go five miles south on Highway 61 to the town of **Homer.** There you'll find the **Bunnell House,** one of the finest examples of Gothic

An Ecological Oasis

The Upper Mississippi National Wildlife and Fish Refuge includes 200,000 acres of wooded islands, backwaters, and marshes that extend for more than 260 miles from Wabasha, Minnesota, to Rock Island, Illinois. This wild portion of the river is home to an astonishing variety of wildlife: Some 270 species of birds, 57 species of mammals, 45 species of amphibians and reptiles, and 113 species of fish make their home here.

While the refuge provides a haven for many animals, it is particularly important as a bird sanctuary. The refuge is part of the Mississippi Flyway, a major migration path from the Gulf of Mexico to Canada. The river is an ideal route for traveling birds: It provides ample food, contains no geographical obstacles, such as mountains or deserts, and is a direct path between the northern and southern reaches of the continent.

Among the more spectacular birds often seen in the refuge is the bald eagle. During the winter eagles fly south as their primary feeding areas in Canada and Alaska begin to freeze. As many as 2,500 of the magnificent birds winter along the Mississippi between the Twin Cities and St. Louis. They can often be seen near the river's locks and dams, which keep the water from freezing and thus make it easier for the birds to catch fish.

Revival architecture in Minnesota. Built in the 1850s by Willard Bunnell, the first permanent white settler in Winona County, the house contains pioneer artifacts and displays. It's open from Memorial Day through Labor Day, Wednesday through Sunday. Call (507) 454–2723 for information.

From Homer continue south on Highway 61 for 4 miles and then head west on County Road 7 for 2 miles to the small village of **Pickwick.** There you'll find the **Pickwick Mill,** a restored, six-story mill built in 1858. Constructed of local stone and timber, the mill produced Itasca Flour, a brand that was sold as far away as Europe and South America.

Southeastern Minnesota was part of the wheat belt, and farmers hauled grain over many miles of primitive roads, often staying overnight in the mill's on-site hotel. During the 1860s, the mill operated day and night to supply flour to the Union army and also to meet the demands of England's growing urban population. Though almost destroyed by a flood in 1980, the mill now houses a museum of nineteenth-century flour milling. It's open on Saturday and Sunday from 11:00 A.M. to 5:00 P.M., May through October. Call (507) 452–9658 for information.

For your last stop in Minnesota, take the scenic **Apple Blossom Drive,** which winds through the many orchards that line the bluffs here along the Mississippi between Dresbach and La Crescent. Blossoms blanket the hillsides in spring, but the views along the drive are lovely at any time of year. In the fall roadside stands sell fresh apples, cider, Indian corn, and pumpkins. Watch for the signs off Highway 61 for the entrance to the drive.

FOR MORE INFORMATION

Minnesota Office of Tourism (800) 657–3700

Minnesota Department of Natural Resources (612) 296–0568

Bemidji (800) 458–2223, ext. 50

Brainerd (800) 950–1162, ext. 30

Grand Rapids (800) 472–6366

Little Falls (612) 632–5155

St. Cloud (612) 251–2940

Minneapolis (612) 661–4700

St. Paul (800) 627–6101

Red Wing (800) 762–9516

Wabasha (612) 565–2585

Winona (800) 657–4972

Wisconsin

In Wisconsin the Mississippi flows through a land of deep valleys and dramatic bluffs, past some of the most beautiful countryside along the entire river road. The southwestern corner of the state was spared the enormous glaciers that once covered much of the rest of Wisconsin. The floodwaters of the melting glaciers to the north, however, eroded the gorge of the Mississippi, creating the spectacular bluffs through which the river runs. In some areas, the bluffs rise more than 500 feet above the Mississippi. River towns are often built on the narrow banks between the bluffs and the water; some are only a few streets wide, but several miles long.

Aside from La Crosse and Prairie du Chien, the river towns in Wisconsin are primarily small villages of only a few hundred people. Many prospered during the steamboat era and then slipped back into a sleepy existence. Fishing is the primary activity now, and most of the villages have a laid-back, casual atmosphere that makes for relaxing touring.

PRESCOTT TO LA CROSSE

The northernmost river town in Wisconsin is **Prescott,** located at the confluence of the St. Croix and Mississippi rivers. The city dates from 1839 and is one of the oldest river towns on the Wisconsin shore. Stop for a picnic at **Mercord Mill Park,** where you can see the line in the water where the blue waters of the St. Croix meet the muddy Mississippi. A historic gear house in the park still contains the hand-operated machinery used to raise and lower

N

W   E

S

Wisconsin

• Prescott

•Stockholm
 • Pepin
  •Alma

      • Trempealeau
      • La Crosse

Mississippi River

• Prairie du Chien

    • Cassville
      • Dickeyville

the lift bridge that once stood here; the building is open weekends from spring through autumn.

Stop at the **Welcome and Heritage Center** in Prescott's Old City Hall for visitor information and to see local history displays. The center (715–262–3284) is at 233 Broad Street.

The **Oak Street Inn** offers inviting accommodations for visitors touring the area. The Italianate home was built in 1854 by one of the town's early settlers and has at various times housed a church, piano factory, and hospital annex. Its front porch is filled with wicker furniture, perfect for socializing. Three comfortable rooms, furnished with antiques, are available to guests. You'll find the inn (715–262–4110) at 506 Oak Street.

From Prescott travel south on Highway 35 for 35 miles through a lovely expanse of bluffs and river vistas to the small village of **Stockholm.** The settlement was founded in 1854 by a group of Swedish immigrants, and begin-

Steps on the River

Early in the nineteenth century, the federal government began assuming responsibility for maintaining the nation's waterways for boat traffic. Although the Lower Mississippi was navigable in all seasons, the Upper Mississippi was much more temperamental, and during long dry spells many parts of the river were too shallow for large boats.

Between 1930 and the early 1950s, the U.S. Army Corps of Engineers constructed twenty-nine locks and dams on the Upper Mississippi to maintain a 9-foot-deep channel from St. Louis to St. Paul. Behind each dam a lakelike area called a pool is formed. Because there is often a considerable difference between the water levels above and below a dam, the gravity-powered locks provide passage from one level to another, alternately lifting vessels to upstream pools and lowering them downstream. The dams are not a flood-control device; they exist solely for the purpose of maintaining a deep channel.

In effect, the system turns the Upper Mississippi into a series of steps. In the 670 miles between St. Paul and St. Louis, the locks and dams lower the river through 420 feet of elevation. Below St. Louis the river is deep enough for barge traffic in its natural state.

The Upper Mississippi's lock and dam system is an engineering marvel that maintains a 9-foot-deep channel from St. Paul to St. Louis.

ning in the early 1970s, the village became the destination for a new wave of immigrants—professional artists who were attracted to its picturesque surroundings and historic buildings. Today several galleries sell original paintings, pottery, jewelry, and other works of art. Don't miss browsing through **Amish Country Quilts and Furniture** (800–247–7657), which is housed in an old general store at 119 Spring Street. Inside are more than a hundred exquisite Amish quilts plus hand-crafted furniture of pine, oak, and cherry.

Across the street is the quaint **Merchant's Hotel,** which was built in the mid-1800s and offers three guest rooms to visitors. An adjoining building that once housed a harness shop is now an antiques store. Call (715) 442–2113 or 448–2508 for reservations.

Just up the street the town's old post office now houses the **Stockholm Institute,** a small museum that chronicles local history, including Stockholm's days as a steamboat port. The museum (715–442–2093) is open on Saturday and Sunday from noon to 5:00 P.M.

From Stockholm travel south on Highway 35 for 7 miles to **Pepin,** which is proud of its status as the birthplace of Laura Ingalls Wilder, author of the enormously popular "Little House" books. Wilder lived in Pepin for just a few years, however, before her restless father took the family to new territories. The Ingalls family spent time in Kansas, Minnesota, and Iowa before finally settling near DeSmet, South Dakota. There Laura met and married Almanzo Wilder, and the two moved to Missouri in 1894. As a farm wife, Laura's writing career began with articles for farm magazines. Later her daughter, Rose Wilder Lane, encouraged her to write about her family's pioneer experiences, and thus began her famous series of books.

To view a replica of the "Little House in the Big Woods," described in Wilder's books, take County Road N north from Pepin for 7 miles. The **Little House Wayside** marks the homestead of Charles Ingalls and the spot where Laura was born in 1867. The wayside's log cabin houses a display of Wilder memorabilia. While the "big woods" Wilder wrote about are now rolling farmland, it's still possible to get a feel for the pioneer life lived by the Ingalls family.

Return to Highway 35 and visit the town of Pepin. The **Pepin Historical Museum** has a more extensive collection of artifacts relating to the famous author's life, including rooms furnished in pioneer style. The museum (715–442–2461) is at 306 Third Street and is open from 10:00 A.M. to 5:00 P.M. daily, from mid-May to mid-October.

The **Depot Museum,** at the north end of Pepin on Highway 35, gives information on railroad and river history. Housed in a restored 1886 train depot, the museum has artifacts from early steamboats and vintage photographs of river pilots as well as a potpourri of railroad memorabilia. The museum is open from 8:00 A.M. to 5:00 P.M., May through late October.

Next continue south on Highway 35 for 15 miles to **Alma.** Nestled between scenic bluffs and the Mississippi, Alma is only two streets wide, but it's 7 miles long. Settled by Swiss immigrants, Alma was once a major center for the logging industry. Today the town is known for its charming waterfront shops, stone retaining walls, terraced gardens, and elegant, turn-of-the-century homes, which cling to the bluff's edge. More than 250 of its buildings are listed on the National Register of Historic Places. Drive up to **Buena Vista Park** for a lovely view of the river. Its viewing platform is 500 feet above the city, and on a clear day you can see for 30 miles.

The downtown also has an observation deck at Lock and Dam Number 4, and the **Alma Museum** (608–685–4975) at 505 South Second Street houses displays of local history. It's open Sundays from 1:00 to 4:00 P.M., May to October.

The **Gallery House** offers bed-and-breakfast accommodations as well as an art gallery and a spice and candy shop. Built in 1861 as a mercantile establishment and family home, this cozy inn is run by Jan and Joe Hopkins, a nurse and a college professor, respectively. Three guest rooms are available, and the rates include use of a tree-shaded deck. You'll find the inn at 215 North Main Street; call (608) 685–4975 for information.

Two other historic structures on Main Street offer lodging. One is the **Burlington Hotel,** which was built in 1891 and includes a supper club as well as six guest rooms furnished with antiques. You'll find it at 809 North Main Street; call (608) 685–3636 for information. The **Laue House Inn** (608–685–4923), an 1863 structure located at 1111 South Main Street, also offers accommodations.

Each Labor Day weekend Alma hosts the **Mark Twain River Festival,** when Mark Twain and Becky Thatcher stroll the streets, and Tom Sawyer invites children to join a fence-painting contest. There are also frog-jumping and seed-spitting contests, a parade, theater performances, food stands, live music, and an arts and crafts fair. Call (608) 685–3511 for information.

From Alma continue south on Highway 35 for 35 miles to **Trempealeau,** where the 1871 **Trempealeau Hotel** offers hearty, moderately priced meals as well as guest rooms. In June, the hotel (608–534–6898) hosts a renaissance festival with games, musicians, actors, artisans, and medieval foods.

West of Trempealeau is **Perrot State Park,** which is named after the French explorer Nicholas Perrot, who built a trading post here in 1665. Located where the Trempealeau and Mississippi rivers meet, the park's 500-foot bluffs offer panoramic views of the river. The park also contains Indian burial and ceremonial mounds as well as petroglyphs marking the vernal equinox and summer solstice. Early explorers and traders used Trempealeau Mountain as a navigation landmark. The mountain was considered sacred ground by the Native Americans of the area.

From Trempealeau continue south on Highways 35 and 53 for 15 miles to **La Crosse,** Wisconsin's largest river city. Located at the confluence of three rivers, the city spreads out on a broad plain, which was a natural rendezvous site for Indians and fur traders. Its name is of French origin and was given to the settlement by traders who saw local Indians playing a ball game with long-handled racquets that was similar to the game of lacrosse. La Crosse soon became a focal point for stage routes, the railroad, and river traffic, and hundreds of boats passed through its harbor each month.

Majestic Bluffs

T*he majestic bluffs that overlook the river, along through this region, charm one with the grace and variety of their forms and the soft beauty of their adornment. The steep verdant slope, whose base is at the water's edge, is topped by a lofty rampart of broken, turreted rocks, which are exquisitely rich and mellow in color—mainly dark browns and dull greens, but splashed with other tints. And then you have the shining river, winding here and there and yonder, its sweep interrupted at intervals by clusters of wooded islands threaded by silver channels; and you have glimpses of distant villages, asleep upon capes; and of stealthy rafts slipping along in the shade of the forest walls; and of white steamers vanishing around remote points. And it is all as tranquil and reposeful as dreamland, and has nothing this-worldly about it—nothing to hang a fret or a worry upon.*

Mark Twain
Life on the Mississippi

The city became a major lumber center in the mid-1800s, and when that industry declined, the city turned to beer making. During the late 1800s and early 1900s, the Gund, Monitor, Bartl, Ziegler, and Heileman breweries were catalysts for the city's economic growth. Today only the Heileman Brewing Company remains. Call 608–782–2337 to arrange a tour of their operations.

A good place to begin your tour of La Crosse is at the **Riverside Museum** in Riverside Park. The museum has a variety of displays that explain the history of the Mississippi in this area, including a replica of a fur trading post and a slide show on the city's heritage. The museum (608–782–1980) is open from Memorial Day to Labor Day, from 10:00 A.M. to 5:00 P.M. daily.

The La Crosse County Historical Society also operates the **Hixon House,** at 429 North Seventh Street. This graceful Italianate house was built in 1859 by lumber baron Gideon Hixon and contains the family's original nineteenth-century furnishings. The house (608–782–1980) is open from Memorial Day to Labor Day, from 1:00 to 5:00 P.M. daily.

For a tour of the Mississippi around La Crosse, step on board the *La Crosse Queen,* a paddlewheeler that offers a variety of sightseeing, luncheon, and dinner cruises. The boat docks at Riverside Park, at the end of State Street; call (608) 784–2893 for information.

Downtown La Crosse includes one of the largest historic districts in the state. Take special note of Christ Episcopal Church, at 111 North Ninth Street, an 1898 structure with a magnificent Tiffany window. For a walking tour map, call the historical society at (608) 782–1980.

To tour another beautiful church, visit St. Rose Convent, at 715 South Ninth Street. Its **Mary of the Angels Chapel** was consecrated in 1906 and is considered one of the loveliest churches in the United States. Built in Romanesque style, the chapel has altars of Italian marble, onyx pillars, and inlaid mosaics of green and gold Venetian glass and mother-of-pearl. Since 1878 at least two Franciscan Sisters have maintained a twenty-four-hour prayer vigil at the convent. Tours are given daily; call (608) 784–2288 for information.

La Crosse hosts many events and festivals each year, including a **Log Boom and Prairie La Crosse Rendezvous** in August. Visitors can step back into the city's lumberjack era and watch logrolling tournaments and lumberjack exhibitions and stroll through an early trader encampment in

La Crosse's Cass Street Bridge connects Wisconsin and Minnesota.

Pettibone Park. Call (800) 658–9424 for information.

One of La Crosse's finest dining establishments is the **Freighthouse Restaurant** (608–784–6211), at 107 Vine Street. The building was used from 1880 to 1955 as a freighthouse for the Milwaukee Railroad and is listed on the National Register of Historic Places. Prices are moderate to expensive.

For overnight accommodations, the **Martindale House,** at 237 South Tenth Street, offers lodging with a Victorian flair. The 1850s home is built in the Italianate style, complete with a cupola and widow's walk. Call (608) 782–4224 for information.

PRAIRIE DU CHIEN TO DICKEYVILLE

From La Crosse continue south on Highway 35 for 60 miles through a series of small villages to the city of **Prairie du Chien,** which is Wisconsin's second oldest settlement (the oldest is Green Bay). European exploration of the area began in the seventeenth century, but archeological evidence indicates that Native Americans had settled in the area by at least 13,000 B.C. The city's location at the western end of the Fox–Wisconsin waterway, which connects the Great Lakes with the Mississippi River, gave it great strategic importance for both Indians and white settlers.

The French were the first Europeans in the area; they developed a fur trade with the Indians beginning in 1685. The city is named for a Fox Indian chief whose name, *Alim,* meant "dog" in English. When the French saw the prairie land that bordered the river, they called it the "Prairie of the Dog," or *Prairie du Chien* in French. Prairie du Chien soon became a hub of the Upper Mississippi fur trade as well as a strategic site for British and American forts.

In 1826 an enterprising fur trader named Hercules Dousman came here and set up shop as an agent for the American Fur Company. Eventually he made a fortune in the fur trade, railroads, steamboating, and other investments. Less than fifty years after his arrival, his descendants built a luxurious mansion, named **Villa Louis,** atop an ancient Indian burial mound on an island in the river. The cream-colored brick house is maintained to look just as it did during its opulent heyday, in the 1890s. Furnished from top to bottom with many of the Dousman family's original heirlooms, it is among the most authentically furnished Victorian houses in the nation. Guides wearing

1890s fashions take visitors through the rooms and explain the history of the family and customs of the day.

Villa Louis's thirteen acres include other historic structures. The former carriage house is now home to the **Museum of Prairie du Chien,** with displays on the town's early history. An 1850 stone general store houses the **Fur Trade Museum,** which documents the fur trade in the Upper Mississippi River Valley. The grounds also include the site of the only battle of the War of 1812 fought in Wisconsin and the ruins of old Fort Crawford.

The Villa Louis hosts a number of annual festivals, including a **Carriage Classic** in September. It's the state's largest horse-and-carriage driving event, where superb examples of many horse breeds are shown in both arena events and cross-country obstacle driving events. The mansion is located on St. Feriole Island and is open daily from 9:00 A.M. to 5:00 P.M., May 1 through October 31. Call (608) 326–2721 for information.

Each Father's Day weekend St. Feriole Island is the site of the **Prairie Villa Rendezvous.** Participants dress in frontier style from the period 1800–1850 and live in canvas tents while trading, bartering, and demonstrating frontier skills and pastimes. Stagecoach rides, music, and food are also part of the festivities. There is no admission charge for visitors; call (608) 326–8555 for information.

Another historic landmark in Prairie du Chien is the **Fort Crawford Medical Museum,** a three-building complex that includes the reconstructed 1831 military hospital of the second Fort Crawford. The museum chronicles the development of medicine over the past 150 years and displays Indian herbal remedies, an 1890s drugstore, and a dentist's and a physician's offices. The site is owned and maintained by the State Medical Society of Wisconsin and is guaranteed to make you thankful you live in the twentieth century. The medical museum (800–545–0634) is at 717 South Beaumont Road and is open daily from 10:00 A.M. to 5:00 P.M., May 1 through October 31.

The **Wisconsin Tourism Information Center** off Highway 18 between Iowa and Wisconsin streets offers extensive information about the region and is also the site of a 1910 statue of Father Jacques Marquette, the first European to view the Upper Mississippi. Phone (800) PDC–1673 for information.

From Prairie du Chien head south on County Road A to **Wyalusing State Park,** a 2,700-acre oasis at the confluence of two magnificent rivers, the Mississippi and the Wisconsin. Indian mounds line the Sentinel Ridge Walk and hiking trails lead to interesting rock formations and canyons.

The Man with the Hole in His Stomach

While serving at Fort Crawford, in Prairie du Chien, Dr. William Beaumont wrote his definitive study of the human digestive system with the invaluable assistance of a French-Canadian named Alexis St. Martin—a man Beaumont called a "dirty, slovenly fellow, unreliable and given to drink."

St. Martin had another attribute that made him attractive to the curious doctor: a gunshot wound in his stomach that refused to heal. Beaumont realized that the injury presented a unique opportunity to study the workings of the stomach. Beginning in 1825, the doctor conducted a series of experiments that involved dropping bits of food tied onto a string into St. Martin's stomach, and then gauging the time it took for them to be digested. Beaumont dropped items ranging from a thermometer to a dozen raw oysters into the hole. Over the course of seven years, he performed more than 200 experiments on the unfortunate French-Canadian. The doctor thus gained information that revolutionized the medical study of the stomach and digestive system. As for the irascible St. Martin, he lived into his eighties and fathered seventeen children.

There's also a marked canoe route, which winds through 10 miles of river islands. For information, call (608) 996–2261.

Next continue south on Highways 35 and 133 for 33 miles to **Cassville.** The town is best known for its **Stonefield Village Historic Site.** Located within Nelson Dewey State Park and operated by the State Historical Society of Wisconsin, the site was named Stonefield in honor of Governor Nelson Dewey's circa 1860 estate, on which the park is situated. (Dewey was Wisconsin's first governor.)

The village is a re-created, turn-of-the-century farming community. It includes a general store, church, saloon, photography studio, and the shops of blacksmiths, printers, and other tradespeople—all surrounding a parklike town square. More than thirty buildings, staffed by historical interpreters, bring to life a bygone era.

Nearby is the **State Agricultural Museum,** which describes the history of farming in Wisconsin through dioramas and exhibits of historic farm tools, agricultural implements, and domestic items. A short walk takes you to the home site of Nelson Dewey, who was one of the state's first large-scale farmers. Stonefield Village and the State Agricultural Museum are open daily from Memorial Day through early October. Admission is $5.00 for adults, $2.00 for children. Call (608) 725–5210 for information.

Cassville itself has a number of nineteenth-century structures, including several historically significant churches. It's also the site of the **Geiger House** (608–725–5419), at 401 Denniston Street, an 1855 Greek Revival home with accommodations in four guest rooms. The **River View Bed and Breakfast** (608–725–5895) was built in 1856 by a riverboat captain and also offers four rooms. You'll find it at 117 Front Street.

The **Cassville Ferry** has been a town institution for many years. For $5.00 you can take your car from Cassville across the river to Millville, Iowa, or go on foot for just $1.00. The ferry departs from Riverside Park daily between Memorial Day and Labor Day. Phone (608) 725–5180 for information.

Mississippi Clamming

Clamming has long been an important river industry. At the turn of the century, the demand for mother-of-pearl buttons made from clam shells fueled a lucrative trade that made great fortunes and depleted the river's extensive beds. On a good day, an experienced clammer could harvest 800 to 1,000 pounds of shells, using a crowfoot dredge that scraped the river bottom where the mussels rested in sand and mud.

During the past 30 years, clamming has experienced a rebirth along the Upper Mississippi, and clam barges and divers once again search for mussels with such colorful names as elephant's ear, sheepnose, mucket, heel-splitter, and warty-back. Today most of the clam shells are shipped to Japan, where they are ground into small pellets and inserted into saltwater clams to start the formation of pearls. Occasionally, clammers find pearls in the clams themselves, though most are asymmetrical and quite small.

From Cassville travel south on Highway 133 for 20 miles to **Potosi,** the "catfish capital of Wisconsin" and the center of what was once a major lead mining area. During the Civil War much of the lead used by the Union army came from the five-county area around Potosi. You can learn more about the region's history at the **St. John Lead Mine.** The mine was in operation from 1827 to 1870 and is one of the oldest mines in the state. The mine, which is listed on the National Register of Historic Places, was known as Snake Cave when the Indians showed it to explorer Nicholas Perrot in 1690. Tours today provide visitors with a glimpse of the equipment and mining techniques used 150 years ago. Check with the mine about an additional, self-guided tour of forty area sites dating back to the great "lead rush." The mine (608–763–2121) is at 129 South Main Street and is open daily from 9:00 A.M. to 5:00 P.M., May through October.

From Potosi head south on Highway 61 for 8 miles to **Dickeyville,** your last stop on Wisconsin's portion of the river road. Here you'll find the **Dickeyville Grotto,** a wonderfully odd, folk-art masterpiece constructed of stone, glass, and shells from around the world by Father Mathias Wernerus. You'll find the grotto at 305 West Main Street; free tours are given daily from June through August. Call (608) 568–7519 for information.

FOR MORE INFORMATION

Wisconsin Division of Tourism (800) 432–TRIP

Wisconsin Department of Natural Resources (608) 266–2181

Prescott (715) 262–3284

Pepin (715) 442–2461

Alma (608) 685–3511

La Crosse (800) 658–9424

Prairie du Chien (800) PDC–1673

Cassville (608) 725–5399

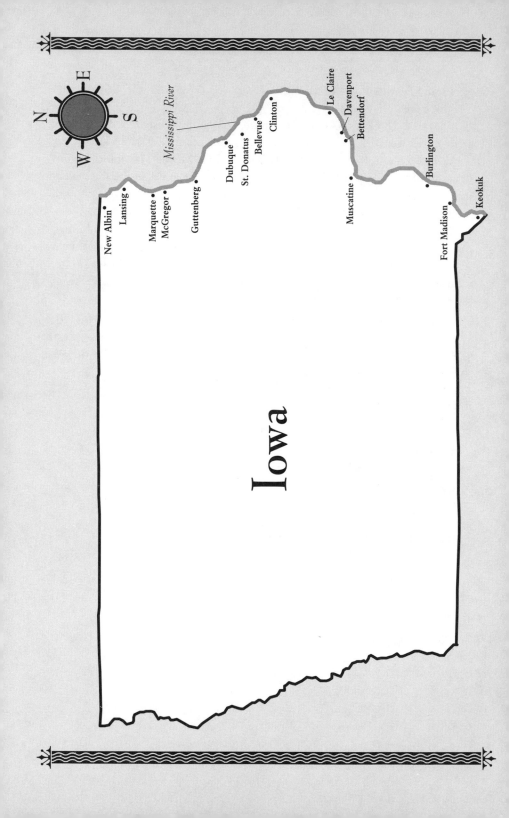

Iowa

he Mississippi borders the state of Iowa for 300 miles, forming its eastern border and flowing past rugged bluffs, deep woods, and a host of picturesque towns. The state's major river ports include Dubuque, once a lead mining boom town and later a center for the lumber and boat-building industries, and Davenport, where dangerous rapids once threatened steamboats and the first railroad bridge crossed the Mississippi in 1853. Iowa's first settlements were founded along the Mississippi, and these towns and cities continue to have unique characters that set them apart from the rest of the state. Rich in history and often filled with magnificent, century-old buildings and homes, these towns draw life and spirit from the water in countless ways.

NEW ALBIN TO DUBUQUE

The Mississippi enters the state at New Albin and flows southward through a part of Iowa known as Little Switzerland, a region marked by beautiful bluffs, forested hills, roller-coaster roads, and meandering rivers and streams. Because the area escaped the leveling effect of the glaciers, its varied landscape belies the state's flat reputation.

Just south of New Albin on Highway 26 is **Fish Farm Mounds,** a 500-acre state preserve containing prehistoric Native American burial mounds in a quiet forest glade near the river. Captain Nathan Boone, the son of Daniel Boone, surveyed this area in 1832. The present Soo Line Railroad follows the approximate route of Boone's survey downriver to a spot called Paint Rock Bluff, near Waukon Junction.

Continue south on Highway 26 for 6 miles to **Lansing,** a quiet river town that contains a number of historic buildings. Two bed-and-breakfasts offer accommodations with a Victorian atmosphere. **Fitzgerald's Inn** (319–538–4872), at 160 North Third Street, was built in 1863 and is tucked into a hillside on the bluff above the river. The **Lansing House** (319–538–4263), at 291 North Front Street, sits right on the bank of the Mississippi, just south of the Blackhawk Bridge, and offers fine views of the river.

You can explore the mazelike backwaters of the Mississippi on board the *Sand Cove Queen,* a paddlewheeler that offers narrated, two-hour cruises as well as private charters. Pilot Les Colsch takes passengers off the main channel into the quiet and scenic backwaters of the Upper Mississippi Wildlife Refuge. The refuge is a haven for wildlife and waterfowl, and in late July and early August, you can see lily pads and lotus blossoms in magnificent bloom. Tickets are $7.50 for adults; $4.00 for children. Call (319) 538–4497 for information.

Before leaving Lansing, take a drive up the bluff to **Mt. Hosmer Park,** which sits atop a 450-foot bluff and offers a spectacular view of the Mississippi River valley in three states.

From Lansing continue south on Highway 364 for 13 miles to **Harpers Ferry,** which began as the site of a ferry service to Wisconsin. The 6,000-acre Yellow River State Forest is located south of town and contains lovely woodlands and excellent trout streams.

From Harpers Ferry continue south on Highways 364 and 76 for 10 miles to the **Effigy Mounds National Monument.** This 1,500-acre area preserves outstanding examples of over 2,000 years of prehistoric Indian mound building. Within its borders are nearly 200 known burial mounds, 29 of which are in the shape of bears or birds (most of the rest are conical or linear in form). The Great Bear Effigy is one of the most impressive mounds—137 feet long and over 3 feet high. The mounds are all the more impressive when you realize that their builders didn't have the ability to see the giant shapes from the air, but instead worked out all the shapes from the ground level.

The visitors center at the monument has exhibits explaining the mounds and the artifacts found within them plus a film on the culture of the Indians who lived here along the banks of the Mississippi. There are also 11 miles of fine hiking trails in the surrounding woods. The center (319–873–3491) is open 8:00 A.M. to 7:00 P.M. from Memorial Day through Labor Day and from 8:00 A.M. to 5:00 P.M. the remainder of the year.

From Effigy Mounds continue south on Highway 76 for 3 miles to **Marquette,** a little town that takes its name from the explorer Jacques Marquette, who traveled through the area in 1673. The paddlewheeler *Miss Marquette* docks at the town's riverfront and offers a variety of gambling cruises. For information, call (800) 4–YOU–BET.

Then continue south a mile to **McGregor,** a charming river town whose restored Main Street has a turn-of-the-century flavor. There you'll find the **McGregor Historical Museum,** which has exhibits on river history and the founding of the community as a ferry boat landing in 1837 as well as information on how a famous circus had its beginning in a McGregor back yard. The museum (319–873–2186) is open Tuesday, Thursday, and Saturday from 2:00 to 5:00 P.M.

The Greatest Show on Earth

In 1860 a couple named August and Salome Ringling moved from Baraboo, Wisconsin, to McGregor, where August found work as a harness maker. The Ringling family lived here for twelve years in a house that still stands today on the road to Pike's Peak.

The family's five boys were skilled acrobats from a young age, and after seeing a traveling circus perform one day, they declared that they could put on just as good a show. Their first circus consisted of one brother doing acrobatics and trapeze tricks, another playing the trumpet, and another putting their elephant (who looked remarkably like a goat) through its paces. About sixty people attended their first show, for which the boys charged an admission price of ten straight pins.

In 1872 the family moved back to Baraboo, and by 1884 the brothers had saved up enough money to start a wagon show with a trained horse and a dancing bear. Today the tradition they began in McGregor is still going strong . . . as the Ringling Brothers Barnum & Bailey Circus.

McGregor is also home to the **River Junction Trade Company,** at 312 Main Street. The atmosphere inside is like that of a general store from a century or more ago, with a tin-plate ceiling, potbellied stove, and counters stacked with bolts of cloth and old-fashioned implements and articles of clothing. Its owner is Jim Boeke, a man who has been fascinated by the Old West ever since he was a boy. All the items in the store are accurate replicas of nineteenth-century clothing and equipment, including riverboat gambling vests, Abe Lincoln hats, gunbelts, sunbonnets, Shawnee tomahawks, leather boots, and calico dresses. The company (319–873–2387) also has a thriving mail-order business, and its illustrated catalog sells for $5.00.

McGregor's **Little Switzerland Inn** offers accommodations overlooking the river in an 1862 structure that once housed Iowa's oldest weekly newspaper. Guests can also stay in a log cabin that was built at Wexford, Iowa, in 1848 and moved into the yard next to the inn in 1987. For information call (319) 873–2057.

For one of the most scenic views along the entire river, drive to **Pike's Peak State Park,** located 2 miles south of McGregor on Highway 340. Here you can stand on a 500-foot bluff overlooking the meeting of the Mississippi and Wisconsin rivers. This is the place where in 1673 the explorers Marquette and Joliet first set foot on land west of the Mississippi. The peak was named for Zebulon Pike, who came through the area in 1805 on an expedition to explore and map the river.

From McGregor head south on Highways 340 and 52 for 20 miles to **Guttenberg.** When French missionaries canoed this portion of the river, they called it *Prairie La Porte,* meaning "door to the prairie." The area was opened for white settlement after the last Fox Indian settlement was abandoned in 1832, and the town's first residents were Germans. They named the town after Johannes Gutenberg, the fifteenth-century inventor of movable type. The town's ethnic heritage is reflected in streets with names like Mozart, Schiller, and Goethe, and the town's library has a bust of Gutenberg and a replica of his famous Bible. Its downtown is listed on the National Register of Historic Places and is a good spot to view the workings of Lock and Dam Number 10.

Displays on the Mississippi's lock and dam system plus information on local history can be found at the **Lockmaster's House Heritage Museum** in Guttenberg. The site is located in the former lockmaster's house, where the lockmasters and their assistants were required to live prior to 1972. The house is the last remaining lockmaster house on the Upper Mississippi and is listed on the National Register. Inside you'll find vintage furnishings and information on the engineering system that makes the upper river navigable for large-scale barge traffic. The museum is located next to the lock and dam; call (319) 252–2068 for information.

Another historic attraction in Guttenberg is the **Old Brewery,** an 1858 limestone structure that houses an art gallery, beer and wine room, and bed and breakfast. Artists Naser and Pat Shahrivar purchased the building in 1987 and have done most of the extensive renovation work themselves. Their two guest rooms are cozily furnished, and downstairs you can enjoy their award-winning artwork while sipping Iowa–made beer and wine. For more information, call (319) 252–2094.

From Guttenberg head south on Highway 52 for 6 miles to Millville, then take County Road C9Y for 15 miles to Balltown, home of **Breitbach's Country Dining.** Breitbach's likes to boast that it's the only restaurant in the world to be visited by both the outlaw Jesse James and the actress Brooke Shields, but that's not the restaurant's only claim to fame: Breitbach's

Breitbach's Country Dining is a former stagecoach stop once visited by Jesse James.

has been refreshing weary travelers since 1852, making this the oldest bar and restaurant in continuous operation in Iowa. The Breitbach family has owned this former stagecoach stop for the past century, and if you stop by today you're likely to be greeted with a hearty welcome by fifth-generation owner Mike Breitbach. The key to the restaurant's longevity is simple: delicious homemade food, reasonable prices, and a cozy atmosphere. Be sure to note the beautiful mural in the bar, which was painted by a traveling gypsy artist in 1934 in exchange for $15 and two weeks' room and board. Breitbach's (319–552–2220) is open for breakfast, lunch, and dinner from 7:00 A.M. to 10:00 P.M. daily. (Closed Mondays during the winter.)

Just north of the restaurant is a particularly fine view of the river valley, where you can rest while digesting the bountiful meal you've just eaten.

From Balltown continue south on Road C9Y for 15 miles to **Dubuque.** The city is named after Julien Dubuque, a French-Canadian fur trader who received permission in 1788 from the Fox Indians to work the lead mines in the area. The territory was opened to white settlement in 1833, and soon hundreds of new residents—many of them immigrants—were pouring into the young town. The next one hundred years saw the decline of mining and the growth of the lumbering, boatbuilding, shipping, and meatpacking industries. During that time Dubuque became one of the most important boatbuilding centers on the Mississippi. As the city grew rich, its citizens filled its streets with magnificent homes and buildings, structures that stand today as eloquent reminders of the city's past.

Begin your stay in Dubuque with a visit to the **River Museum,** a fascinating complex of six sites that explore the rich heritage of America's historic inland waterways. Inside are exhibits on the Indians, explorers, gamblers, adventurers, and steamboat pilots who lived and worked on the Mississippi. Among the highlights are tours of the 227-foot sidewheeler *William H. Black,* which is permanently docked near the museum, and the National Rivers Hall of Fame, a facility honoring such river heroes as Mark Twain, explorers Lewis and Clark, and inventor Robert Fulton. The complex forms one of the largest river museums in the country and gives a comprehensive and absorbing introduction to the history of the Mississippi as well as that of Dubuque.

The River Museum is located next to the Mississippi in the Ice Harbor area of downtown Dubuque. Admission is $6.00 for adults; $3.00 for children ages 7 to 15 (tickets good for two days). The museum (319–557–9545) is open daily from 10:00 A.M. to 6:30 P.M. from May through October.

A Riverman's Contempt

Great fortunes were made and lost during the nineteenth-century lumber trade along the Upper Mississippi, and hard feelings were often the result. The River Museum in Dubuque has the original of the following letter, which is dated October 12, 1904, and is addressed to a Mr. Elmer McCraney of Lansing, Iowa.

In common with people generally, I have always known you was a treacherous sneak, but didn't know how complete a stinker you could make of yourself until I learned of your action regarding the raft I brought to Dubuque. I am rather old to plan much but think I will live long enough to play even with you—as a starter, I will say that if you run the Joyce logs another year, you will do it for $800.00 per raft.

Yours with contempt,
Geo. Winans

From November through April it's open from 10:00 A.M. to 4:00 P.M., Tuesday to Sunday.

The **Mathias Ham House Historic Site,** at 2241 Lincoln Avenue, will give you more information on the city's past. The 1856 Italianate house was built by a man who grew rich off the area's lead mines and reflects the splendor of antebellum Dubuque. Also located on the site is a one-room schoolhouse and a log house that's the oldest building in Iowa. Tours of the site are given daily from June 1 to October 31 from 10:00 A.M. to 5:00 P.M. Phone (319) 557–9545 for information.

Next take a ride on the city's **Fenelon Place Elevator,** which bills itself as the world's shortest, steepest scenic railway. The quaint little elevator was built in 1882 by J. K. Graves, a businessman who worked in downtown Dubuque but liked to return home each day for lunch and a nap. The problem was that it took him a good hour to drive his horse and buggy home and back again. To solve the problem he commissioned a small cable car modeled after those he had seen on trips to Europe and had it installed on the bluff near his home. Graves's neighbors started asking permission to use the elevator, and soon it became a fixture of the city. In the intervening years the cars and support structure have been rebuilt several times, so even if it *seems* as if you're going to tumble to the ground as you're riding it, rest assured that the cars are safe. The elevator is even listed on the National Register of Historic Places—quite an honor for a machine designed to give a businessman time enough for a nap. The railway elevates passengers 189 feet up a steep hillside, from which you can see a lovely view of Iowa, Illinois, and Wisconsin. It's located at 512 Fenelon Place and is open from 8:00 A.M. to 10:00 P.M., April 1 to November 30.

After you've ridden the elevator, browse through the nearby Cable Car Square shopping district, an area of renovated homes and buildings that now house gift shops, antiques stores, and boutiques.

The **Grand Opera House** is another Dubuque landmark. Built in 1889, the theater hosted such greats as George M. Cohan, Lillian Russell, Ethel Barrymore, and Sarah Bernhardt in its early years, and today offers repertory productions from June through August and a number of other shows and productions during the rest of the year. Call (319) 588–1305 for ticket information. **Five Flags Theater** (319–589–4254) at Fourth and Main streets is another restored performing arts showplace. It was built in 1910 and is modeled after the famous music halls of Paris.

A number of Dubuque's grand old mansions offer lodging; call the city's convention and visitors bureau at (800) 798–8844 for a brochure. One of the loveliest is the **Redstone Inn,** a wine-colored mansion built in 1894 by a prominent Dubuque industrialist as a wedding present for his daughter. The house is now an intimate, fifteen-room Victorian hotel with towers, turrets, and cupids frolicking across the ceiling in the front parlor. You'll find the inn (319–582–1894) at 504 Bluff Street.

Another lovely place to stay in Dubuque is the **Hancock House Bed and Breakfast** at 1105 Grove Terrace. This gracious Queen Anne home perches on a bluff overlooking the city and river and offers nine guest rooms furnished with antiques. Call (319) 557–8989 for reservations.

Dubuque offers several unique ways to sample its historic attractions. One is the **Victorian House Tour and Progressive Dinner.** Guests stop at four of Dubuque's finest mansions (including the Redstone House and the Mathias Ham House) and enjoy a five-course dinner along the way. The four-hour dinner tour is available on Friday evenings from June through October as well as during the Christmas season. The cost is $36 per person, and reservations are required. Phone (319) 557–9545 for information.

You can also tour the city on the old-fashioned **Trolleys of Dubuque,** which offer a narrated hour-long tour of the city at 12:30 P.M. each day from May through October. The tour begins at the Iowa Welcome Center in the Ice Harbor area; tickets are $7.50 for adults, $4.00 for children. Call (800) 408–0077 for information.

Another way to see the city is on a **Rustic Hills Carriage Tour,** a horse-drawn carriage ride that operates out of Cable Car Square. The service (319–556–6341) operates daily from April 1 through October 31.

Other historic structures in Dubuque include the **Shot Tower,** on the riverfront, which produced lead shot during the Civil War; the **Old County Jail,** at Eighth Street and Central Avenue, which now houses the Dubuque Museum of Art; and the **Julien Dubuque Monument** on a high bluff overlooking the Mississippi in the Mines of Spain State Recreation Area.

Dubuque is also the site of Lock and Dam Number 11, which offers free tours Sundays at 2:00 P.M., Memorial Day through Labor Day. Another way to see the river is on board the two gambling boats that operate in the area, the *Diamond Jo Casino* (800–582–1683) and the *Silver Eagle Casino Cruise Ship* (800–723–2453). For a nongaming cruise, board the *Spirit of Dubuque,* a paddlewheeler that offers sightseeing excursions and lunch and dinner cruises. Call (800) 747–8093 for information.

A good time to visit Dubuque is during **Riverfest,** held each year during the second weekend in September. The city hosts a variety of free family entertainment, including a Dragon Boat Festival, with brightly painted, hand-carved Chinese dragon boats that race on the Mississippi River. Call (319) 557–9200 for information.

ST. DONATUS TO MUSCATINE

From Dubuque head south on Highway 52 for 11 miles to **St. Donatus,** a small village famous for its Old World architecture and traditions. Its settlers were immigrants from Luxembourg who tried to duplicate the architecture and customs of their native land in their new home. The town's primary landmark is its Catholic church, which was built in 1858 in the Luxembourg tradition of stone walls covered with a thin coat of stucco. Behind the church is what is believed to be the oldest outdoor Way of the Cross in North America. The winding path leads up a hill, past the fourteen Stations of the

Cross. At the top is the Pietà Chapel, a small stone building modeled after a church in Luxembourg.

Other attractions in St. Donatus include the **Gehlen House and Barn,** a structure built in 1848 that is listed on the National Register of Historic Places and now houses a doll museum with over 4,000 dolls and toys. The museum (319–773–2405) is open daily from 8:30 A.M. to 5:30 P.M.

Next continue south on Highway 52 for 10 miles to the aptly named town of **Bellevue,** French for "beautiful view." The town was founded in 1853, making it one of the oldest settlements in the state, and was once the county seat of Jackson County. One of its prominent early settlers was Elbridge Gerry Potter, who in 1843 built a grist mill at the south end of town and a homestead he called Paradise because he "went through Purgatory to find it." His large stone home, which still stands on Mill Creek Road, housed Iowa's first lending library.

Bellevue's history is preserved at the **Young Museum,** at 410 North Riverview Street. The museum, which overlooks the river, is furnished with turn-of-the-century antiques and is known for its fine displays of china and Victorian memorabilia. It's open 1:00 to 5:00 P.M. on Saturdays and Sundays during the summer months.

Bellevue is also the site of Lock and Dam Number 12 and its downtown is lined with century-old stone and brick buildings, many of which now

The Bellevue War

Peaceful Bellevue was the site of a one-day battle in 1840 that has come to be known as the Bellevue War. The fighting took place between a posse of local citizens and hotel owner William Brown and his gang of thieves and robbers. Determined to rid the town of their presence, Bellevue residents offered Brown and his gang a fair trial in exchange for surrendering. The offer was refused and gun fighting broke out. In the end, seven men lay dead in the street. The remainder of Brown's gang were whipped, set adrift on the Mississippi, and forever banned from the town. Since then, Bellevue's streets have been relatively quiet.

house stores selling antiques, collectibles, and arts and crafts. A brochure on the town's historic buildings is available from the chamber of commerce (319–872–5830) at 210 North Riverview Street.

Two of those historic structures now house distinctive bed-and-breakfasts. The **Spring Side Inn** has been known as "the castle" to local residents for many years. It was named for the seven springs that surround it and was built of native limestone around 1850 in the Gothic Revival style. Each of its six guest rooms has a river view and is named after an American author who was writing at the time the house was built. The inn (319–872–5452) is located on Ensign Road, overlooking the town.

Another restored gem is **Mont Rest,** a home built in 1893 on a wooded hillside overlooking the town and river. Its five guest rooms include a tower room that was once a gambling den for the home's original owner, Seth L. Baker, who lost the home in a card game two years after he built it. The room has a panoramic view of the Mississippi and its own private deck. You'll find the inn (319–872–4220) at 300 Spring Street.

Before leaving Bellevue, pay a visit to **Bellevue State Park,** south of town. The 547-acre park is known for its high bluffs and scenic views of the river and also for its Butterfly Garden, a one-acre plot that is carefully planned to provide food and habitat for nature's most beautiful and delicate creatures. Near the garden is the South Bluff Nature Center, which contains dioramas and natural history displays relating to the area.

From Bellevue follow Highway 52 for 20 miles to the quiet island town of **Sabula,** where the **Castle Bed and Breakfast** (319–687–2714) offers overnight accommodations in a stone-faced, turn-of-the-century home overlooking the river.

Next head south on Highway 67 for 15 miles to **Clinton,** a city that grew rich during the nineteenth century as a transportation and lumber center. The city is also the site of Lock and Dam Number 13, which marks the southern end of one of the widest pools on the river. Here the Mississippi and its marshes stretch for nearly 4 miles between the Iowa and Illinois shores. A good place to view the river is from **Eagle Point Park and Nature Center,** a recreation area on North Third Street. Adjacent to the park and nature center is a children's zoo.

Clinton celebrates its river heritage each summer with the **Clinton Area Showboat Theatre.** Performances are held on board the *City of Clinton* showboat, a restored paddlewheeler permanently dry-docked in the city's

Riverview Park. The theater recalls the days when lavish showboats plied their way up and down the river and is the perfect place to complete a day's touring along the Mississippi. A professional acting company performs a variety of musicals, comedies, and dramas each season; call (319) 242–6760 for information.

The **Clinton County Historical Society Museum** at 708 Twenty-fifth Avenue North tells the story of the area's early settlers, its river history, and its once-booming lumber trade. Its hours are Saturday and Sunday, 1:30 to 4:30 P.M., and Wednesday 1:00 to 3:00 P.M. Call (319) 242–1201 or 242–6769 for information.

To get a closer view of the river and try your luck at riverboat gambling, book a cruise on the *Clinton Riverboat Casino.* Call (800) 457–9975 for information.

Just south of Clinton is Camanche, where the **Camanche Depot and Museum** is housed in a restored 1899 railroad depot and 1951 Milwaukee/Soo caboose. The museum (319–259–1268) is located at 102 Twelfth Avenue, and is open Sundays from 1:00 to 4:00 P.M., from June through September.

Continue on Highway 67 for 20 miles to **Le Claire,** which marks the beginning of what was once one of the most dangerous passages along the entire Mississippi. Treacherous rapids stretched for 13 miles from Le Claire to Rock Island, Illinois, an area that at low-water periods was impassable by anything larger than a small boat. Even during normal conditions it took an experienced and knowledgeable pilot to safely negotiate the rapids, and Le Claire was home to many steamboat pilots who made their living guiding boats through this short stretch of river.

Though the rapids have been tamed by the U.S. Army Corps of Engineers, you can still enjoy a trip back to the golden age of steamboating on board the *Twilight.* The beautifully appointed, 150-passenger paddlewheeler offers two-day cruises that depart from Le Claire and run upriver to Galena, Illinois. Passengers stay overnight at Chestnut Mountain Resort, spend the morning touring Galena's historic attractions, and then have a relaxing afternoon and evening back on board as the *Twilight* returns to Le Claire. The boat's owner, Captain Dennis Trone, is a former navy officer who gave up his military career to pursue his dream of a life on the river. Throughout the cruise, passengers are treated to entertaining tidbits of Mississippi lore and history along with delicious food and incomparable views of the river out every window. The *Twilight* offers one of the best cruises on the river, particularly for anyone with an interest in the steamboat era. Tickets are $200 per person, double occupancy. Call (800) 331–1467.

Another attraction in Le Claire is the **Buffalo Bill Museum.** William F. Cody was born on a farm near Le Claire in 1846, became a Pony Express rider at the tender age of fourteen, and later gained fame as a buffalo hunter who supplied meat for the workers building the railroad lines. In 1872 he began his long career as a showman, taking his Wild West show to all parts of the United States and Europe.

The Buffalo Bill Museum pays tribute to the man and his legend and also contains exhibits on early pioneers and the history of Le Claire, particularly its steamboat industry. The sternwheeler *Lone Star,* which is believed to have been the last working steamboat on the Upper Mississippi, is permanently docked next to the museum. The museum (319–289–5580) is on the river bank. To reach it, turn east off Jones Street. Its hours are 9:00 A.M. to 5:00 P.M. daily, May 15 through October 15.

The **Buffalo Bill Cody Homestead** is located about 10 miles northwest of Le Claire near the town of McCausland. The house is furnished in period style, and buffalo, burros, and longhorn cattle graze on the land surrounding it. The site (319–225–2981) is open daily from 9:00 A.M. to 6:00 P.M., April through October.

In August Le Claire and its sister town across the river in Illinois, Port Byron, stage the **Great River Tug Fest,** which includes a tug-of-war across the Mississippi. Fireworks, music, food, and arts and crafts are part of the celebration. Call (309) 523–3312 for information.

On your way out of town, stop by the **Mississippi Valley Welcome Center,** just off of I–80, south of Le Claire. The center gives comprehensive information on this stretch of the river road.

DAVENPORT TO MUSCATINE

From LeClaire continue south on Highway 67 for 3 miles to **Davenport** and **Bettendorf**, which along with the Illinois cities of Moline and Rock Island form the **Quad Cities.** The area has been an important river port for hundreds of years. It began as a trading center for the American Fur Company and was a battleground during the War of 1812. Davenport was the first city in Iowa to have railroad service, and it was here that the first train crossed the Mississippi in 1853. During the Civil War a prison camp for Confeder-

The Quad Cities' nineteenth-century past is recalled in the Village of East Davenport.

ate soldiers was located in the area, and nearly 2,000 southern soldiers were buried here, far from their homes. (*Gone With The Wind* fans will recognize this as the place where Ashley Wilkes was held prisoner.) In the years following the war, the area became a major port for river travel once again.

Arsenal Island, the largest island in the upper Mississippi, is an excellent place to learn more about the history and military importance of the Quad Cities. The Rock Island Arsenal was built during the Civil War to meet the Union's needs for artillery equipment and continues to manufacture weapons parts and military supplies. With its 9,000 civilian and military workers, the arsenal is the area's largest employer.

You can visit several historic sites on Arsenal Island. The **Arsenal Museum** is the second oldest U.S. Army museum (West Point is the oldest) and contains one of the largest military arms collections in the nation. The museum (309–782–5021) is open daily from 10:00 A.M. to 4:00 P.M.

The **Colonel Davenport House** showcases the life and times of the Quad Cities' first permanent white settler. A former Army officer, Davenport built a lucrative trading empire and in 1833 constructed this impressive Federal-style home, which must have been a big change from the log cabin

Lincoln and the Rock Island Bridge

I n 1853 East met West at Davenport with the first crossing of the Mississippi by train. The bridge's construction ignited bitter opposition from powerful river interests, who rightfully saw the railroad as a great threat to their virtual monopoly on transportation.

Tensions flared even higher in 1856, when the steamboat *Effie Afton* struck one of the bridge's piers and was totally destroyed by the ensuing fire. The owners sued the railroad, who maintained that the so-called accident was intentional. The best legal talent in the state was recruited by both sides—including a lawyer named Abraham Lincoln, who acted as counsel for the railroad. Arguing that "one man had as good a right to cross a river as another had to sail up or down it," Lincoln eloquently defended the railroad's interests. Though the case was left unresolved when the jury failed to agree on a verdict, Lincoln's words helped lay the legal groundwork for the nation's rapidly expanding transportation system. The case was finally settled in the railroad's favor by the Supreme Court in 1862. It was a verdict that marked a significant turning point in the rise of the railroad and decline of the steamboat.

he and his family had lived in since their arrival on the island in 1816. Much of the planning for the future Quad Cities region was completed in the Davenport house. Unfortunately, Davenport didn't live to see the area grow and prosper, for he was murdered by river bandits in his home in 1845. The crime so shocked the region that it led to the formation of its first criminal justice system. The Colonel Davenport House (309–786–7336) is open Tuesday through Sunday from May through October.

While you're on Arsenal Island, take the time to wander through the tranquil **Confederate Cemetery.** The orderly rows of headstones are a sobering reminder of the human toll taken by the War Between the States. This is the largest Confederate cemetery north of the Mason–Dixon Line, and a national cemetery for veterans and their families is nearby.

The island is also the site of the **Mississippi River Visitor Center,** which offers a bird's-eye view of the workings of Lock and Dam Number 15, plus displays on river navigation and the work of the U.S. Army Corps of Engineers that tamed the dangerous rapids here. Phone (309) 794–5338 for information.

An excellent way to tour Arsenal Island is on a narrated **Trolley Tour.** The tours are operated by Carnival Cruise Line, which also offers boat cruises on the Mississippi. Call (800) 227–9967 for information.

Next travel to the **Village of East Davenport,** which was founded in 1851 and soon became a thriving logging, sawmill, shipping, and mercantile center. Today the area is a 120-acre historic district that includes over 500 homes and businesses, many dating from the pre–Civil War era. The business district along East Eleventh and Twelfth Streets includes dozens of unusual specialty shops, artists' studios, and restaurants. Just east of the village is Lindsay Park, once the site of a major Civil War training camp for Union soldiers. It's now a quiet, tree-shaded area offering a lovely view of the Mississippi River and Arsenal Island from its 50-foot bluff.

Each year on the third weekend in September, the village brings to life the 1860s during **Camp McClellan Civil War Days.** Activities include a Civil War encampment, a battle reenactment, and a full-dress military ball. For information contact the Village of East Davenport Association at (319) 322–0546.

The **Bix Beiderbecke Memorial Jazz Festival** is another Quad Cities event worth attending. It pays tribute to the memory of Davenport-born jazz great Leon "Bix" Beiderbecke. For three days and four nights in July, the Quad Cities are filled with the toe-tapping sounds that are Bix's legacy. The celebration also includes arts, crafts, and food. Call (309) 324–7170 for information.

Another Davenport attraction is the **Putnam Museum of History and Natural Science,** which gives a comprehensive introduction to the history and wildlife of the Quad Cities and the Upper Mississippi River Valley. It's open Tuesday through Sunday; call (319) 324–1922 for information.

Walnut Grove Pioneer Village allows you to wander through history yourself, through a late 1800s settlement of nearly two dozen buildings. A highlight is the beautiful St. Ann's Church, built in 1853. The village is at the north edge of Scott County Park, located 9 miles north of Davenport on Highway 61. It's open daily from April through October. Phone (319) 285–9903 for information.

There are a number of fine bed-and-breakfasts in the Quad Cities. One of the grandest is the **River Oaks Inn,** an 1850s mansion perched atop a bluff overlooking the Mississippi. Five guest bedrooms are available and a carriage house with hot tub. The inn (319–326–2629) is at 1234 East River Drive in Davenport.

Another unique place to stay is the **Abbey Hotel,** a Romanesque structure overlooking the river that was for many years a cloistered Carmelite monastery. The hotel offers nineteen luxuriously appointed guest rooms (considerably changed from the days when nuns and monks made their home here). For information call (800) 438–7535.

Riverboat gambling is another popular attraction in the Quad Cities. The *President Riverboat Casino* (800–BOAT–711) and *Jumer's Casino Rock Island* (800–477–7747) offer gaming cruises. **Celebration Cruises** (800–227–9967) offers a variety of sightseeing and theme cruises.

From the Quad Cities head west on Highway 22 for 25 miles to the city of **Muscatine.** White settlers first came to the area in 1835, and two years later James Casey started a trading post here to service the flourishing river-

Muscatine Buttons

John Boepple is credited with launching the turn-of-the-century pearl button industry. Not satisfied with the quality of buttons he could make out of animal horns in his native Germany, Boepple experimented with the freshwater clams that were shipped to him from the Illinois River. He was pleased to find that their iridescent interior produced a sturdier and more attractive button, and eventually he immigrated to Muscatine, where he had heard that there was a rich supply of clams that collected naturally along this stretch of the Mississippi River.

Boepple opened Muscatine's first mother-of-pearl button factory in 1897, and by 1905 the area was producing over one-third of the world's buttons. Button making was a labor-intensive operation requiring a great deal of handwork. More than forty factories employed 3,500 people—over 50 percent of the local workforce—and Muscatine became known as the pearl button capital of the world. The industry thrived until zippers became widespread and plastic buttons flooded the market.

Today all but three of the factories are gone, but the memory of the industry's boom days linger—and in countless attics across the country, Muscatine buttons still adorn clothing from years past.

boat industry. Soon people began calling the area Casey's Wood Pile, though by 1850 the growing town had adopted the more elegant name of Muscatine. The word was taken (depending upon whom you believe) either from the Mascoutin Indians who once lived here or else from an Indian word meaning "burning island."

The first major industry in Muscatine was lumber, but by the late 1890s button making had become the city's main source of revenue. The city's **Pearl Button Museum** chronicles the development of the industry and is the only museum in the world dedicated to this unique enterprise. Here you can see the complete button-making procedure, from collecting the shells in the river through processing, cutting, and dying. You'll find the museum (319–263–8895) in downtown Muscatine at the corner of Iowa Avenue and Second Street; its hours are 1:00 to 4:00 P.M. on Saturdays.

You can learn more about area history at the **Muscatine Art Center,** a combination museum and art gallery at 1314 Mulberry Avenue. The facility is housed in a 1908 mansion with a contemporary addition. It has an excellent collection of decorative arts and works by such noted European and American artists as Matisse, Chagall, Renoir, Grant Wood, and Georgia O'Keeffe. Of particular interest is the Art Center's "Great River Collection," which includes paintings, drawings, prints, and maps relating to the Mississippi. The center (319–263–8282) is open daily except Monday.

Lock and Dam Number 16 is in Muscatine and includes an observation deck for viewing its operations. Another good place to see the river and city is from the **Mark Twain Overlook,** off Highway 61 (about one block northeast of the Norbert Beckey Bridge). The site includes a picnic area and an historical marker with information on the formation of the Great River Road.

Downtown Muscatine (an area roughly bounded by Fourth Street, Pine Street, Orange Street, and the Mississippi River) contains many vintage buildings, and other parts of the city have historic homes built during the city's glory days. The chamber of commerce (800–25–PEARL), at 319 East Second Street, has information on walking tours.

On the third weekend in August, Muscatine hosts **Great River Days,** a riverfront community celebration, that includes fireworks, live entertainment, and a carnival. Call (319) 264–5666 for information.

Muscatine is also well known for the melons grown on Muscatine "Island," a former Mississippi island (now silted in and part of the mainland) with fertile, sandy soil. Follow Highway 61 south to Fruitland, where farmer's markets sell watermelon, cantaloupe, and other produce as well as locally made crafts and other souvenir items.

From Muscatine take Highways 61 and 99 south for 30 miles to **Toolesboro,** site of the **Toolesboro Indian Mounds.** This National Historic Landmark includes one of the largest Indian mounds in the state. The mounds are the work of Hopewell Indians who lived in the area from 200 B.C. to A.D. 400. Their elaborate death ceremonies included building mounds for their dead and surrounding them with pottery, pipes, tools, weapons, and ornaments. The Hopewell people prospered in the area but seem to have disappeared by the sixth century for reasons unknown to archeologists. The site's visitors center (319–523–8381) is open daily from Memorial Day through Labor Day from noon to 4:00 P.M.

BURLINGTON TO KEOKUK

From Toolesboro continue south on Highway 99 for 25 miles to **Burlington.** Native Americans knew this part of the river as *Shoquoqon,* meaning flint hills. Flint deposits were plentiful in the limestone bluffs in the area, which was a favorite hunting site. The region was first seen by the French explorers Marquette and Joliet in 1673, was visited by Zebulon Pike in 1805, and was the site of a trading post in 1808. It was eventually named Burlington by early settler John Gray after his Vermont home, and the town grew up along the river bank in a valley encircled by hills. The city was an important frontier settlement and was the second capital of the Wisconsin Territory as well as the first capital of the Iowa Territory. As Mark Twain commented in *Life on the Mississippi:* "In Burlington, as in all these upper-river towns, one breathes a go-ahead atmosphere which tastes good in the nostrils."

Begin your tour at the **Port of Burlington Welcome Center,** a 1928 riverside structure that was built to load barges with coal by means of an overhead conveyor. The building was renovated through local donations and is now an Iowa welcome center, a port of call for riverboats, and the site of town festivals. Inside the building you can see historic displays and a video of local attractions and obtain tourist information. The center (319–752–8731) is located at 400 North Front Street and is open daily.

No visit to Burlington would be complete without a walk down **Snake Alley,** a street that connects the Heritage Hill historic district with downtown businesses. The zigzagging cobblestone lane has been called the

Snake Alley

Building towns on the steep hillsides that border much of the Upper Mississippi required considerable ingenuity. Burlington's Snake Alley is among the most creative solutions. It was constructed in 1894 as an experimental street connecting the fashionable Victorian neighborhood of Heritage Hill to the downtown. The 275-foot-long winding street rises steeply for nearly 60 feet up the bluff and is constructed of tilted bricks designed to allow better footing for horses. The design was not completely successful, however. Drivers often lost control of their horses on its steep curves, and plans to construct more streets on its model were abandoned.

Snake Alley nevertheless proved to be a useful landmark for the city. Horses were "test driven" up the winding curves at a gallop, and if they were still breathing when they reached the top, they were deemed fit enough to haul the city's fire wagons. When cars were first offered for sale, they had to endure the same test. Auto dealers used Snake Alley to show off the vehicle's power, with prospective buyers clinging nervously to their seats.

crookedest street in the world and is the city's most famous landmark. You'll find it between Washington and Columbia streets on Sixth Street.

From Snake Alley, take a stroll through the Victorian Heritage Hill neighborhood; many of its structures were constructed during Burlington's building boom following the Civil War. Its hillside setting, numerous limestone retaining walls, brick sidewalks, garden walls, narrow passageways between buildings, and cobblestone and brick alleys provide a picturesque setting for the many architecturally significant buildings here, including numerous churches. Nearly 160 structures reflect a variety of periods and styles, including Greek and Gothic Revivals, Italian Villa, Queen Anne, and Georgian. Take special note of the Burlington Free Public Library, at 501 North Fourth Street, which houses its own art collection and is constructed in an eclectic blend of the Italian Villa, Renaissance Revival, and Georgian Revival styles.

The district is also home to the **Phelps House Museum,** at 512 Columbia Street. Located at the top of Snake Alley, this elegant Victorian home features furnishings dating from 1774 and a "medical memories" display describing the years the building housed Burlington's first Protestant hospital. The museum (319–753–2449) is open Wednesday and Sunday, 1:30 to 4:30 P.M., May through October.

Two other museums operated by the Des Moines County Historical Society are worth visiting. The **Apple Trees Museum,** at 1616 Dill Street, houses Burlington memorabilia, Native American artifacts, and an extensive doll collection. The **Hawkeye Log Cabin,** in Crapo Park, features pioneer-era furniture and tools in an historic structure in Burlington's oldest and largest park. The cabin is located on a bluff overlooking the Mississippi at the spot where Zebulon Pike raised the American flag for the first time on what would become Iowa soil. Both museums are open Wednesday and Sunday, 1:30 to 4:30 P.M., May through October. Phone (319) 753–2449 for information.

Another Burlington attraction is the *Catfish Bend Casino,* a paddle-wheeler that spends the winter in Burlington and the summer in nearby Fort Madison. The 560-passenger boat offers dockside gambling from November through April; call (800) 372–2WIN for information.

The **Schramm House Bed and Breakfast** offers overnight accommodations with a Victorian ambiance. The Queen Anne home was built in the 1870s by John Schramm, a prominent dry goods retailer. Two guest rooms are offered by innkeepers Sandy and Bruce Morrison; call (319) 754–0373 for information.

Another historic bed-and-breakfast is the **Mississippi Manor,** an Italianate structure built in 1878 that offers four guest rooms, each named after a Mark Twain character. It's located at 809 North Fourth Street; call (319) 753–2218 for information.

Burlington's downtown also contains many well-preserved historic structures and is lined with trees, shrubs, and benches. Its most distinctive characteristic is its many imposing churches. Nine houses of worship can be found within one or two blocks of Jefferson Street, creating a lovely panorama of steeples and spires. The West Jefferson antiques district is located in the 800 block and is also a pleasant area for a stroll.

While you're downtown, stop by **Big Muddy's,** Burlington's only riverfront restaurant. It's housed in an 1898 structure at 710 North Front Street that was once a railroad freight station and is open daily at 11:00 A.M. The restaurant (319–753–1699) is a popular spot for boaters; prices are moderate to expensive.

Burlington hosts a number of annual events, including the Snake Alley Criterium, a bike race held Memorial Day Weekend, and a Dragon Boat Festival in July. Best known is the **Burlington Steamboat Days,** a musical festival held during the third week in June that attracts nationally known rock, country, jazz, big band, and other musical groups, who perform daily on outdoor stages. The regional event attracts more than 100,000 visitors and includes fireworks, a parade and carnival, and many other attractions. For more information call the Burlington Area Convention and Tourism Bureau at (800) 827–4837.

From Burlington head south on Highway 61 for 18 miles to **Fort Madison.** The town was founded in 1808 as a government trading post and was the site of the first U.S. military post on the Upper Mississippi River. **Old Fort Madison** is a reconstructed replica of the frontier fort, which was attacked and burned by Indians in 1813. History comes alive here daily with the roar of cannons and the crack of flintlock muskets, and costumed interpreters can lead you on a tour of buildings that includes the officers' quarters, enlisted men's barracks, and blockhouses. The fort hosts a number of living-history events throughout the year and is located in Riverview Park, on the Mississippi. The fort (319–372–7700) is open daily from 9:00 A.M. to 5:00 P.M., Memorial Day through September.

Also on the riverfront is the **North Lee County Historical Museum,** which is located in the town's 1909 Mission-style railroad station, a building listed on the National Register of Historic Places. Displays here include information on the ice gathering that was done on the Mississippi in the days before refrigerators, plus railroad, pioneer, and Native American history. The museum (319–372–7661) is open daily from April through September, and on weekends in October.

Next door is Fort Madison's newest museum, the **Flood Museum.** Citizens of the town have turned tragedy into tourism by creating displays centered the 1993 Mississippi flood, which devastated much of the Midwest. Photos, newspaper articles, quotes from those who experienced the flood, and television footage help tell the story of the disaster. There's also a trashed-out, flooded kitchen that shows the mess faced by many homeowners. The museum celebrates the courage and spirit of those who worked together to survive the summer of 1993 along the river. It's open April through October, from 9:00 A.M. to 4:00 P.M., Monday through Saturday, and 1:00 to 4:00 P.M. on Sunday. Call (319) 372–7661 for information.

Fort Madison's downtown riverfront district has a number of antiques and specialty shops, as well as the elegant **Kingsley Inn.** This renovated, turn-of-the-century showplace is named after Lieutenant Alpha Kingsley, who supervised the construction of the original Old Fort Madison. The inn offers fourteen luxurious rooms decorated with Victorian antiques, including nine rooms overlooking the Mississippi and the reconstructed fort. Adjacent to the hotel is **Alpha's,** a moderately priced restaurant serving excellent food. Both the inn and the restaurant can be reached at (319) 372–1411.

From May through October the *Catfish Bend Casino* offers riverboat gambling in Fort Madison. The boat docks in Riverview Park; call (800) 372–2WIN for information.

From Fort Madison continue south on Highway 61 for 25 miles to **Keokuk,** the last stop along the Mississippi in Iowa. Keokuk was once the site of dangerous rapids located at the point where the Des Moines River met the Mississippi. In the early days of settlement, steamboats were unable to go beyond these rapids, and all passengers had to disembark here to either continue their journey on land or board another boat upriver.

Mark Twain lived in Keokuk for two years as a young man and worked in the printing shop of his brother, Orion Clemens. Most of the type for the city's first directory was set by Twain, who listed himself in its pages as an "antiquarian." When asked the reason for this, he replied that he always thought that every town should have at least one antiquarian, and since none had appeared for the post, he decided to volunteer.

Though far removed from the South, Keokuk played a vital role in the Civil War. The city was the central swearing-in point for all the Iowa volunteers, and it was a major medical center for the wounded. Soldiers injured on southern battlefields were transported up the Mississippi River on hospital boats and treated at the seven hospitals located in Keokuk. Often the trip was futile, and many soldiers—both Union and Confederate—found their final resting place in Keokuk's National Cemetery, one of the original twelve established by Congress in 1862.

Those Civil War days live again each year on the last weekend in April during the **Battle of Pea Ridge Civil War Reenactment.** The event is one of the largest reenactments in the Midwest and includes mock battles, a military ball, period foods and music, theater productions, buggy rides, and many other events. (One interesting tidbit of Civil War history is that Iowa had more volunteers per capita than any other state.) Call (800) 383–1219 for information.

The *George M. Verity* **Riverboat Museum** will take you back to the days when Keokuk was a busy river port. Built in 1927, the *Verity* was the first of four steamboats built to revive river transportation on the Mississippi. In 1960 it was retired and given to the city of Keokuk for use as a river museum. Today it contains many old-time photographs and other riverboat memorabilia as well as other historic artifacts. The *Verity* (319–524–4765) is berthed in Victory Park at the foot of Main Street on the Mississippi River. It's open daily from April through November, 9:00 A.M. to 5:00 P.M.

Keokuk is also the site of Lock and Dam Number 19, a 1,200-foot lock that is the widest on the Mississippi. The dam's electric generating plant was the largest in the world when it was built in 1913. Visitors are invited to tour the plant's operations from Memorial Day to Labor Day; call (319) 524–6363 for tour information.

Because the lock and dam keep the water open for fishing during the cold months, Keokuk is an important feeding area for bald eagles in winter.

Steamboat Designs

Robert Fulton invented the first commercially successful steamboat in 1807, but Henry Shreve is credited with establishing the basic design that later boats would follow: his boat *Washington* had a shallow draft that could clear snags and sandbars, side paddlewheels, and a "floating wedding cake" design of two decks surmounted by a boxlike pilothouse with chimneys on either side.

Later boats typically were of two general types. Sternwheelers were powered by one paddlewheel at the back of the boat, and sidewheelers had paddlewheels on each side somewhere between midship and the rear. The latter were easier to maneuver, as one wheel could turn forward while the other turned reverse for sharper turns. Sidewheelers were faster and thus preferred by passengers, and sternwheelers were often used to push barges filled with cargo.

Early steamboats were simple, no-frills vessels, but later they became increasingly elaborate, as their owners attempted to lure passengers away from the railroads that were offering faster and more comfortable travel accommodations.

In January the city hosts **Bald Eagle Appreciation Days,** with shuttle-bus service to and from observation areas and seminars, exhibits, and films on the magnificent birds.

Among the many historic structures in Keokuk is the **Samuel F. Miller House and Museum.** Miller was appointed to the Supreme Court by Abraham Lincoln, and his home is now owned and operated by the Lee County Historical Society. The museum (319–524–7283), at 318 North Fifth Street, is open Thursday through Sunday, 1:00 to 4:00 P.M., from Memorial Day to Labor Day.

The Keokuk Convention and Tourism Bureau (800–383–1219), at Fourth and Main streets, offers brochures that will guide you through the city's historic areas. The Lee County Courthouse, St. John's Episcopal Church, and the mansions on Grand Avenue are especially noteworthy.

Overlooking the Mississippi at 816 Grand Avenue, you'll find the **Grand Anne Bed and Breakfast,** a twenty-two-room showplace built in 1897. Owners Bob Diefenbach and Dana McCready moved here from California in 1992 after falling in love with the home's stately grandeur, and they spent seven intensive months restoring its interior. Today the Queen Anne mansion is a cozy B & B that offers three guest rooms furnished with period antiques; freshly baked cookies and apple cider are served at bedtime. Call (319) 524–6310 for information.

Another of the city's historic mansions is the site of a cooking school and gourmet restaurant called **Liz Clark's.** The home, at 116 Concert Street, was built by a lumber magnate in 1847 and was a stop on the Underground Railroad before the Civil War. Liz Clark bought the property in 1971; her seven course meals (reservations only) are exquisitely prepared and served and cost about $25 per person (far less than what you'd pay for a similar meal in any large city). For reservations, call (319) 524–4716.

A fun way to tour the Keokuk area is on the **Trans-Mississippi Trolley,** which operates out of the Keokuk Union Depot, at 200 Water Street. Two 1927-era trolley cars travel along the waterfront, cross the Mississippi, and then wind through the scenic woodland near Hamilton, Illinois. The trolleys operate on weekends through October; departure times are 12:30, 2:00, and 3:30 P.M. Fares are $7.00 for adults and $5.00 for children ages 4 to 18. Call (319) 524–2085 for information.

The trolley's route across the Mississippi is a two-lane, swing-span bridge, which is also a good spot for viewing the river on foot. A marine radio at the end of the deck allows listeners to hear the towboat captains communicating with officials at the locks as the tows ease in and out. Rand Park, which contains the burial site of the famous Sac Chief Keokuk, is another favorite spot for viewing the river.

FOR MORE INFORMATION

Iowa Division of Tourism (515) 242–4705

Iowa Department of Natural Resources (515) 281–5145

McGregor (319) 873–2186

Guttenberg (319) 252–2323

Dubuque (800) 798–8844

Bellevue (319) 872–5830

Clinton (319) 242–5702

Quad Cities (800) 747–7800

Muscatine (800) 25–PEARL

Burlington (800) 82–RIVER

Fort Madison (319) 372–9582

Keokuk (800) 383–1219

THE MIDDLE
CHANNEL

Illinois and Missouri

Illinois

T he Illinois portion of the Great River Road extends for over 500 miles, though only about 50 of them directly border the Mississippi. Much of the river's course through Illinois is through unpopulated, peaceful countryside, past woodlands little changed in the past century, and through some of the nation's most productive farmland. In the north, the beautiful bluffs that have lined much of the upper river are still common, but as the river flows southward the topography changes into expansive lowlands.

The river's long journey through Illinois takes travelers on a trip back in time from the French colonial period of the eighteenth century to the painful divisions of the Civil War. Towns like Galena, Nauvoo, Quincy, and Cairo echo with the ghosts of times past.

EAST DUBUQUE
TO MOLINE

The Mississippi enters Illinois at **East Dubuque,** a little town that clings to the bluffs and spreads along the river flats. Sinsinawa Avenue (also known as Sin Street) is East Dubuque's main street and includes a lively array of honky-tonks and taverns left over from the Prohibition era and the years when neighboring Iowa was dry. Al Capone did business in East Dubuque, and the Mississippi once transported many barrels of bootleg whiskey distilled in the area. Illegal gambling was also commonplace here, and so many people say

71

that the rebirth of riverboat gambling in the area is just a legal version of what has long been a part of East Dubuque's history. Today the *Silver Eagle Casino Cruiser,* which docks on Frentress Lake, just east of town, offers gambling cruises on the river; call (800) 745–8371 for information.

East Dubuque is also home to the **Captain Merry Guest House.** The river once lapped at the front steps of this elegant 1867 Italianate mansion; today, it's contained a block away by a levee. Captain Merry was a steamboat captain with an unsavory history; local lore says that he captured runaway slaves and kidnapped free black men and sold them back down the river. The house was once the site of large Victorian soirées, and Abraham Lincoln is said to have danced in its parlor. Architecturally the house is one of the most interesting in the region, with cavernous underground tunnels, Tuscan marble fireplaces, elaborate plaster ceilings, and a widow's walk on top. Joe and Madi Schlarman saved the grand old mansion from the wrecking ball and have restored the home to its original elegance. Five guest rooms are available; call (815) 747–3644 for reservations.

From East Dubuque take Highway 20 south for 14 miles as it winds through scenic Jo Daviess County, which has been called the New England of the Midwest because of its winding country roads, charming villages, rugged hills, secluded valleys, and magnificent vistas. The county is named after Joseph Hamilton Daviess, a Kentucky politician and folk hero who died in the 1811 Battle of Tippecanoe. Its centerpiece is **Galena,** one of the most picturesque towns along the entire Mississippi.

Galena's history is intimately tied to the lead deposits that were found in its surrounding hills. The region was once one of the richest sources of lead ore in the world. Even before the arrival of white settlers, Sac and Fox Indians mined the deposits, and the French mined lead here throughout the eighteenth century. In 1807 Congress created the Upper Mississippi Lead Mine District, and in the 1830s Galena was the site of the nation's first large mineral rush—two decades prior to California's gold rush. (The word *Galena* itself is Latin for lead.)

The boom made Galena a major commercial center. Fortunes were made not only in mining but also in steamboating, banking, and merchandising. The city reached its zenith in the 1850s, when its population grew to more than 14,000 and Galena became the busiest Mississippi River port between St. Louis and St. Paul. Lovely architectural showplaces were built on Galena's steep hills, and substantial commercial buildings lined its downtown.

Downtown Galena is a time capsule of beautiful nineteenth-century architecture.

The arrival of the railroad in 1854 signaled the beginning of the city's decline, as trains gradually replaced steamboats and the Galena River silted in from soil erosion caused by mining and farming. During the Civil War Galena hoped for better times, due to wartime demands for lead and because of its status as the hometown of General Ulysses S. Grant. The town never regained its antebellum prosperity, however, and its population dwindled as the steamboats stopped running and lead was no longer in demand.

The decline was actually a blessing in disguise because economic stagnation prevented Galena's magnificent architecture from being razed or modernized. In the 1960s the town was rediscovered by a new generation of people eager to restore its old buildings, fueling a renaissance that has continued to grow. In particular, Galena has attracted many artists who now live and work in the area.

Today Galena manages to combine small town friendliness with a cultured sophistication; it's known for its many antiques stores, specialty shops, and art galleries. A sense of history is omnipresent here as well. More than 85 percent of the town's buildings are listed on the National Register and include impressively restored examples of the Federal, Greek Revival, Italianate, Gothic Revival, Second Empire, and Queen Anne styles. The entire downtown is annexed as a historic district and is under strict signage, construction, renovation, and design regulations.

Galena's ties to the Civil War era are especially strong. The town has the honor of claiming an incredible nine Civil War generals as former residents. By far the most famous was Ulysses S. Grant, whose home can be toured at 500 Bouthillier Street. **The Ulysses S. Grant Home State Historic Site** contains the structure's original furnishings with items belonging to the Grant family. The decor has been restored to resemble engravings from the 1868 presidential campaign. The home is open 9:00 A.M. to 5:00 P.M. daily, April through December, and Thursday through Monday, January through March. Phone (815) 777–0248 or 777–3310 for information.

The **Galena–Jo Daviess County History Museum** is a good spot to learn more about the area. Housed in an 1858 Italianate mansion at 211 South Bench Street, the museum includes exhibits on the Civil War, the city's mining and steamboat history, and the geology of Jo Daviess County. A highlight of its collection is the original of Thomas Nast's painting *Peace in Union,* which depicts Lee's surrender to Grant. There's also an audiovisual show of Galena history. The museum (815–777–9129) is open daily from 9:00 A.M. to 4:30 P.M.

The **Old Market House State Historic Site** is a Greek Revival structure built between 1845 and 1846 that was the hub of community life during Galena's most prosperous era. Today it houses historical and architectural exhibits and features a short audiovisual architectural show every thirty minutes. During the summer and fall, it's also the site of an open-air farmer's market each Saturday morning. The Old Market House is located one block off Main Street at 423 North Commerce Street and is open daily from April through December and Thursday through Monday from January through March. Call (815) 777–2570 or 777–3310 for information.

The **Old General Store Museum** re-creates a nineteenth-century general store, complete with cracker barrel, potbellied stove, and backroom

Grant in Galena

While Galena rightly takes great pride in its most famous former citizen, Ulysses S. Grant was far from a leading citizen during his early years in the city. After failing to make a living elsewhere at several occupations, he came to the area with his family in 1860 and went to work as a clerk in his father's leather goods store.

Grant had lived in Galena for less than a year when Fort Sumter fell. As a former army officer, he helped muster the local regiment and led the men to Springfield, where he was appointed quartermaster for the Illinois troops. From there he rose through the ranks and eventually led the Union Army to victory. (His supporters said his initials stood for "Unconditional Surrender.") In 1865 he returned to Galena in triumph, and grateful Galena citizens presented Grant and his family with a two-story Italianate brick house on a hilltop on the town's east side.

The Grants, however, spent little time in their new home. After being elected to the presidency in 1868, Grant made Washington, D.C., his home, and after his second term, he eventually settled in New York. The house stayed in the Grant family until 1904, when the late president's children gave it back to the city of Galena.

bar. It represents the lifetime collection of local resident Marie Duerrstein, who left it to the Illinois Historic Preservation Agency when she died. Much of the collection came from the attics of downtown shops. Before the construction of Galena's flood wall in 1951, its main street was often flooded. Merchants would haul merchandise up to the top floors of buildings, and some of the goods never came back down. When people began restoring the buildings in the 1960s and 1970s, they found the old treasures and gave them to Marie. The museum (815–777–9129) is at 223 South Main Street. It is open 10:00 A.M. to 4:00 P.M. daily from June through October and on weekends in November and December.

The **Vinegar Hill Historic Lead Mine and Museum** will give you an introduction to the difficult conditions endured by the region's early miners. The mine is owned by the Furlong family, who are descendants of the Irish-born miner who originally prospected the claim in 1822. The tour begins in a mining shed and then proceeds into the mine itself, which includes an underground lake. Hard hats are provided; be prepared to walk stooped over for much of the tour. The mine is at 8885 North Three Pines Road, 6 miles north of Galena on Highway 84, and is open 9:00 A.M. to 5:00 P.M. daily from June through August and on weekends in May, September, and October. Call (815) 777–0855 for information.

Also open for tours is the **Belvedere Mansion and Gardens** at 1008 Park Avenue. The Belvedere is one of the most imposing structures in Galena, an Italianate, twenty-two-room mansion built in 1857 for J. Russel Jones, steamboat magnate and ambassador to Belgium. It's furnished with an eclectic mixture of Victorian pieces, items purchased by its owners from Liberace's estate, and several props used in *Gone With the Wind,* including the famous green drapes that Scarlett turned into a dress.

For $5.00 you can combine your tour of the Belvedere with a visit to the **Dowling House,** at 220 Diagonal Street, at the north end of the downtown. Built of native limestone in 1826, it is Galena's oldest home still in existence and once housed a general store on its first floor and living quar-

The Italianate Belvedere Mansion was built in 1857 by steamboat magnate J. Russel Jones.

ters on the second. Faithfully restored, it gives a sense of life during Galena's earliest years as a rough mining boomtown. Both homes are open daily, Memorial Day through December, and on weekends, January through April. For information call the Belvedere at (815) 777–0747 and the Dowling House at (815) 777–1250.

While you're downtown, don't miss the **Toy Soldier Collection,** at 302 Main Street. The store is owned by W. Paul LeGreco, who dresses as General Grant and is happy to pose for a picture. He also casts, paints, and sells toy soldiers from ancient times to Desert Storm and willingly chats about the famous Civil War general.

The **DeSoto House Hotel** (800–343–6562), at 230 South Main Street, is another downtown landmark. Built in 1855, the brick structure underwent an $8-million restoration in the mid-1980s and offers fifty-five rooms furnished with period reproductions (plus such modern amenities as TVs and phones). It also houses an atrium restaurant called The Courtyard and a dinner establishment called The Generals' Dining Rooms. Prices are moderate to expensive.

Other lodgings with a Victorian flair can be found in the nearly sixty bed and breakfasts that operate in Jo Daviess County. **Renaissance Riverboat Suites and Rooms** is one of the finest. Former mayor Terry Cole and his wife, Victoria, bought a historic brick commercial building one block from the Galena River and converted it into luxurious guest accommodations. Each suite is named after a famous riverboat from Galena's history and most have double whirlpools, fireplaces, and stained glass windows. In the back there's a year-round hot tub tucked into a cavern in the rock bluff. Call (815) 777–0123 for reservations.

Rates at Galena bed and breakfasts are generally lower in the off-season of November through March and on Sunday through Thursday nights. A two-night minimum stay is usually required on weekends. Call (800) 747–9377 for more suggestions for lodgings and other information on Galena and Jo Daviess County.

From Galena head south on Highways 20 and 84 for 30 miles to **Savanna.** Just north of town is the **Mississippi Palisades State Park,** where magnificent views of the river can be seen from atop limestone bluffs. The park's 2,550 acres contain some of the loveliest countryside along the Upper Mississippi, with sheer cliffs, deep ravines, and excellent hiking.

Savanna is a quiet river town that draws its name from the plains extending southward from here. The **Pulford Opera House Antique Mall**

(815–273–2661), at 330 Main Street, is a turn-of-the-century structure that houses over a hundred antiques dealers as well as an 1880s-era saloon.

The town is the northern end of a 90-mile hiking and biking trail called the **Great River Trail,** which will one day stretch to Rock Island, Illinois. Although portions of the trail are still under development, much of the section from Savanna south to Thomson is already in place and provides a lovely way to see the river. For a brochure describing the route, call the Quad Cities Convention and Visitors Bureau at (800) 747–7800.

You can get more information about the area at the **Savanna Train Car Museum,** a 1940s-era Hiawatha passenger train car on South Main Street that houses displays of railroad memorabilia as well as the town's chamber of commerce. The museum (815–273–2722) is open Monday through Friday, 9:00 A.M. to 3:30 P.M.

From Savanna continue south on Highway 84 for 9 miles to Thomson, home to the **Thomson Burlington Depot Museum** (815–259–2155), located just off Route 84. The depot was built in the late 1800s and contains railroad history exhibits and memorabilia. It's open on weekends from Memorial Day through October 1, from 1:00 to 4:00 P.M.

From Thomson continue south on Highway 84 for 8 miles to **Fulton,** a town named after Robert Fulton, the inventor of the steamboat. Lock and Dam Number 13 is located just north of the city and marks the beginning of one of the river's widest areas, nearly 4 miles across. Don't miss **Heritage Canyon** when you're in the Fulton area. Located in an old stone quarry surrounded by twelve wooded acres, the site features a re-created pioneer village with a swinging bridge, 1860 home, church, schoolhouse, blacksmith shop, doctor's office, and log cabins. The complex has been developed by Harold and Thelma Wierenga over several decades and is located at 515 North Fourth Street. Heritage Canyon (815–589–2838) is open daily from April 1 through December 15 from 8:00 A.M. to 5:00 P.M.

Next continue south on Highway 84 for 7 miles to Albany, where you'll find the **Albany Mounds State Historic Site** on South Cherry Street. The mounds date back to 2000 B.C. and were made by Hopewell Indians who lived here along the banks of the Mississippi. There are trails to the mounds, and the site (309–887–4335) is open daily from sunrise to sunset.

History from more recent days is commemorated at the **Tri-Township Heritage Museum,** on Lime Street. Local history exhibits and antiques are found within. The museum (309–887–4085) is open on Saturday mornings from Memorial Day through Labor Day.

From Albany continue south on Highway 84 for 15 miles to **Port Byron,** named after the poet Lord Byron. The town was founded in 1828 by Archie Allen, who operated a ferry across the river. One of the town's early mansions, at 502 North High Street, now operates as a bed-and-breakfast called **The Olde Brick House.** Built in the 1850s, the Greek Revival mansion overlooking the Mississippi once served as a summer home to Cyrus McCormick, the founder of the International Harvester Company. A station on the Underground Railroad during the Civil War, the fourteen-room home is now owned by Fred and LaVerne Waldbusser, who have beautifully restored its nineteenth-century charm. Four guest rooms are available; call (309) 523–3236 for information.

Each August, Port Byron and its sister town of LeClaire, on the Iowa shore, participate in the **Great River Tug Fest.** A 2,400-foot rope is stretched across the river, and teams vie to see who has the strength to pull the other into the water. Fireworks, music, food, and arts and crafts are also part of the occasion. Call (309) 523–3312 for information.

From Port Byron continue south on Highway 84 for 5 miles to **Hampton. Black's Store** is an 1849 general store that houses the Hampton Historical Society, which has displays on the early settlement of the area. The store was once a busy trading post and provided fuel for firing steamboat boilers as well as goods for local farmers. It's located at 601 First Avenue and is open from 2:00 to 4:00 P.M. on summer weekends. Phone (309) 755–0362 for information.

MOLINE TO NAUVOO

From Hampton continue south on Highway 84 for a mile to the **Quad Cities,** which include Moline and Rock Island in Illinois and Davenport and Bettendorf in Iowa. The area is one of the Mississippi's major tourism, commercial, and manufacturing centers with a rich history that lives on in many attractions. (For a complete introduction to the Quad Cities, see the sections on Davenport and Bettendorf beginning on page 55.)

Riverboat gambling is a major draw in the Quad Cities, with two boats offering passengers the chance to try their luck: the *President Riverboat Casino* (800–BOAT–711) and *Jumer's Casino Rock Island* (800–477–7747). The **Celebration Cruise Line** offers a variety of nongaming sightseeing cruises and also operates a trolley tour of Arsenal Island, which lies between the cities. Call (800) 227–9967 for information.

Riverboat Gambling

While a nineteenth-century riverboat gambler would undoubtedly be amazed at a modern casino boat, there is indeed a long tradition of gaming on the Mississippi. Even before the steamboat era, gambling was a common pastime on the keelboats that hauled cargo up and down the Mississippi and its tributaries. The lives of the deckhands were hard, their pleasures were few, and gambling was a popular way to pass the time on long journeys. When the boats were docked, the gambling continued in gaming houses and taverns that catered to the rowdy river men.

On steamboats gambling was also common. Though steamboat authorities discouraged the practice, most boat owners turned a blind eye to the games of poker, whist, brag, and euchre played by passengers. Professional gamblers and shysters also frequented the riverboats and often found easy marks among their fellow travelers. Those who were caught cheating, however, faced an unpleasant punishment: steamboat captains would strip them of their winnings and leave them stranded on the nearest sandbar.

The **Great River Trail** that begins in Savanna continues through Moline and Rock Island, providing a scenic route for hikers and bikers. As you enter Moline from the north, you'll pass the portion of the trail known as the Ben Butterworth Memorial Parkway. For a brochure describing the entire route system, call the Quad Cities Convention and Visitors Bureau at (800) 747–7800.

You can learn more about the history of the Quad Cities at the **Rock Island County Historical Society,** at 822 Eleventh Avenue. This 1877 mansion houses museum exhibits and includes a carriage house and historical library. Its hours are Thursday through Monday, 9:00 A.M. to 5:00 P.M., and Sunday, 1:30 to 4:30 P.M. Phone (309) 764–4673 for information.

Moline has many stately homes built during the city's nineteenth-century boom years. Among them is the **Deere–Wiman House,** built in the 1870s by Charles Deere, who headed the famous John Deere tractor and implement manufacturing company, founded by his father. The house, at

817 Eleventh Avenue, is open for tours and includes such amenities as an Art Deco enclosed swimming pool, underground tunnels connecting various outbuildings, and a series of formal gardens. Call (309) 765–7961 for hours and information.

Across the street is another home of equally grandiose proportions, a mansion known as the **Butterworth Center.** It was built in 1892 as a wedding gift from Charles Deere to his daughter Katherine and her new husband, William Butterworth. Its interior features an organ that can still fill the bilevel living room with music, a library decorated in Italian Renaissance style, a greenhouse, and formal gardens. For hours and information, call the Deere–Wiman House at (309) 765–7961.

The **Hauberg Indian Museum** provides fascinating insights into the Native American history of the area. Founded in 1939 by Dr. John Hauberg, the museum celebrates the culture of the region's first inhabitants. On display are full-sized models of Sauk and Mesquakie dwellings, dioramas showing daily activities of the tribes, and many artifacts from the period 1750 to 1800. The museum is part of the **Black Hawk State Historic Site,** which is located near what was once the capital of the Sauk nation. The westernmost battle of the American Revolution was fought here; colonists destroyed a portion of the village in retribution for the Sauks' military assistance to the British. The site is named after the warrior who led the Indians in the Black Hawk War of 1832 and includes 205 acres of rolling woodlands with over 4 miles of hiking trails. The museum (309–788–9536) is at 1510 Forty-sixth Avenue (Blackhawk Road), in Rock Island, and is open daily from March through November.

The **Center for Belgian Culture,** at 712 Eighteenth Avenue in Moline, celebrates the ethnic heritage of the Belgian immigrants who founded the city with an Old World lace exhibit and displays of pioneer memorabilia. The center (309–762–0167) is open 1:00 to 4:00 P.M. on Wednesday and Saturday.

From the Quad Cities head west on Highway 92 for 25 miles and then south for 15 miles to **New Boston.** The Sauk and Mesquakie Indians called this region of the Mississippi "Yellow Banks," after its yellow, sandy soil. Abraham Lincoln entered military service in this area as a captain in the Black Hawk War of 1832, which drove the Indians farther westward and opened up the region for white settlement. Early settler Levi W. Meyers wrote that "the country was so rich and beautiful, it was so near an earthly paradise that it would seem as if every settler would have chosen it as his permanent home."

Though the area's early river settlements did indeed thrive as steamboat ports, today they are quiet villages. New Boston was first surveyed in 1834 by Abraham Lincoln and was established as a town that same year. It has a number of historic buildings, including the 1856 Levi Willits home that's now the **New Boston Museum.** Located one block from the river at the corner of Second and Main streets, the museum houses displays of local history. It's open Saturday from 9:00 A.M. to 5:00 P.M. and Sunday from 1:00 to 5:00 P.M., April through November. Phone (309) 587–8643 or 587–8217 for information.

Next continue south for 8 miles to **Keithsburg.** In 1986 its commercial district, with over a dozen significant structures, was put on the National Register of Historic Places. The **Sharon L. Reason–Keithsburg Museum** (309–374–2659), at Fourteenth and Washington streets, contains information on local and river history plus a room dedicated to those who served in the military. It's open from 1:00 to 5:00 P.M., Wednesday through Sunday, from April through November.

From Keithsburg drive south for 12 miles through the 3,000-acre Big River State Forest to **Oquawka,** named after the Indian word for "yellow banks." The town is the county seat of rural Henderson County and is home to one of the oddest landmarks along the river road: the **Grave of Norma Jean the Elephant,** on Fifth Street, between Clay and Mercer. During a terrible thunderstorm on July 17, 1972, a lightning bolt struck the tree where Norma Jean was chained. The elephant, who was in town with a traveling circus, was killed instantly. Norma Jean was buried on the spot, all 6,500 pounds of her, and her grave is marked with a large boulder.

The Henderson County Courthouse is also worth noting. Built in 1842, the brick structure is the second oldest courthouse in Illinois and is still in use today. You'll find it at the corner of Fourth and Warren streets.

Three miles south of Oquawka on Highway 164 is the **Henderson Covered Bridge,** which was erected in 1866 and is one of the few remaining covered bridges in the state. During a flood of Henderson Creek in 1982 the bridge was washed away, but it has been completely restored and rebuilt on its original site. Cars are prohibited, but foot traffic is welcome.

Continue south on Highways 164, 34, and 96 for 45 miles to **Nauvoo,** one of the best preserved and most historically significant settlements along the Mississippi. During the 1840s Nauvoo was the site of a Mormon settlement led by Joseph Smith and was the second largest city in Illinois. After Smith's murder in 1844 and the Mormon exodus that followed, French Icarians came to Nauvoo and established a short-lived experiment in communal living from 1849 to 1856. Though later settlers made their home here, the quiet town never regained its former prominence and remains today a kind of nineteenth-century time capsule.

In the 1950s the Mormon descendants of the town's original residents returned to Nauvoo and undertook a mammoth restoration project. Today the Mormon village lives again, with over two dozen buildings open to visitors. Old-time crafts are demonstrated by skilled artisans and costumed interpreters bring the daily routines of the early settlers to life. Among the buildings lining the village's quiet streets are homes once occupied by Joseph Smith and Brigham Young, a blacksmith shop, log cabin schoolhouse, bakery, cultural hall, and newspaper office. The **Joseph Smith Historic Center,** near the riverfront, offers walking tours of the Smith Homestead, Grave

The Mormons at Nauvoo

The Mormons came to Nauvoo in 1839 seeking a place where they could live in peace, far from the intolerance and persecution they had endured in other settlements. Their charismatic prophet and leader, Joseph Smith, named this scenic bend in the Mississippi *Nauvoo,* which means "beautiful place" in Hebrew. During the 1840s the community flourished and became the tenth largest city in the nation, with a charter from the state legislature that made Nauvoo virtually an autonomous state.

The Mormons did not find the peace that they sought, however. Internal divisions appeared within the community, and a rising tide of political and social antagonism from the surrounding settlers erupted in violence in 1844, when a mob attacked and killed Joseph Smith and his brother Hyrum in nearby Carthage. The Mormon community scattered, with the largest contingent traveling west to Utah under the leadership of Brigham Young. Another group followed Joseph Smith III, who became leader of a separate Mormon denomination called the Reorganized Church of Jesus Christ of Latter-Day Saints, whose headquarters are now in Independence, Missouri. Nauvoo, once a bustling city, became a ghost town.

Site, and Mansion House. The **Latter-Day Saints Visitors Center,** on the north side of the village, gives further information about the Mormon settlement. Both centers are open daily, year-round.

Old Nauvoo celebrates its heritage each summer with the **City of Joseph Outdoor Musical.** Its story is based on journals kept by the original settlers and includes sixteen original musical numbers. A cast of more than 300 fills the five-level outdoor stage; the pageant is held in late July and early August, and admission is free.

Another part of Nauvoo's heritage is celebrated during the **Nauvoo Grape Festival,** held on Labor Day weekend. After the flight of the Mormons, a wave of French, German, and Swiss immigrants began a wine industry in Nauvoo, which continues to this day. A highlight of the annual festival is the Wedding of Wine and Cheese, a centuries-old custom borrowed from Roquefort, France. In addition to regional wine, it features the delicious, locally made Nauvoo blue cheese. Other activities include a buckskinner rendezvous, flea market, arts and crafts show, grape stomp, and live entertainment.

At any time of the year, you can visit **Baxter's Vineyards,** at 2010 East Parley Street. Established in 1857, Baxter's is Illinois' oldest winery and is open daily for tours and wine samples. For information call (217) 453–2528.

In the present-day town of Nauvoo, which is located on a hill above the original settlement, you can browse through antiques, crafts, and specialty shops. Also take note of the site of the **Nauvoo Temple,** which was once one of the largest structures in the Midwest. The building was damaged by a fire in 1848 and destroyed by a tornado three years later.

For overnight accommodations, try **Hotel Nauvoo,** an 1840 inn at 1290 Mulholland Street that also offers dining (217–453–2211).

HAMILTON TO ALTON

From Nauvoo follow Highway 96 south for 11 miles to Hamilton. There a spur on the river road passes through **Warsaw,** a pleasant little river town with many buildings listed on the National Register of Historic Places. During the early 1800s two forts were built here on the Mississippi bluffs. Fort Johnson was constructed in 1814 under the command of Major Zachary Taylor, who later became president of the United States. After the fort was abandoned for several years, a new post named Fort Edwards was built on the same site to protect the movement of supplies on the Mississippi. The fort was later taken over by the American Fur Company and became a central trading post for exchanges with the Sauk and Mesquakie Indians. In 1914 a monument was erected on the bluff where the forts had once stood.

From Warsaw return to Highway 96 and continue south for 35 miles to the historic river city of **Quincy.** Founded in 1818, the town was christened Quincy in 1825 in honor of newly elected President John Quincy Adams. Its abundant timber, fertile soil, plentiful game, and prime location on the Mississippi all contributed to its rapid growth. Sawmills flourished as the rich surrounding forests were cleared for farming, and flour mills and meat-packing plants shipped their products from the growing riverfront. By the 1850s Quincy had become Illinois' third largest city. During the steamboat era as many as 2,500 ships a year passed through the Quincy harbor, which is the largest natural harbor on the Mississippi.

Quincy's location across the river from the slave state of Missouri made the city a hotbed of controversy during the years leading up to the Civil War. In 1858 the town was the site of one of the famous debates between U.S. Senator Stephen Douglas and his challenger, Abraham Lincoln. The first antislavery society in Illinois was founded here, and Quincy was an important stop on the Underground Railroad.

The city still retains much of the flavor of a nineteenth-century river town and boasts the state's largest variety of significant architecture outside of Chicago. Its centerpiece is the seven-square-block downtown historic district, which includes Washington Park, the city's original central square, laid out in 1825. The park is home to a sculpture by Lorado Taft commemorating the Lincoln–Douglas debate that took place here, and long rows of Victorian storefronts line the square and extend five blocks to the east.

A good place to begin your tour is at the **Villa Kathrine,** a wonderfully odd mansion that houses Quincy's Tourist Information Center. Located on a bluff overlooking the river, the Moorish-style villa, built in 1900, is one of the few examples of Mediterranean architecture on the Mississippi. The home was built by the wealthy and eccentric George Metz, who based its design on his sketches and photos of villas in North Africa. After many years of neglect, the villa is gradually being restored. You'll find the Villa Kathrine (217–224–3688) on the river road at 532 Gardner Expressway. It is open 9:00 A.M. to 5:00 P.M., Monday through Saturday, and 1:00 to 5:00 P.M. on Sunday.

Another Quincy landmark is the **Governor John Wood Mansion,** at 425 South Twelfth Street. The fourteen-room structure is the restored home of John Wood, Quincy's founder and one of Illinois' first governors. An outstanding example of Greek Revival architecture, the mansion was built between 1835 and 1838. The adjacent visitors center is home to the Historical Society of Quincy and Adams County and houses a library containing early manuscripts and documents. The mansion (217–222–1835) is open 1:00 to 4:00 P.M. on Saturday and Sunday, year-round, with additional weekday hours during the summer.

The **Gardner Museum of Architecture and Design** celebrates Quincy's outstanding architectural heritage and is the nation's only community-based architectural museum. Housed in Quincy's Old Public Library, an 1889 Richardsonian Romanesque landmark, the museum shows how the history of Quincy is revealed through its architecture. During the summer "Quincy Characters," dressed in period costume, are on hand to explain the exhibits. The museum (217–224–6873) is located at Fourth and Maine streets and is open 1:00 to 5:00 P.M., Tuesday through Sunday.

The **Quincy Museum of Natural History and Art** is housed in one of the city's most impressive Victorian homes, the 1891 Newcomb–Stillwell mansion, at 1601 Maine Street. Its first floor has been restored to the style of the 1890s, and its second and third floors display exhibits on Native American and natural history. The museum (217–224–7669) is open Tuesday through Sunday, from 1:00 to 5:00 P.M.

More Victorian-era history is on display at the **Pharmacy Museum,** at Fifth and Chestnut streets. The building was home to the Heidbreder Hagemann Drug Store for nearly eighty years and retains its original tin ceilings, oak showcases, and a large collection of apothecary artifacts. The museum (217–224–1000) is open 1:00 P.M. to 4:00 P.M., Saturday and Sunday, from May through September.

Quincy's **All Wars Museum** is appropriately located on the grounds of one of the nation's largest and oldest veterans homes, the Illinois Veterans Home, at 1707 North Twelfth Street. The museum (217–222–8641) has exhibits on military history from the American Revolution to Desert Storm. It's open 1:00 to 4:00 P.M., Monday through Friday, and 9:00 A.M. to 11:00 A.M. on Saturday and Sunday.

The **Lincoln–Douglas Valentine Museum,** at 101 North Fourth Street, is located in the restored Lincoln–Douglas Building (named for the famous debate held across the street in Washington Park). The museum features a large collection of antique and unusual valentines, including boxes manufactured at Quincy Paper Box, which was once one of the country's most prominent makers of valentine heart candy boxes. The museum is open daily from 9:00 A.M. to 9:00 P.M. by appointment; call (217) 224–3355 or 224–5767 to schedule a tour.

For overnight accommodations in Quincy, try the **Bueltmann Gasthaus,** a bed-and-breakfast in the East End historic district. The B & B is housed in an 1880s mansion originally built in Queen Anne style, though later renovations added an overlay of English Tudor Revival. Owners Charlotte and David Bueltmann offer four guest rooms furnished with period antiques; call (217) 224–8428 for information.

From Quincy take Highways 57 and 96 south for 65 miles through rural countryside to **Kampsville,** where you'll continue south on Highway 100 for 20 miles to the 8,000-acre **Pere Marquette State Park,** the largest state park in Illinois. The park is named after Father Jacques Marquette, the French Jesuit missionary priest who, along with the explorer Louis Joliet, first explored the area in 1673. The centerpiece of the park is a recently refurbished, massive stone-and-timber lodge built in the 1930s by the Civilian Conservation Corps. Call (618) 786–3323 for information.

Continue on Highway 100 for 5 miles to the town of **Grafton,** a pretty little river town that suffered considerable damage during the 1993 flood. A number of its antiques stores, specialty shops, and restaurants remain closed as a result, but the town is rebounding and many businesses will likely reopen.

From Grafton the river road becomes a four-lane highway that hugs the bank between the Mississippi and beautiful 400-foot bluffs. The route is one of the most scenic along the river and includes a separate bike and walking path. Just a few miles down the road from Grafton, you'll find lovely **Elsah,** a little village of fewer than 200 people that is one of the most picturesque towns on the Great River Road. Elsah is a former steamboat port that got bypassed by the modern world until just a few decades ago, and was the first village to be placed in its entirety on the National Register. Tucked into a valley between the river bluffs, Elsah has the feel of a New England village.

The **Elsah Museum,** on Mill Street, has displays on the town's early days as a steamboat port. The museum is open Thursday through Sunday from 1:00 to 4:00 P.M., April through October. The major commercial establishment in the village is **Elsah Landing,** a restaurant and bakery housed in an 1880s–era building at 18 LaSalle Street. For over twenty years the restaurant has prepared all of its soups, breads, and desserts from scratch daily, using fresh local ingredients whenever possible. The recipient of many awards, Elsah Landing has also produced three cookbooks. After a long day

The Great Flood of 1993

As early as 1796, the French historian Constantin Volney observed that "this great, this magnificent Mississippi . . . is a very bad neighbor." Those who lived through the flood of 1993 would undoubtedly agree. The flood was the most destructive in the river's recorded history, killing 50 people, devastating 55,000 homes, and costing over $15 billion in destroyed property and crops.

The flood began slowly. The Mississippi normally rises as the spring thaw sends millions of gallons of snowmelt down the river. But the spring and summer also brought an unusual weather pattern: The jetstream that brings cold air from the Arctic traveled much farther south than was usual and remained stationary over the Midwest. When hot, humid air from the southeast met the cold air from the far north, endless rain was the result. From June through August, the record water levels topped levees up and down the river, flooding towns, cities, farmsteads, and thousands of acres of the world's most productive cropland. Sandbag operations helped save many areas, but in other places the river was an inexorable force.

By September, the river had receded below flood stage, and the long and backbreaking cleanup began in earnest. Once again, the mighty Mississippi had proven its awesome power.

of touring, the restaurant's homey, old-fashioned dining rooms offer a wonderful place to unwind. Elsah Landing (618–374–1607) is open 11:30 A.M. to 7:30 P.M., Tuesday through Sunday. Prices are inexpensive.

For overnight accommodations overlooking the river, try the **Corner Nest Bed and Breakfast,** at 3 Elm Street. The 1883, Franco-American home offers four inviting guest rooms furnished with a mixture of period antiques and modern conveniences. Guests are also welcome to use a cozy screened porch with wicker furniture. Although their home was damaged by the flood, owners Judy and Bob Doerr look on the bright side, saying that it gave them the chance to completely refurbish the first floor of their house. You'd never guess that their beautiful home had suffered any damage. Call (618) 374–1892 for information. Also in Elsah are the **Maple Leaf Cottage Inn** (618–374–1684), which offers accommodations in charming cottages surrounded by gardens, and the **Green Tree Inn** (618–374–2821), a modern building with nine guest rooms designed in the style of an 1850s inn.

From Elsah continue on Highway 100 for 5 miles to **Alton.** On a bluff north of town you'll see the **Piasa Bird,** a reproduction of a prehistoric painting described by the explorers Marquette and Joliet in 1673. Just below the mouth of the Illinois River, they reported seeing the images of two large monsters painted on a bluff. According to Marquette's diary, "each was as large as a calf with horns like a deer, red eyes, a beard like a tiger's, a face like a man, the body covered with green, red and black scales, and a tail so long that it passed around the body, over the head and between the legs, ending like a fish's tail." The Illini Indians called the birds *piasa,* and according to legend the fearsome creatures devoured human flesh. The original pictograph was destroyed by quarry activity in 1870, but this reproduction continues to bid a unique welcome to travelers along the river road.

The city of Alton dates back to 1818, when land speculator Colonel Rufus Easton plotted its streets and named the new settlement after his oldest son. The town thrived with the blossoming of the steamboat era, and during the Civil War was a main supply point for the Union armies and a key stop on the Underground Railroad.

On your way into Alton you'll pass a monument relating to the town's Civil War history. In the early 1800s, Alton became the site of the first Illinois State Penitentiary, which was later targeted by the reformer Dorothea Dix as being particularly inhumane, even by the standards of the day. By 1860 all of its prisoners had been transferred elsewhere, but the facility was soon occupied again by thousands of Confederate prisoners, who during 1862 and 1863 suffered a terrible smallpox epidemic. Near the corner of Broadway and Williams streets, you'll find the **Civil War Prison Monument,** a neatly stacked pile of limestone rock that is all that remains of the infamous prison.

Today downtown Alton retains a nineteenth-century river town flavor with the modern addition of a large riverboat gambling complex along its waterfront. The *Alton Belle Casino* offers a variety of cruises each day; call (800) 336–7568 for information. The adjoining **Alton antiques district** has more than 60 shops, which make this a center for the antiques trade in the Midwest.

Each June the riverfront area hosts the **Alton Landing River Festival,** which celebrates the city's river history with arts and crafts, food and entertainment. Call (800) 258–6645 for information. Another downtown attraction is the **Alton Museum of History and Art,** which contains exhibits on the town's Civil War history and the steamboat era. The museum (618–462–2763) is housed in an 1850 structure at 121 East Broadway Street and is open 1:00 to 4:00 P.M., Thursday through Sunday.

Another piece of Alton history is marked by the **Lincoln–Douglas Square,** at Broadway and Market streets. Abraham Lincoln and Stephen Douglas held their seventh and last senate debate here in 1858. The *Alton Daily Courier* reported that Mr. Douglas was "thrashed out" by Mr. Lincoln, and though Lincoln lost the senate race, he became known throughout America by the media who covered the debates, and he went on to win the presidential election two years later.

More Civil War–era history is commemorated by the **Lovejoy Monument** in the Alton City Cemetery, at 1205 East Fifth Street. The abolitionist Reverend Elijah P. Lovejoy was shot by a proslavery mob in Alton in 1837 as he and his defenders guarded his printing press. Lovejoy became a national martyr for both the abolitionist and free press movements, and the monument was dedicated to him in 1897.

From Alton continue south on Highway 3 through the adjoining cities of Wood River and Hartford. Just south of Hartford is the **Lewis and Clark State Historic Site,** a monument that marks the point from which Lewis and Clark set off on their epic journey to explore the West in 1804. Their expedition built its first camp here at the mouth of Wood River Creek and spent the winter of 1803–4 preparing for the trip west. The monument also overlooks the confluence of the Mississippi and Missouri rivers.

COLLINSVILLE TO CAIRO

From Hartford continue on Highway 3 as it enters the greater St. Louis metropolitan area. The river road travels along a number of different highways through this area, but the route is clearly marked with signs bearing the familiar green pilot's wheel.

West of **Collinsville,** don't miss the **Cahokia Mounds World Heritage Site.** The site includes the remains of the most sophisticated prehistoric Indian civilization north of Mexico and is one of the most impressive and fascinating stops along the river. From about A.D. 700 to A.D. 1500, a city of 20,000 people flourished here on the fertile banks of the Mississippi—a settlement larger than that of London at that time. Its people built over one hundred massive earthen mounds, of which about sixty are preserved within the site's 2,200 acres. The largest, Monk's Mound, covers over fourteen acres and rises in four terraces to a height of 100 feet, making it the largest prehistoric earthen construction in the New World. About 1300 the city's population began to decline for reasons not well understood, and by 1500 Native Americans abandoned the settlement, leaving the mounds as an enigma to be discovered by the European settlers who came to the region.

Today the site includes a superb visitors center that brings the culture of this civilization to life. Included is a walk-through model of a "neighborhood" of the city that once stood here. Visitors are also welcome to climb to the summit of Monk's Mound. The center (618–346–5160) is open 9:00 A.M. to 5:00 P.M. daily and is located at exit 24 off Interstate 255.

From Cahokia Mounds return to Interstate 255 and travel south to the Highway 157 exit, which will take you to the town of **Cahokia.** Cahokia

Mississippian Mounds

Cahokia Mounds is one of many sites along the Mississippi once inhabited by a vanished group of Native Americans that archeologists have named the Mississippian Indians. Beginning about A.D. 800 these Indians founded settlements along the great rivers of the eastern United States. The soils along the river bottoms were rich and easily farmed, and the Mississippian Indians came to rely on domesticated crops for their food supplies, particularly maize, beans, and squash.

Most of the Mississippian settlements were built around a central ceremonial plaza, which included one or more large earthen mounds topped by a chief's house or temple. Many of the mounds were constructed in stages over a period of many years and were the products of an artistically sophisticated and highly organized culture. The Mississippians were part of a trade network that stretched across the continent. Some of their settlements, like that at Cahokia, had populations numbering in the thousands.

By A.D. 1500 the Mississippian Indians had deserted the great mound centers of the Mississippi Valley for reasons largely unknown. Today only their mounds remain, mute reminders of the people who flourished along the river many centuries ago.

begins a 50-mile stretch of land known as the **French Colonial District,** a region that was once the heart of France's vast colonial holdings in the middle of the continent.

The **Cahokia Courthouse Historic Site** is a major landmark from those days. Built around 1740, it is an excellent example of a type of early French construction called *poteaux-sur-solle,* meaning "post-on-foundation." Its walls are constructed of upright hewn logs, with stone and mortar chinking in between. Originally built as a private residence, the structure became the county courthouse in 1793, after the region became part of the country's Northwest Territories. For twenty-four years the Cahokia Courthouse was an important political center for a territory that extended to the Canadian border. After recurrent flooding in the area led to the county seat's move to Belleville, the house became, over a period of time, a town hall, storehouse, saloon, and again a home. In 1940 it was finally restored and is now furnished as it was during the days when it was a center for government in the new territory. The courthouse (618–332–1782) is located at 107 Elm Street and is open from 9:00 A.M. to 5:00 P.M., Tuesday through Saturday.

From Cahokia continue south on Highway 3 for 17 miles to **Waterloo,** a town with a strong German ethnic identity and over 200 buildings dating back to the nineteenth century. Among its historic attractions is the **Peterstown House,** at 275 North Main Street. The structure was built in the 1830s as a stagecoach stop on the Kaskasia–Cahokia Trail. Today it's furnished in the style of the mid–1800s and includes displays on local history. Call (618) 458–6422 for information.

From Waterloo you have a choice of two routes south. The more direct route follows Highway 3 for 30 miles to Ellis Grove. The alternative route heads southwest on the Maeystown Road for 8 miles to the quaint village of **Maeystown.** Like Elsah to the north, all of Maeystown has been placed on the National Register of Historic Places. The settlement was founded in 1852 by German immigrants and includes over fifty structures dating back to the 1800s. The 1833 **Corner George Inn** (618–458–6660) at Main and Mill streets offers overnight accommodations in seven guest rooms, and a number of the town's other buildings house antiques and gift shops.

Continue southwest on the Maeystown Road for about a mile and then head south on the Bluff Road for 13 miles to **Prairie du Rocher.** Settled in 1722, the village is the oldest town in southern Illinois, a quiet oasis reflecting the townspeople's great pride in their French heritage. Its historic buildings include the 1863 St. Joseph Church and the **Creole House** on

Market Street, an excellent example of French Colonial architecture, constructed around 1800. The house is open by appointment; call (618) 282–2245 to arrange a tour.

While you're in town, pay a visit to **La Maison du Rocher Country Inn.** The stone structure was built in 1885 as a hotel and has been extensively remodeled into a cozy bed-and-breakfast offering two upstairs bedrooms decorated in French Victorian style. Downstairs is an award-winning restaurant that's open for breakfast, lunch, and dinner (prices are inexpensive to moderate). There's also a small gift shop adjoining the restaurant with visitor information. Owner Jan Kennedy knows everything there is to know about Prairie du Rocher and its history, including the heroic efforts that saved the town from the 1993 flood. For information about the inn and restaurant, call (618) 284–3463.

The French Legacy in Illinois

Shortly after Marquette and Joliet's exploration of the Mississippi River in 1673, the French explorer Sieur de La Salle laid claim to the entire river valley in the name of France. Settlers came to this part of Illinois hoping to grow wealthy off the region's fur trade and the gold and silver they believed lay within the river bluffs. Though those riches proved elusive, the colonists did find wealth of another sort: The fertile bottomlands of the region became the breadbasket that fed the rest of New France.

The French built a series of forts near the Mississippi to protect their interests in the area. The first and second were wooden structures that fell victim to the river's frequent floods, and so in the 1750s a massive stone fortress named Fort de Chartres was constructed near Prairie du Rocher ("prairie by the rock").

Though the region's colonial settlements flourished, France itself became embroiled in a series of wars that eventually resulted in the loss of its North American empire to England. Even after the government changed hands, however, the French settlements retained much of their original culture, traditions, language, and architecture. These remnants of France linger to this day along the Illinois banks of the Mississippi.

From Prairie du Rocher follow the signs to **Fort de Chartres,** an impressive reconstruction of the stone fort that was built here between 1753 and 1756. For more than half a century, the fort was the seat of political and military power for a large portion of the French colonial empire. Its thick walls were constructed of limestone quarried from the bluffs near Prairie du Rocher and laboriously conveyed several miles to the fort's site on the Mississippi. Surrounding the fort was a dry moat, and inside were buildings that included the commandant's house, storehouse, guardhouse, and jail. In 1765 the fort was the last French fortification to be surrendered to the British, who renamed it Fort Cavendish. It was the seat of English government in the area until 1772, when it was partially destroyed by floodwaters and abandoned.

During the next century the remaining walls of the fort were decimated by continued floods and by local citizens scavenging for building materials. (You can see some of the original fort's stone, for example, in the walls at La Maison du Rocher Country Inn.) In 1913 the state of Illinois acquired the property, and later constructed a replica of the fort. Today Fort de Chartres lives again, with tours conducted by interpreters in period attire and frequent living history reenactments. The largest is the **Fort de Chartres Rendezvous,** which is held on the first weekend in June. More than 1,000 participants dressed as fur trappers, Indians, craftsmen, and soldiers bring to life the eighteenth century with military displays, crafts, music, dancing, and food. The site itself is open daily from 9:00 A.M. to 5:00 P.M. Call (618) 284–7230 for information.

From the fort return to Prairie du Rocher and take the Bluff Road south through Modoc and Roots for 12 miles to the town of **Ellis Grove.** There a spur on the river road takes you past more remnants of the French colonial empire, including the **Pierre Menard Home,** which is considered the finest example of French Colonial architecture in the Midwest. The graceful, low-slung house was built about 1800 by the first lieutenant governor of Illinois and depicts the lifestyle of the region's upper-class French-American citizens. The home (618–859–3031) is open daily from 9:00 A.M. to 5:00 P.M.

Above the hill from the Pierre Menard home is the **Fort Kaskaskia State Historic Site,** which offers a beautiful view of the river valley. The fort was built on a high bluff during the French and Indian War to protect the French citizens of the nearby village of Kaskaskia from British attack. In 1766 the townspeople destroyed the fort rather than allow it to be occupied by the British, who had gained control of the entire region. Today only the earthworks that supported the fort's palisades remain.

The town of **Kaskaskia,** which served as the first Illinois capital from 1818 to 1820, suffered a similarly unfortunate fate. Successive spring floods eventually destroyed the original capital, and the river later orphaned the modern town of Kaskaskia, making it the only community in Illinois to lie west of the Mississippi. Mark Twain had a philosophical approach to the river's roving ways: "The Mississippi is a just and equitable river; it never tumbles one man's farm overboard without building a new farm just like it for that man's neighbor. This keeps down hard feelings."

To reach Kaskaskia Island from the Illinois side, travelers must cross the bridge at Chester, Illinois, and then head north for 4 miles past St. Mary, Missouri. The town's major historic site is the **Kaskaskia Bell,** a 650-pound bell cast in France and given by King Louis XV to the village church in 1741. The bell is also called the Liberty Bell of the West, having rung on July 4, 1778, to celebrate the capture of Kaskaskia by Colonel George Rogers Clark. Clark's victory removed the territory from British hands and made it part of the commonwealth of Virginia.

From Fort Kaskaskia return to Highway 3 and head south for 5 miles to **Chester.** The city was founded in 1819 and later became a busy river port and agricultural center. The **Randolph County Museum and Archives,** an 1864 stone structure at 1 Taylor Street, houses local history displays and information on the French colonial period. The museum (618–826–2510) is open daily; call for hours. Next to the museum is the Randolph County Courthouse, which includes a visitors center and observation deck overlooking the river.

From Chester continue south on Highway 3 for 30 miles as it winds through the southern portion of Illinois, past the Shawnee National Forest, which stretches from the Ohio River to the Mississippi. At **Grand Tower,** a short detour off the main highway lets you view the river landmark that gave the town its name, a 60-foot pillar of limestone that juts out of the Mississippi close to the Missouri shore. The swirling waters at its base made this a particularly dangerous stretch of river for steamboats.

South of Grand Tower the road enters a portion of Illinois known as Little Egypt, a designation given by early settlers who compared the region's fertile delta to that of the Nile River. In tiny **Thebes,** 30 miles south of Grand Tower, the Greek Revival **Thebes Courthouse** overlooks the river and recalls a bit of Civil War–era history. The slave Dred Scott is said to have once been imprisoned here while awaiting trial in the famous case that galvanized the abolitionist movement in the 1840s and 1850s. Local lore also says that Abraham Lincoln once practiced law here.

From Thebes continue south on Highway 3 for 23 miles to the last stop on Illinois' portion of the Great River Road, the historic river city of **Cairo** (pronounced CARE-oh). Located where the Ohio River meets the Mississippi, Cairo was one of the nation's most important river ports during the steamboat era. The city played a crucial role during the Civil War, when General Ulysses S. Grant directed the assault on the South from here. After the war the city became a boomtown, with taverns and gaming houses crowding its rowdy riverfront and elegant mansions lining its streets.

Despite its prosperous beginnings, Cairo's glory days were numbered. The decline of river and rail traffic nudged the city into a slow decline, from which it has never fully recovered. But while its downtown has seen better days, the town has a somnolent charm of its own, and a number of structures recall the days when it was one of the most significant ports on the river.

Hell-Roaring Cairo

"Whatever nation gets the control of the Ohio, Mississippi, and Missouri Rivers will control the continent," General William Tecumseh Sherman wrote in 1861. The fortification of Cairo, which sat at the confluence of the Mississippi and Ohio, was a crucial part of the Union's strategy to keep control of the western rivers. At a time when good roads and rail lines were scarce, the Mississippi provided a direct route into the heart of the Confederacy, and Cairo's position made it the natural launching point for the campaigns into the states of Tennessee and Mississippi.

Within two days of Fort Sumter's surrender in April 1861, Union soldiers occupied Cairo just hours ahead of an advancing Confederate force. Fort Defiance was hurriedly constructed over the following months, and in September General Ulysses S. Grant arrived to take command of the soldiers who were pouring into the formerly small town.

Some 200,000 people passed through Cairo during the war years, creating an economic boom that built huge fortunes for many local citizens—and provided plenty of temptations for soldiers. One captain referred to the town as "hell-roaring Cairo," and noted that "the many places of amusement, gambling, and worse kept the Provost Marshall busy and the Guard House full."

Begin your tour at the **Cairo Custom House,** a Romanesque building at Fourteenth Street and Washington Avenue that houses the town's history museum. The structure was built in 1872 after Congress designated Cairo as a port of delivery and once held a post office and federal court in addition to customs offices. Inside the museum are displays relating to Cairo's river history and its role in the Civil War. Its collection includes the desk used by General Ulysses S. Grant during the Union army's stay in Cairo. The museum (618–734–1019) is open from 10:00 A.M. to 3:00 P.M., Monday through Friday.

Across the street from the Custom House is the stately **Cairo Public Library,** built in 1884 of red brick in the Queen Anne style. With its many art pieces and historical displays, the building functions as both a museum and library. Its ornate furnishings include original stained glass windows and wainscoting of carved walnut and oak. In the reference room take special note of the replica of the steamboat *City of Cairo,* which was carved by a river pilot in 1876. The reading room has a round oak table that was used as a gaming table on a steamboat: The hole in the top was for raking in chips and money. The library (618–734–1840) is at 1609 Washington Avenue and is open Monday through Saturday.

Continue north on Washington Avenue, which was once known as Millionaire Row because of its many elaborate mansions. At 2700 Washington Avenue you'll find **Magnolia Manor.** Its original owner, Charles Galigher, was a friend of General Grant and made a fortune during the Civil War by selling flour for hardtack. Galigher built this four-story, Italianate mansion between 1869 and 1872. Its fourteen rooms are filled with period furnishings, many of them from the Galigher family. The manor (618–734–0201) is open for tours from 9:00 A.M. to 5:00 P.M., Monday through Saturday, and from 1:00 to 5:00 P.M. on Sunday.

Next door to the Magnolia Manor is its "sister" house, the **Windham Bed and Breakfast.** The home was constructed in 1876 in a similar Italianate style and now is a B & B offering three guest rooms. The Windham (618–734–3247) is located at 2606 Washington Avenue.

Before leaving Cairo, visit **Fort Defiance State Park** at its southern tip (which is also the southernmost point in Illinois). The park is named after the Civil War military post commanded by General Grant and offers an expansive view of the meeting of the blue waters of the Ohio River with the brown Mississippi.

FOR MORE INFORMATION

State of Illinois Tourism Information (800) ABE–0121

Illinois Department of Conservation (217) 782–7454

Northern Illinois Tourism Council (800) 248–6482

Western Illinois Tourism Council (800) 232–3889

Central Illinois Tourism Council (800) 262–2482

Southern Illinois Tourism Council (800) 342–3100

Galena (800) 747–9377

Quad Cities (800) 747–7800

Nauvoo (217) 453–6648

Quincy (800) 458–4552

Alton (800) ALTON IL

Maeystown (618) 458–6660

Prairie du Rocher (618) 284–3463

Chester (618) 826–2721

Cairo (618) 734–2737

Missouri

outh of Keokuk, Iowa, the Mississippi begins to form the eastern border of Missouri. On its course through the state the river flows by many of the Mississippi's most historically significant towns, including St. Louis, a city that played a major role in the settlement of the West, and Hannibal, the most famous river town of them all.

Missouri is significant in other ways as well. As the Mississippi winds its way south, the bluffs that have lined its banks all the way from the Twin Cities give way to the lowlands that characterize the Lower Mississippi. Missouri is also a transition state between the North and South. As you travel downriver, the customs, climate, and architecture will remind you more and more of Dixie.

ALEXANDRIA TO HANNIBAL

The Mississippi enters the state at Alexandria, a small village of a few hundred people that was hard hit by the 1993 flood. From Alexandria the river road follows Highway 61 west for 7 miles and then turns south to parallel the Mississippi, winding through rural countryside for 17 miles until it meets the river again at **Canton,** the site of Lock and Dam Number 20. Canton is a peaceful town connected by ferry service to Illinois and is also home to the **Golden Eagle Showboat** at Second and Green streets. The landlocked replica of a nineteenth-century sidewheeler steamboat offers dinner theater performances of comedies and musicals. Its season runs from late May to

Alexandria •

Canton •

Palmyra •
Hannibal •

Mississippi River

Louisiana •
Clarksville •

St. Louis •

Missouri

Kimmswick •

Ste. Genevieve •

Jackson •
Cape Girardeau •

Charleston •

New Madrid •

Caruthersville •

N
W E
S

early September, and tickets are about $18. For information, call (314) 288–5273.

Follow Route B to the south edge of Canton and you'll find the **Remember When Toy Museum.** Filled with a collection of more than 10,000 antique toys, the museum is owned by Robert and Carol Wyatt, a librarian and an elementary schoolteacher, respectively. The museum includes every kind of toy you had as a child—plus thousands more you wish you could have had. The Wyatts are in the process of building a pioneer village adjacent to their museum, and they also operate a manufacturing company that reproduces antique toys and weapons that are used in historical reenactments across the country. The site is popular with Civil War craftsmen/reenactors, who often camp near the museum on summer weekends. The museum (314–288–3995) is open Monday through Saturday during the summer months, from 9:00 A.M. to 5:00 P.M., and on Saturdays only during the rest of the year.

From the toy museum continue south on Route B for 5 miles to La Grange, where the river road rejoins Highway 61. Continue south for 15 miles past West Quincy, an unfortunate town devastated by the 1993 flood, to **Palmyra.** The town was founded in 1819 and was for many years the northernmost town on the Salt River Trail that ran from St. Charles, Missouri, to the Des Moines River. Palmyra was settled largely by southerners and during the Civil War was the site of what Presidents Lincoln and Davis both called the "darkest act" of the war. In 1862 ten Confederate prisoners being held for minor offenses were executed here when a Confederate officer refused to release a citizen sympathetic to the Union cause. A monument on the Marion County Courthouse lawn commemorates the "Palmyra massacre."

More than 200 antebellum structures remain in Palmyra, including the 1828 **Gardener House** (314–769–3076), a former stagecoach stop and hotel at Main and Hamilton streets that serves as a visitors information center and local history museum. The house has brochures describing a walking tour of Palmyra's historic buildings.

From Palmyra head south on Highway 168 for 10 miles to **Hannibal,** the classic river town immortalized by Mark Twain. Twain spent his boyhood years here along the Mississippi in the 1840s and later featured the town in many of his writings. Though today this city of 18,000 may seem a bit too ready to exploit its most famous citizen with attractions like Tom 'N Huck Motel and Injun Joe Campground, at its heart it remains a quiet, small river town. Stroll its historic district down by the riverfront, where it's not hard to imagine how the town must have looked to a small boy growing up here a century and a half ago.

Mark Twain, whose given name was Samuel Langhorne Clemens, was born in the nearby settlement of Florida, Missouri, in 1835, six months after the Clemens family had moved to the state from Tennessee. "I was postponed—postponed to Missouri," Twain later explained. "Missouri was an unknown new state and needed attractions." In 1839 the Clemens family moved to the more prosperous town of Hannibal, where Twain's father operated a store, practiced law, and later served as a justice of the peace. Twain lived in Hannibal until he was seventeen, when he left to become a journeyman printer in St. Louis.

For the rest of his life, Twain looked back on his boyhood days in Hannibal with great affection and drew upon them in countless ways for literary inspiration. The area was a young boy's adventure land: The surrounding hills had cliffs, caves, and dense woods to explore, and the mighty river

Hannibal's Favorite Son

Samuel Clemens led an adventurous life after leaving Hannibal at the age of seventeen, becoming a printer, steamboat pilot, Confederate soldier (for a brief two weeks), Nevada gold and silver miner, day laborer, and later a newspaper reporter and travel writer. In 1863 he adopted the pseudonym of Mark Twain, river men's jargon for water 2 fathoms deep.

Twain's first national literary success came in 1865 with his story "The Celebrated Jumping Frog of Calaveras County," followed by *Innocents Abroad*, a best-selling book describing his travels in Europe and the Holy Land. His later books and lecture tours solidified his international fame.

Though Twain eventually made his home in Connecticut, he returned many times to Hannibal, the river town he remembered so fondly. During an interview in India he once observed, "All that goes to make the me in me is in a small Missouri village on the other side of the globe."

beckoned just two blocks away from Twain's home. Though his early years were not without difficulties and tragedy (including the death of his father when Twain was twelve), the author's years in Hannibal were some of the happiest of his long life and sparked a love affair with the Mississippi River that continued to his death.

Much of the pleasure of a visit to Hannibal comes from following in Twain's footsteps. Begin your tour with a visit to the historic district next to the river. The **Mark Twain Boyhood Home and Museum,** at 208 Hill Street, preserves the small white clapboard home where Twain lived for nine years. Twain would later use the house as a model for the home of Tom Sawyer. He based Tom on himself, Aunt Polly on his mother, and Sid and Mary after his brother and sister. Other characters, including Huck Finn and Becky Thatcher, were patterned after childhood friends. On a tour through the house, it's easy to imagine young Tom sneaking out of his bedroom window for a night of adventures with Huck, or tricking the neighborhood kids into whitewashing the picket fence that surrounds the home's garden.

The museum complex also includes a building across the street, where Twain's father served as a justice of the peace in the 1840s and the family lived during a time of financial difficulties. The courtroom became the inspiration for a number of scenes in Twain's works, including the trial of Muff Potter in *Tom Sawyer.*

The Mark Twain Boyhood Home and Museum preserve memories of the famous author's childhood along the Mississippi.

103

Inside the home's annex and museum is a treasure trove of Twain memorabilia, including first editions of his books, one of his trademark white
suits, and the robes worn by the famous author when he received an hon-
orary degree from Oxford. The home and museum (314–221–9010) are
open daily year-round. Its summer hours are from 8:00 A.M. to 6:00 P.M. Call
for off-season hours.

Down the street from Twain's home is the **Cardiff Hill** described in his
works. At its base stands a statue of Tom and Huck, with Tom striding
eagerly into adulthood and Huck gently trying to hold him back. At the top
of the hill stands the **Mark Twain Memorial Lighthouse,** which was dedicated in 1935 to celebrate the hundredth anniversary of the author's birth.

No visit to Hannibal would be complete without a paddlewheeler cruise
on the Mississippi. The *Mark Twain Riverboat* docks at the landing at the
foot of Center Street and offers sightseeing and dinner cruises along with a
commentary on river history, legends, and sights. The cruises offer a lovely
view of Hannibal, which is nestled into a valley surrounded by wooded hills.
Another highlight of the trip is prime viewing of Jackson's Island, a spot that
is featured prominently in Twain's works. During the summer months the
400-passenger boat offers one-hour cruises at 11:00 A.M., 1:30 P.M., and 4:00
P.M., and dinner cruises at 6:30 P.M.; cruises are less frequent during the
spring and fall. Call (314) 221–3222 for information.

Another evening entertainment in Hannibal is **The Reflections of
Mark Twain,** a two-hour, outdoor pageant presented by twenty-five local
actors. The show consists of excerpts from *Tom Sawyer, Huckleberry Finn,* and
Life on the Mississippi and presents Hannibal through Mark Twain's words.
Performances begin at 8:30 P.M., May through September. Call (314)
221–2945 for information.

Before you leave the historic district, you might want to sample several
other attractions, most of which have similar hours to the Twain home. The
Becky Thatcher Bookshop, at 211 Hill Street, is the former home of
Laura Hawkins, who attended school with the young Twain and later
became the model for Becky Thatcher. The downstairs houses a fine book-
store (314–221–0822) with an excellent Twain collection, and the upstairs
parlor and bedroom are restored to their 1840s appearance.

The **Haunted House on Hill Street Wax Museum,** at 215 Hill Street,
has lifesize wax figures of Mark Twain and his family and twelve of his famous
characters plus several "haunted" rooms. Twain's work is also commemorated

at the **Tom Sawyer Dioramas Museum,** at 323 North Main Street, which features sixteen hand-carved miniature scenes from his works.

Several companies in Hannibal's historic district offer enjoyable touring options. The **Hannibal Trolley** (314–221–1161) departs from 301 North Main Street for a 14-mile, narrated tour. The **Twainland Express** (800–786–5193) is based at 400 North Third Street and offers two different tours of the area. The **Mark Twain Clopper** (314–439–5054) takes visitors on a horse and buggy ride through the streets of Hannibal. The twenty-minute, narrated tour begins at Hill and Main streets.

Another Hannibal landmark is the **Rockcliffe Mansion,** a turn-of-the-century home at 1000 Bird Street built by lumber magnate John J. Cruik-shank. Once one of the finest river estates in America, Rockcliffe played host to Mark Twain on his final visit to his hometown in 1902, when he addressed 300 members of Hannibal society from its magnificent stairway. The home has been restored to its former Victorian splendor and includes a fine collection of antique dolls on its third floor. Rockcliffe is open for daily tours from 9:30 A.M. to 5:00 P.M. (Hours are shorter during the winter months.) For information, call (314) 221–4140.

On the outskirts of Hannibal is another Twain landmark: the large cave that Twain explored as a boy and that later was a model for the fictional place where Tom and Becky were lost, buried treasure was found, and Injun Joe was trapped and died. The **Mark Twain Cave** is a National Historic Landmark that includes miles of passageways carved out of limestone by an underground stream. Guides take visitors on an hour-long, circular tour of the cool recesses of the cave. The site is open year-round, with summer hours from 8:00 A.M. to 8:00 P.M. Admission is $8.00 for adults, $4.00 for children. The cave (800–527–0304) is located 1 mile south of Hannibal on Highway 79. Adjacent to the Mark Twain Cave is **Cameron Cave,** which also offers guided tours during the summer months.

Two restaurants in Hannibal offer dining in historic buildings. The **Missouri Territory Restaurant** is housed in the town's nineteenth-century former post office, at 600 Broadway. The restaurant (314–248–1440) is open for lunch and dinner; prices are inexpensive to moderate. In the historic district, try the **Ole Planters Restaurant,** at 316 North Main Street. The restaurant (314–221–4410), known for its German chocolate pie, is housed in an 1856 building that once housed a general store and tailor's shop. Prices are inexpensive to moderate.

Overnight guests in Hannibal can choose their accommodations from several distinctive properties. The **Garth Woodside Mansion** has been rated as one of the Midwest's ten best country inns by the *Chicago Sun Times.* The Victorian showplace was built in 1871 as a summer home for businessman John Garth and his wife, Helen, and is surrounded by thirty-nine acres of woodlands. The Garths were childhood friends of Twain, and the author spent many nights at their lovely estate. A centerpiece of its interior is a beautiful walnut "flying staircase" that vaults upward for three stories with no apparent support. The renovated home is owned by Irv and Diane Feinstein, who offer eight guest rooms. Rates include a full breakfast and a Victorian-style nightshirt to wear to bed. If you're lucky, you'll get the room where Twain stayed during his visits to Hannibal. The inn is located south of town off of Highway 61; for information, call (314) 221–2789.

Another B & B with a Garth connection is the **Fifth Street Mansion,** an 1858 Italianate home, at 213 South Fifth Street, that was once the townhouse of John and Helen Garth. The mansion (314–221–0445) offers seven guest rooms. The 1880s-era **Queen Anne's Grace,** at 313 North Fifth Street, also offers Victorian-style accommodations. Call (314) 248–0756 for information.

Hannibal hosts a number of annual events that are particularly good times to sample its small town attractions, including the **National Tom Sawyer Days** held over the July 4th weekend. The festival features such activities as a frog jumping contest, the National Fence Painting Championships, and Mississippi Mud Volleyball. Each year the town also selects two children who will be its Tom Sawyer and Becky Thatcher Goodwill Ambassadors for the coming year. On the third weekend in October, the **Autumn Historic Folklife Festival** is held, with artisans demonstrating crafts of the mid-1800s, and street musicians and storytellers entertaining visitors.

For your final stop in Hannibal, drive to **Riverview Park,** a 400-acre park with scenic overlooks that provide wonderful views of the Mississippi. There you'll also find a statue of Mark Twain, standing on top of a 300-foot bluff and looking down on the river he loved. It's still possible to view the scene through Twain's eyes: "After all these years I can picture that old time to myself now, just as it was then: the white town drowsing in the sunshine of a summer's morning . . . [and] the great Mississippi, the majestic, the magnificent Mississippi, rolling its mile-wide tide along, shining in the sun."

The National Fence Painting Championships celebrate one of the best loved passages in all of Mark Twain's books.

LOUISIANA TO ST. LOUIS

From Hannibal head south on Highway 70 for 32 miles to the town of **Louisiana** along a route that is one of the loveliest segments of the river road. The highway winds through steep, thickly forested hills with magnificent trees that at one point meet in an archway over the road. Three scenic overlooks provide wonderful views of the river and its islands, little changed from when Mark Twain traveled along it here.

Louisiana is a charming town that was founded in 1818 by southerners from Kentucky, Virginia, Tennessee, and the Carolinas. It retains a southern feel to this day, with many gracious antebellum homes, and a downtown that has one of the most intact Victorian streetscapes in Missouri. For the best views of the Mississippi, follow Georgia Street east to the riverfront area, or drive to Henderson–Riverview Park at the crest of Main and Noyes streets. Visitor information and local history exhibits can be found at the **Louisiana Historical Museum,** at 116 South Third Street. The museum (314–754–4443) is open 9:00 A.M. to 1:00 P.M., Monday through Friday.

The Kings of the River

"Your true pilot cares nothing about anything on earth but the river, and his pride in his occupation surpasses the pride of kings," wrote Twain in *Life on the Mississippi*.

Such pride was well-earned, for a pilot needed skill, guts, and a prodigious memory to navigate the constantly changing river. Most began as deckhands and worked their way up to pilot after a lengthy apprenticeship. Working with few navigational aids and very few channel markers, a pilot depended upon his own memory of landmarks to alert him to treacherous sandbars, dangerous shallows, and snags that could sink his boat. He also needed to be master of a complicated system of bells and pulleys to communicate with the crew, and strong enough to handle the huge pilot wheel that turned the boat's rudders.

The depth of the river was determined by a technique called sounding. A pole or weighted rope was lowered into the water until it touched bottom, and the depth was signaled up to the pilothouse. "Mark twain" indicated a depth of 2 fathoms (12 feet), which was more than deep enough for a steamboat.

Louisiana is home to **Stark Bro's Nurseries,** one of the oldest and largest commercial nurseries in the world. In 1816 horticulturalist and early settler James Hart Stark began grafting apple cuttings from trees in his native Kentucky onto wild crab apple trees that grew in the rich soil along the Mississippi River; his descendants carried on his successful experiments with many other plant varieties. The company's most notable achievement was the development in 1893 of the Red Delicious apple, the world's most popular variety. The Stark Bro's Nursery worked with famed scientist Luther Burbank on other plant experiments and obtained the first patent granted a fruit variety in 1934. The nursery's garden center at the west end of Georgia Street contains exhibits of Burbank memorabilia and antique equipment once used by the company. Across the street is the **Pioneer Stark Cabin,** built by James Hart Stark. Call (800) 325–4180 for information.

A five-block area of Louisiana's downtown is listed on the National Register of Historic Places, and includes many antiques and gift shops housed in historic properties. For overnight accommodations, book a room at the **Riverview Bed and Breakfast,** at 403 North Main Street. The 1880s home (314–754–4270) is built on a bluff overlooking the Mississippi. Another Victorian bed-and-breakfast is **Serandos House** (314–754–4067), at 918 Georgia Street, which also offers dinners, by appointment, for guests.

From Louisiana continue south on Highway 79 for 8 miles to **Clarksville,** the site of Lock and Dam Number 24. Settled in 1817, much of this small town of 500 people is listed on the National Register. In 1987 Clarksville launched a major drive to restore its architectural treasures. Private donations have purchased almost a dozen vacant commercial buildings and funded a restoration program for the business district.

Begin your tour of Clarksville at the **Great River Road Tourist Information Center** on the north end of town on Highway 79. The new structure overlooks the lock and dam and includes visitor information as well as a river museum on its lower floor, where there are displays on the 1993 flood, the work of the U.S. Army Corps of Engineers, and the ecosystem of the Mississippi. The center (314–212–3132) is open year-round, and the grounds are a prime spot for eagle-watching during the winter.

For an even better view of the river, ride the **Clarksville Skylift** to the top of a 600-foot bluff, supposedly the highest point on the Mississippi. The lift (314–212–3132) operates daily during the summer and fall months.

For overnight accommodations, try the **Russell–Carroll House** (314–242–3854), an 1877 home with three guest rooms, or the **Daniel Douglass House** (314–242–3939), an 1859 Italianate home on South Second Street with three guest rooms. Both B & Bs are located on Highway 79, which runs through downtown Clarksville.

From Clarksville continue south on Highway 79 for 60 miles to **St. Louis,** one of the river's greatest cities. St. Louis is a crossroads in two important ways. The city marks the end of the Upper Mississippi, which is kept navigable by locks and dams, and the beginning of the Lower Mississippi, whose channel is naturally broad and deep enough for boat traffic. St. Louis was also the "jumping off" point for the West, the place where settlement ended and the frontier began.

St. Louis's position overlooking the confluence of the Missouri and Mississippi rivers made it a natural location for a city. In 1764 a French fur trapper named Pierre Laclede saw the site's potential and founded a settlement here that he named after the French monarch Louis IX, the Crusader King. The city first became a center for the fur trade, then an outfitting post for the thousands of immigrants traveling overland to the West. By the late 1800s, the city had become a thriving industrial hub and one of the nation's major commercial centers.

Today St. Louis has grown far beyond its frontier roots into a major metropolitan area, but it has not forgotten its historic ties to the river. Begin your tour in the downtown riverfront area, where the **Jefferson National Expansion Memorial** pays tribute to the huge migration that settled the West and to the genius of the president who shaped so much of the character of the young nation.

The memorial's centerpiece is the nation's tallest monument, the dramatic **Gateway Arch,** a gleaming curve of stainless steel that rises 630 feet above the banks of the Mississippi. The monument was designed by the Finnish-American architect Eero Saarinen as a tribute to the soaring mind of Thomas Jefferson; it is also a graphic representation of St. Louis's historic

Exodus to the West

During the nineteenth century, St. Louis witnessed an unprecedented exodus, the largest peacetime migration that the world has ever seen. Its vanguards were Lewis and Clark, intrepid explorers sent by President Thomas Jefferson to map the newly acquired Louisiana Purchase. Their reports of a country rich in fur-bearing animals lured trappers to follow in their footsteps.

Gradually word of the frontier's riches filtered back to the East, where thousands of land-hungry settlers pulled up stakes and came to St. Louis to be outfitted for the long and arduous journey across the plains and mountains to the West Coast. In 1848 gold was discovered in California, and the flow of emigration became a flood.

Ironically, the Great Plains—through which all the pioneers had passed on their way west—was the last region to be settled. "Sodbusters" built houses of earth and plowed the fertile prairie, enduring the plain's extremes of weather as they forged a life on what was once considered the Great American Desert. In 1890 the census bureau made it official: The frontier was no more, and the Louisiana Purchase was truly part of the nation.

role as the gateway to the West. A tram (314–425–4465) carries visitors to an observation room at the top of the structure, offering visitors an unparalleled view of the city and river.

Beneath the arch is the **Museum of Westward Expansion,** which describes the experiences of the pioneers on their long journey and the growth and development of the western United States during the nineteenth century. Also featured is a film describing the mammoth construction project that built the arch. The museum (314–425–4465) is open daily from 9:00 A.M. to 6:00 P.M. during the winter and from 8:00 A.M. to 10:00 P.M. in the summer.

The **Old Courthouse** is also part of the Jefferson National Expansion Memorial. Built between 1839 and 1862, the Greek Revival structure was the site of many impassioned debates prior to the Civil War. It was also the venue where the slave Dred Scott sued for his freedom in 1847. His case drew national attention, and the ruling against Scott by the U.S. Supreme Court in 1857 fanned the flames that would later erupt in the Civil War. Inside the courthouse you'll find two restored courtrooms and a museum with five galleries of displays on St. Louis history. Visitors can also view a thirty-minute film on the city's growth from a fur-trading post into a modern city. The courthouse (314–425–4468) is open daily from 8:00 A.M. to 4:30 P.M.

More riverfront history is preserved just north of the arch. **Laclede's Landing** is a nine-block area of century-old buildings with brick and cast

The historic district of Laclede's Landing offers a rich array of entertainment options.

iron facades located in the area where Pierre Laclede founded the city over 200 years ago. The landing's warehouses, which once stored tobacco, cotton, and other commodities shipped on the river, have been renovated into restaurants, shops, offices, galleries, and night clubs. The area's nineteenth-century heritage is recalled with cast-iron street lamps, cobblestone streets, and horse-drawn carriages offering rides. Laclede's Landing is located between Interstate 70 and the Mississippi River, between the Eads and Martin Luther King bridges.

Another historic renovation in the downtown area is the **Union Station,** an 1894 Richardsonian Romanesque train terminal that was once the busiest passenger rail facility in the nation. A $135-million renovation has turned this National Historic Landmark into a festival marketplace filled with over one hundred shops and restaurants plus a beautifully restored central hall with a vaulted ceiling. You'll find Union Station on Market Street between Eighteenth and Twentieth streets.

Before leaving the downtown area, step on board a paddlewheeler to sample the river's charms. The *Huck Finn, Tom Sawyer,* and *Becky Thatcher* are replicas of nineteenth-century steamboats and offer one-hour narrated cruises. The boats are operated by **Gateway Riverboat Cruises** (314–621–4040), and tickets are $7.00 for adults, $3.50 for children.

Riverboat gambling is another popular attraction on the riverfront. The **President Casino on the Admiral** is the state's only permanently moored casino, operating just north of the Gateway Arch. The Art Deco–style riverboat has been a St. Louis landmark for five decades; it offered excursion cruises until it was permanently moored in 1979. After a $40-million renovation, the boat now offers dockside gambling daily. Call (800) 772–3647 for information.

Other gaming boats in the metropolitan area include the **Casino St. Charles** (800–325–7777), which is based in nearby St. Charles and offers cruises on the Missouri River. On the Illinois side of the Mississippi, the **Alton Belle Casino** (800–336–7568) and the **Casino Queen** (800–777–0777) offer daily cruises.

After touring the city's riverfront, drive to Forest Park, a beautiful expanse of greenery that was the site of the 1904 World's Fair. The park now includes many of the city's finest attractions, including the St. Louis Zoo, Art Museum, and Science Center. There you'll also find the **History Museum,** which tells the history of St. Louis with special emphasis on its river roots. Operated by the Missouri Historical Society, the museum's exhibits include "Where Rivers Meet," which looks at the history of St. Louis from 1764 to 1900, and "St. Louis in the Gilded Age," which explores life in the city from the post–Civil War period through the 1890s. The History Museum (314–746–4599) is located at Lindell Boulevard and DeBaliviere Street in Forest Park and is open from 9:30 A.M. to 5:00 P.M., Tuesday through Sunday.

Anyone interested in the steamboat era shouldn't miss the **Golden Eagle River Museum.** Housed in a 1927 mansion built on a high bluff with an exceptional view of the Mississippi, the museum tells the story of the nation's steamboat trade through models, photographs, maps, and original steamboat artifacts and equipment. Other displays describe modern navigation on the river, and the library contains a large collection of books and research materials relating to all aspects of river history. Named after the *Golden Eagle* steamer, the last overnight passenger boat to run out of St. Louis, the museum was founded by many of her regular passengers after the boat sank in 1947. It is located in Bee Tree Park in southern St. Louis County, 4½ miles south of Interstate 270. The Golden Eagle River Museum is open from 1:00 to 5:00 P.M., Wednesday through Sunday, from May through October. For information call (314) 846–9073 or 772–1629.

More steamboat-era history is preserved at the **Jefferson Barracks Historical Park,** a former U.S. Army post overlooking the Mississippi that includes restored military buildings, two museums, and a national cemetery. The park also hosts historical reenactments and military history programs throughout the year. Among the soldiers who served at the post were Ulysses S. Grant, Robert E. Lee, Jefferson Davis, and William Tecumseh Sherman. The park (314–544–5714) is located at 533 Grant Road and is open from 10:00 A.M. to 5:00 P.M., Wednesday through Saturday, and from noon to 5:00 P.M. on Sunday.

Nearly a dozen of the city's nineteenth-century homes are also open for tours. You can learn more about the city's rich musical heritage at the **Scott Joplin House State Historic Site,** at 2658 Delmar Boulevard. The famous ragtime musician lived here from 1900 to 1903; the building includes his restored, turn-of-the-century apartment, information on his life and music, and African-American history galleries. The house (314–533–1003) is open daily.

The **Campbell House Museum,** at 1508 Locust Street, tells the story of the fur trade of the early 1800s. The Victorian mansion was once the home of fur trader and Indian commissioner Robert Campbell and contains most of its original furnishings. The house (314–421–0325) is open daily except Monday.

The **Eugene Field House and Toy Museum,** at 634 South Broadway Street, is the 1845 childhood home of Eugene Field, author of such children's poems as "Little Boy Blue." His father, Roswell M. Field, served as the lawyer for Dred Scott. The museum (314–421–4689) includes a large collection of antique toys and dolls. It is open Wednesday through Saturday, 10:00 A.M. to 4:00 P.M., and Sunday from noon to 4:00 P.M.

The **General Daniel Bissell House,** at 10225 Bellefontaine Road, was built in 1816 by the commanding officer of Fort Bellefontaine, the first American military post west of the Mississippi, and contains original family furnishings. The house (314–868–0973) is open Wednesday through Saturday, from noon to 5:00 P.M.

St. Louis's varied ethnic traditions have given the city a wide assortment of excellent restaurants. Properties with an historic theme include the *Lt. Robert E. Lee,* a sternwheeler permanently docked on the riverfront that houses a restaurant and dinner theater. Prices are moderate to expensive; call (314) 241–1282 for information.

A fine restaurant that also offers lodging is the **Lemp Mansion Restaurant and Inn,** housed in the 1862 mansion that was once the home of a St. Louis beer baron. While the house is said to be haunted, you're likely to be able to enjoy your meal here without supernatural disturbances. The restaurant (314–664–8024) is at 3322 De Menil Place, and prices are moderate to expensive.

Nearby is the **Chatillon–De Menil House,** a three-story Greek Revival mansion built in 1848. The home is open for tours and also offers a moderately priced luncheon. You'll find it at 3352 De Menil Place; call (314) 771–5828 for information.

St. Louis holds a number of annual celebrations that are excellent times to visit its attractions. Each Independence Day, the city throws one of the nation's largest parties on its riverfront, with air shows, free concerts, international food booths, and fireworks. The Old Courthouse contributes to the festivities with its **Victorian Fourth of July Celebration,** which includes interpreters in period clothing and Victorian music and decorations. Call (314) 434–3434 for information.

Each Labor Day weekend, the **St. Louis Blues Heritage Festival** celebrates the city's blues traditions, which traveled upriver from the Mississippi

Delta. Free outdoor concerts are offered at Laclede's Landing. Call (314) 241–BLUE for information.

KIMMSWICK TO JACKSON

From St. Louis take Interstate 55 south for 12 miles to exit 186 and follow the signs to the tranquil little village of **Kimmswick.** Founded in 1859 by German immigrants, Kimmswick became a favorite recreation spot for the elite of St. Louis and a busy steamboat port and railroad depot in the 1880s. The coming of the automobile and modern highways left the town behind, however, until a restoration effort began in 1970. Since then many of the town's nineteenth-century buildings have been renovated, creating a kind of living history museum along its narrow lanes. More than twenty antique stores, gift shops, and restaurants thrive here, but Kimmswick still manages to retain an unspoiled air. Most establishments are open each day except Monday.

You can learn more about the town's history at the **Burgess–How House and Museum** at Third and Elm streets. The log structure is open Sundays from 1:00 to 4:00 P.M., April through October. For information about the museum or about house tours given by the Kimmswick Historical Society, call (314) 464–TOUR.

Another piece of Kimmswick history is commemorated at the **El Camino Real Marker,** off Highway K, which leads into town. The red granite boulder marks the first road that linked St. Louis to southeast Missouri. The road followed Indian and game trails and was called *El Camino Real,* or "the king's highway," by the Spanish. Many river towns still carry variations of the name on their modern streets and roads.

Next door to the Burgess–How Museum is the **Old House Restaurant,** a 1770 log structure that once served as a trading post and later as a tavern and stagecoach stop. Inside is a delightful restaurant whose low ceilings and rustic decor carry through the building's historic theme. The Old House (314–464–0378) is open for lunch and dinner; prices are moderate to expensive.

Another excellent restaurant in town is the **Blue Owl Restaurant and Bakery,** housed in a turn-of-the-century former tavern at Second and Market streets. The Blue Owl's prices are moderate, and its desserts are divine. Call (314) 464–3128 for information. For overnight accommodations, try the **Kimmswick Korner Inn** (314–467–1027) at Front and Market streets. The 1890s-era inn offers two guest rooms and has an adjoining gift shop.

From Kimmswick continue south on either Highway 61 or Interstate 55 for 40 miles to historic **Ste. Genevieve,** which lays claim to being the first permanent European settlement west of the Mississippi. The original village was founded in the early 1700s by French colonists who migrated across the river from the French village of Kaskaskia in what is now Illinois. After a disastrous flood in 1785, the entire town was moved to its present site on higher ground. Ste. Genevieve remained a predominately French settlement for many years, though a later wave of German immigrants broadened its ethnic mix. Today its downtown retains its European ambiance and French flavor, with narrow streets lined with centuries-old homes. The village, in fact, can be thought of as an open-air architectural museum, illustrating the various periods of settlement in the New World.

Begin your tour of Ste. Genevieve at the **Great River Road Interpretive Center,** at 66 South Main Street. The new structure houses information on the town's heritage and attractions and includes displays on the river road and the 1993 flood, which did considerable damage to parts of Ste.

A Civilized Oasis

Travelers accustomed to the rough manners and simple customs of the frontier were often surprised by the cultured atmosphere that prevailed in Ste. Genevieve. The French colonists who settled the town brought with them an appreciation for the finer things in life. Even in the middle of the wilderness, they enjoyed frequent holidays, delicious foods, and wine made from local grapes. Women were often active in business with their husbands, and the wealthier citizens of the town wore stylish clothing shipped upriver from New Orleans.

The French who colonized the Mississippi Valley had a relatively friendly relationship with the native peoples they encountered. In Ste. Genevieve the French traded, lived, and intermarried with the local Peoria Indians, who were often invited to the village's social celebrations. Many settlers wore Indian articles of clothing and adapted foods and cooking techniques taught to them by their Indian neighbors.

Genevieve. The center (314–883–7097) is open Monday through Friday from 9:00 A.M. to 3:00 P.M. and on weekends from 9:00 A.M. to 4:00 P.M.

Next head across the street to the **Bolduc House,** a structure built in 1770 that is regarded as the most authentically restored French Colonial house in the nation. Its builder, Louis Bolduc, was a prosperous lead miner, merchant, and planter during the settlement's early years. The home's vertical-log construction has the heavy look of a medieval fortress, and is a remarkably well-preserved example of the architecture used by the region's earliest European settlers. The site also includes a stockade fence, a frontier kitchen, and eighteenth-century culinary and medicinal herb gardens.

Next door is the **Bolduc–LeMeilleur House,** which was built around 1820 by the husband of Louis Bolduc's granddaughter. The house is an interesting combination of French and American forms of construction and illustrates the ways in which the culture of the French settlement was gradually becoming more Americanized. Both Bolduc homes are open from 10:00 A.M. to 4:00 P.M., Monday through Saturday, and from 11:00 A.M. to 5:00 P.M. on Sunday, April through November. For information, call (314) 883–3105.

Another home dating back to Ste. Genevieve's early years is the **Maison Guibourd–Valle House** at Fourth and Merchant streets. While Bolduc House was built by a middle-class merchant, the 1784 Guibourd–Valle House was owned by a wealthy nobleman, who filled it with furnishings from around the world. Today the site includes a beautiful rose garden. The house is located at Fourth and Merchant streets and is open daily from 10:00 A.M. to 5:00 P.M., April through November.

The **Felix Valle House State Historic Site** shows the rapid change that came to Ste. Genevieve following the Louisiana Purchase in 1803. The Federal-style structure was built in 1818 as a combination store and residence and marks a change from the wooden, vertical-log construction that was used along the Mississippi River during the French and Spanish colonial periods of 1700 to 1790. Its interior contains early Empire furnishings and includes an authentically stocked mercantile store. The site (314–883–7102) is at Merchant and Second streets and is open from 10:00 A.M. to 4:00 P.M., Monday through Saturday, and from noon to 5:00 P.M. on Sunday.

More information about the history of this unique village is recounted at the **Ste. Genevieve Museum,** a handsome stone structure at Merchant Street and Dubourg Square. Its displays include information on local river history, the Native Americans who once lived in the area, and the Spanish and French colonial eras. The museum is open from 9:00 A.M. to 4:00 P.M.

daily; call (800) 373–7007 for information.

Ste. Genevieve has a number of fine bed-and-breakfasts housed in historic buildings, including the **Inn St. Gemme Beauvais.** The white-columned brick structure was built in 1848 and became an intimate inn one hundred years later, making this the oldest bed-and-breakfast in Missouri. Innkeeper Janet Joggerst has been welcoming guests for more than fifteen years and knows how to make them feel pampered and at home. The inn (314–883–5744) is located at 78 North Main Street and offers seven rooms as well as an elegant, moderately priced luncheon from 11:00 A.M. to 2:30 P.M. in its dining room.

Another Victorian lodging establishment in Ste. Genevieve is the **Southern Hotel,** a stately, Federal-style hotel built in the 1820s that lured the river trade with fine food, busy gambling rooms, and the first pool hall west of the Mississippi. The hotel was completely renovated in 1986 by new owners Mike and Barbara Hankins and offers eight guest rooms. The Southern Hotel (314–883–3493), at 146 South Third Street, also operates a gift shop in its lovely back garden.

Ste. Genevieve hosts a number of annual events that showcase its heritage. **French Colonial Days** are held each June and recreate life in the settlement during its earliest years. Included are craft demonstrations, candlelight tours of the historic district, music, and food. On the second full weekend in August, Ste. Genevieve hosts the **Jour de Fête,** "days of celebration," commemorating the town's French and German heritage. The event includes one of the Midwest's largest craft festivals as well as colonial artisan demonstrations, period music, dancing, and entertainment. For information, call (800) 373–7007.

If you're interested in exploring the French colonial district on the Illinois side of the river before traveling farther south, take the **Ste. Genevieve–Modoc Ferry,** which crosses the Mississippi here. The ferry operates from 6:00 A.M. to 8:00 P.M. daily; call (800) 373–7007 for information.

From Ste. Genevieve continue south on Highway 61 or Interstate 55 for 45 miles. At Jackson take in a bit of railroad history on board the **St. Louis Iron Mountain and Southern Railway.** The vintage steam engine takes passengers on a variety of sightseeing and dinner excursions; special events such as train robberies, vintage fashion shows, and murder mysteries are scheduled throughout the year. The train runs on Wednesdays and weekends during the summer months and on weekends during the spring and fall. Fares are $8.00

The Dangers of Steamboats

Although Twain described the steamboats of his day as being "as beautiful as a wedding cake—without the complications," the boats were actually vulnerable to a host of threats: Snags, sandbars, storms, ice jams, rapids, low water, inexperienced pilots, and floods all took their toll.

The greatest danger of all was fire, particularly from boiler explosions. In a few minutes an entire boat could be destroyed and all its passengers killed in a spectacular disaster of flying wreckage, clouds of steam, and fountains of scalding water. Such an explosion killed Twain's younger brother, Henry Clemens, in 1858.

Fires were common even without such explosions. A single spark from a smokestack could easily ignite the cotton and hay that many steamboats carried as cargo. All of these threats made the average life of a steamboat less than five years in the mid-1800s.

for adults, $4.00 for children. For information, call (800) 455-RAIL.

Also in Jackson is the **Oliver House,** once home to Robert Oliver, a Missouri state senator, and his wife, Marie, who designed the official Missouri state flag. The 1880s-era, Federal-style brick house, at 224 East Adams Street, is filled with period furnishings and is open 1:00 to 4:30 P.M. on Saturday from May through December. For information call (314) 243–0533.

From Jackson either head south on Highway 61 for 6 miles to Cape Girardeau or take a detour on Highway 177 for 8 miles to the **Trail of Tears State Park.** The 3,600-acre site includes a portion of the Trail of Tears that was followed by the Cherokee people on their forced march from Tennessee to Oklahoma during the winter of 1838–1839. The 1,200-mile march took a heavy toll on the tribe: Of the 13,000 who began the trip, over 3,000 died along the way. The park's visitors center (314–334–1711) contains information on this tragic chapter in American history and is open daily. The park also includes limestone bluffs that offer a scenic view of the Mississippi below.

CAPE GIRARDEAU TO CARUTHERSVILLE

From the Trail of Tears State Park continue south on Highway 177 for 10 miles to **Cape Girardeau.** The city draws its unusual name from Jean Baptiste Girardot, a French soldier who in the early 1700s established a trading post here on a rock promontory overlooking a natural cove, or "cape," on the Mississippi. The first permanent settlement was founded in 1792 by Louis Lorimier, who was appointed by the Spanish governor general as his representative to deal with local Indian tribes. The Louisiana Purchase brought the settlement into American hands in 1803, and the town grew to be an important shipping and commercial center. During the Civil War, Union forces occupied the town and built four forts to protect the city and the river.

The **Cape River Heritage Museum** is a good place to begin your tour. Its exhibits on river history include hands-on displays for children and information on the town's early years as a steamboat port. The museum also includes a display on the first Missouri state flag and a full-size fire engine, which recalls the days when the turn-of-the-century building served as the town's fire station. The museum (314–335–6333), at 538 Independence Street, is open 11:00 A.M. to 4:00 P.M., Wednesday, Friday, and Saturday from March through December.

Cape Girardeau's **Common Pleas Courthouse** is the centerpiece of its historic downtown area. Built in 1854, the courthouse sits on four acres of land on a bluff overlooking the river and was once a site for Indian council meetings. The surrounding park has an old-fashioned bandstand, a Civil War monument and fountain, and several historical markers. You'll find the courthouse and park at the intersection of Themis and Lorimier streets.

Just across the street from the courthouse are two of the murals for which Cape Girardeau is famous. The two ceramic tile murals on the Southeast Missourian Newspaper Building depict the art of printing and the making of a newspaper. The city's convention and visitors bureau (800–777–0068) has a listing of other murals in the area.

On the south end of the downtown is the 1853 **Old St. Vincent's Church,** an excellent example of the Renaissance-influenced Gothic style. More than one hundred plaster masks on its inside and outside walls depict characters from the medieval mystery and miracle plays. You'll find the church at the corner of Main and William streets.

Another Victorian-era Cape Girardeau landmark is the **Glenn House,** at 325 South Spanish Street. Built in 1883, the house has been elegantly restored with period furnishings and includes a room with river history displays. The house (314–334–1177) is open 1:00 to 4:00 P.M., Thursday through Sunday, April through December.

South of Cape Girardeau you'll find the **American Heritage Museum,** a collection of antique agricultural equipment that includes steam engines, threshers, tractors, and buggies. The museum (314–334–2333) is at the intersection of Interstate 55 and Airport Road and is open from 9:00 A.M. to 5:00 P.M. daily.

If you're hungry after a day of touring, try the **Port Cape Girardeau Restaurant,** which is housed in an 1830s building located at 19 North Water Street, in the heart of the historic riverfront district. When Union forces occupied the city during the Civil War, General Ulysses S. Grant maintained offices on the building's second floor. The restaurant (314–334–0954) is open daily for lunch and dinner; prices are moderate to expensive.

Each June Cape Girardeau celebrates its river heritage with **Riverfest,** when the riverfront comes alive with fireworks, carnival rides, food stands, craft booths, and other entertainment. For information, call (314) 335–1388.

The city is home to several fine bed-and-breakfasts housed in historic mansions. The **Bellevue Bed and Breakfast** (800–768–6822), at 312 Bellevue Street in the downtown area, is an 1890s Second Empire Victorian home with two guest rooms. The **Rivendell Bed and Breakfast** (314–334–5507) is an 1838 home at 151 South Spanish Street that also offers two guest rooms.

From Cape Girardeau you have a choice of two routes south. The direct route runs along Interstate 55 for 50 miles to New Madrid. If you're interested in the alternative route that runs closer to the river, take the Scott City exit off Interstate 55 and then follow Route N for 25 miles to **Charleston.** The town has a southern feel to it, with stately homes surrounded by dogwoods and azaleas. Each year on the third weekend in April, when the flowering plants are at their height, Charleston hosts its **Dogwood and Azalea Festival.** The event includes tours of historic homes, an ice cream social, a parade, and a beauty queen contest. Call (314) 683–6509 for information.

Also in Charleston is the **Mississippi County Historical Museum,** a turn-of-the-century home at 403 North Main Street that houses displays of Indian artifacts, local history, and a collection of military uniforms dating back to the Civil War. The house is open on Tuesday and Thursday; call (314) 683–3837 for information.

At Charleston you once again have a choice of two routes. The shorter one heads west on Interstate 57 for 10 miles to Miner, then south on Interstate 55 for 20 miles to New Madrid. The alternate loop tour takes you closer to the river and runs east on Highway 60/62 for 7 miles to Wyatt and then south on Highway 77 for 12 miles to Wolf Island. From there watch for the sign to **Towosahgy State Historic Site.** The sixty-four-acre site preserves the remains of a fortified village and ceremonial center for a group of Mississippian Indians and includes several earthen mounds.

Return to Highway 77 and head south to Dorena, then north again on Highway 102 for 2 miles to **Big Oak Tree State Park,** a 1,000-acre site that preserves a section of the magnificent swamp forests that once covered the area. A boardwalk gives easy access so that visitors can see the park's huge, towering trees, many over 100 feet tall. Each September the park (314–649–3149) sponsors a **Living History Day,** when artisans and craftsmen demonstrate old-time skills.

Continue north on Highway 102 for 14 miles to East Prairie, and then take Highway 80 back to Interstate 55, which leads south 10 miles to **New Madrid.** This picturesque small town began as a trading post in 1783, and its name recalls its early status as an outpost of Spain. The area became part of the United States in 1803 as part of the Louisiana Purchase and is best known for having lent its name to a series of powerful earthquakes in 1811 and 1812. The main quake registered 8.6 on the Richter Scale and was the strongest ever recorded in North America. The New Madrid Fault is still active today, with over 300 small quakes recorded annually (but with some luck, your visit here won't be unpleasantly interrupted).

The New Madrid region was settled by pioneers from Kentucky, Virginia, and Tennessee, and prior to the Civil War its agriculture was based on slave labor. In 1862 Union forces under General John Pope laid siege to the town for thirteen days, and the Confederate troops evacuated to a nearby island, which was fortified to block the Mississippi River. The island and most of its forces were captured on April 7, 1862.

You can learn more about area history at the **New Madrid Historical Museum,** which has exhibits on Native American, Civil War, earthquake, and river history. The museum (314–748–5944) is housed in an 1886 saloon, which stands at 1 Main Street, and is open from 9:00 A.M. to 5:00 P.M., Monday through Saturday, and from noon to 5:00 P.M. on Sunday.

The **Hunter–Dawson State Historic Site,** at 312 Dawson Road, is a fifteen-acre estate that includes a home built in 1858 by a wealthy merchant, William Washington Hunter. Three major floods on the Mississippi have left

The New Madrid Earthquake

The strongest series of earthquakes ever recorded in North America began at the New Madrid Fault on December 16, 1811, and continued to rumble through the area until February 17, 1812. Though the first shocks were felt during the night, the full force of the quake came at dawn: The earth undulated like ocean waves, throwing up great volumes of water, sulphur, steam, and sand, and opening up huge fissures that stretched for miles. The Mississippi receded from its banks and rose up into a mountain of water, then came crashing down to its banks and actually reversed itself so that it flowed upstream for a time. Shock waves were felt as far away as Montana, New Orleans, Canada, and the East Coast, ringing church bells in Washington and awakening Thomas Jefferson at his Monticello estate in Virginia.

The quakes permanently altered the topography of the region, lowering the land from Cape Girardeau to Helena, Arkansas, from 10 to 50 feet, flooding most of the southern reaches of Missouri, and creating Reelfoot Lake in Tennessee. The area's sparse population prevented massive loss of life, but the series of quakes led to an exodus of terrified settlers. It took several decades before large numbers of people would return, finally trusting the stability of the earth below them once again.

their marks on its walls, an indication of New Madrid's sometimes overly close ties to the river. Furnished with period antiques, the home (314–748–5340) is open Monday through Saturday, 10:00 A.M. to 4:00 P.M., and on Sunday from noon to 4:00 P.M.

A much older historic site can be seen near the junction of Highway 61 and Interstate 55: a **Mississippian Indian mound,** a 1,000-year-old earthen mound where the Spanish explorer Hernando de Soto is said to have held the first Christian religious service west of the Mississippi. Exhibits on the culture of the people who built the mound can be seen at the New Madrid Historical Museum.

A fine place to view the river in New Madrid is from an observation deck located at the end of Main Street on the levee. The deck offers a panoramic view of the river as it winds around the wide New Madrid bend.

From New Madrid continue south on Interstates 55 and 155 for 35 miles to **Caruthersville,** the last major town on Missouri's portion of the river road. In 1794 the Spanish fort of San Fernando was built here as an outpost for the fur trade that flourished in the region's heavily wooded swamps and bayous. After the New Madrid earthquakes of 1811 and 1812, the area was left largely deserted, except for the Walker and Covington families. John Hardeman Walker was an astute young man who recognized opportunity when he saw it. After the quake, the seventeen-year-old gathered up all the loose livestock left behind by frightened settlers and soon acquired vast tracts of land that no one wanted. Walker became such a powerful landowner that he was later responsible for the creation of Missouri's "bootheel," that portion of the state that extends southward into Arkansas. Surveyors had originally marked the state's boundary in a straight line from Kansas to Tennessee, which would have left Walker's extensive holdings in the territory of Arkansas, at that time a wild and lawless area. The indefatigable pioneer traveled to Washington to testify before Congress and successfully argued for the inclusion of the 1,100-square-mile tract of land into the new state of Missouri. In 1851, at the age of sixty-three, Walker laid out the city of Caruthersville and named it in honor of another pioneer citizen, Sam Caruthers. Walker's grave lies behind the Eastwood Memorial United Methodist Church, between Ward Avenue and Fifth Street.

FOR MORE INFORMATION

Missouri Department of Tourism (314) 751–4133

Missouri Department of Natural Resources (800) 334–6946

Canton (314) 288–5215

Palmyra (314) 769–3076

Hannibal (314) 221–2477

Louisiana (314) 754–5921

Clarksville (314) 242–3132

St. Louis (800) 916–0040

Ste. Genevieve (800) 373–7007

Cape Girardeau (800) 777–0068

New Madrid (314) 748–5300

Caruthersville (314) 333–1222

LOWLANDS AND LEVEES

Kentucky, Tennessee, Arkansas, Mississippi, and Louisiana

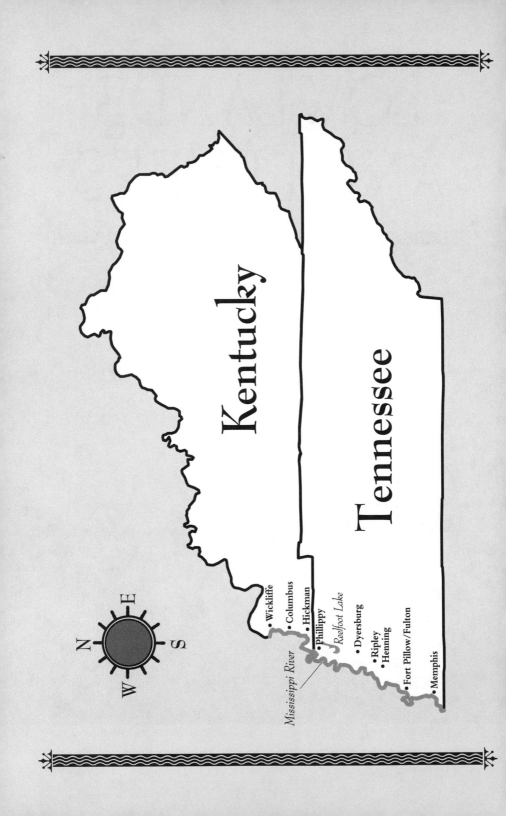

Kentucky and Tennessee

$$\Longleftrightarrow\!\!\!\!\sim\!\!\!\!\sim\!\!\!\!\sim\!\!\!\!\sim\!\!\!\!\sim\!\!\!\!\Longleftrightarrow$$

S outh of Cairo, Illinois, the Mississippi begins to form the western borders of Kentucky and Tennessee. The river is not as strong a presence in this region as it is in most of the other states along its banks. The river road does not for the most part hug the Mississippi, and aside from Memphis, there are no major cities along the route.

The rural counties that border the river offer their own quiet charm, however. Here you'll find an uncluttered countryside of peaceful farms, scenic wild areas, and sleepy small towns. Then head south to Memphis, one of the river's greatest cities, where the rich music, culture, and history of the delta are all celebrated.

KENTUCKY

After crossing the confluence of the Mississippi and Ohio rivers at Cairo, continue south on Highway 51/60 for 5 miles to **Wickliffe.** On the north end of town, you'll find the **Wickliffe Mounds,** once the location of a Mississippian Indian village. As at the better known Cahokia Mounds site in Illinois, the Native Americans here built large earthen mounds that were likely topped by temples or the houses of chiefs and priests. While Cahokia Mounds preserves the remains of a major city, the settlement at Wickliffe was more on the order of a small town. Murray State University now owns the site and operates a museum where you can learn more about the culture of the Indians who lived here some 900 years ago and about the ongoing archeological excavation of the mounds. The museum (502–335–3681) is open daily, March through November, from 9:00 A.M. to 4:30 P.M.

The town of Wickliffe has a fine, brick, white-columned courthouse, a structure that during the Civil War was used as quarters for a company of Union soldiers after Confederate troops evacuated Kentucky.

From Wickliffe follow Highway 51/62 for 9 miles to Bardwell and then head southwest on Highway 123 for 7 miles to **Columbus-Belmont State Park,** a 156-acre site that commemorates an important Civil War battle. In 1861 almost 20,000 rebel soldiers labored to turn Columbus into an impregnable fortress they named Fort De Russey. More than one hundred heavy guns were placed on the bluffs, several steamboats were converted into gun-

Summer Sunrises

I had myself called with the four o'clock watch, mornings, for one cannot see too many summer sunrises on the Mississippi. They are enchanting. First, there is the eloquence of silence; for a deep hush broods everywhere. Next, there is the haunting sense of loneliness, isolation, remoteness from the worry and bustle of the world. The dawn creeps in stealthily; the solid walls of black forest soften to gray, and vast stretches of the river open up and reveal themselves; the water is glass-smooth, gives off spectral little wreaths of white mist; there is not even the faintest breath of wind, nor stir of leaf; the tranquillity is profound and infinitely satisfying. . . . And all this stretch of river is a mirror, and you have the shadowy reflections of the leafage and the curving shore and the receding capes pictured in it. Well, that is all beautiful; soft and rich and beautiful; and when the sun gets well up, and distributes a pink flush here and a powder of gold yonder and a purple haze where it will yield the best effect, you grant that you have seen something that is worth remembering.

Mark Twain
Life on the Mississippi

An enormous anchor that was part of the Confederate attempt to blockade the Mississippi is on display at Columbus-Belmont State Park.

boats, and a huge chain was stretched across the river. A second rebel camp was built on the Missouri side of the river at Belmont, and the heavily fortified site became known as the Gibraltar of the West.

Union general Ulysses S. Grant attacked the Belmont camp in November 1861. After a sharp skirmish the Confederates were forced to retreat, and Grant turned his guns on the main stronghold at Columbus. He was overpowered and withdrew upriver, but only after he burned the camp at Belmont.

By then Grant realized that the fortress couldn't be taken by direct assault, and Union forces proceeded to take positions surrounding Columbus. Severely outflanked, the Confederates evacuated the area in February 1862, leaving the Mississippi open for Union occupation. The Battle of Belmont was highly significant because it marked the beginning of the Union's western campaign, the opening of the Mississippi River to Union supplies, and Ulysses S. Grant's first active engagement in the Civil War.

At the park you can see various relics from the battle, including a network of earthen trenches and the sixteen-ton anchor that held the great chain that stretched across the river. The park also has a magnificent view of the wide channel of the Mississippi. The park's museum (a former army hospital) is open daily from 9:00 A.M. to 5:00 P.M., May through September, and houses information about the battle as well as displays of early Indian artifacts. Call (502) 677–2327 for information.

From Columbus head south on Highways 123 and 239 for 18 miles to Cayce, then west on Highway 94 for 9 miles to the river town of **Hickman.** The town was settled in 1837 during the early years of the westward expansion and became an active steamboat port. The **Old Hickman Historic District** on Clinton Street is being restored to bring back more of its nineteenth-century flavor. Also take note of the 1903 Fulton County Courthouse, at Cumberland and Wellington streets, a structure with towers, turrets, and a working Seth Thomas clock.

From Hickman continue west on Highway 94 for 12 miles through Sassafras Ridge and Miller, which is the southernmost Kentucky town on the river road. The route bypasses a large section of land orphaned from the rest of Kentucky by a huge loop in the Mississippi. The region is called Madrid Bend, and is also referred to as "Kentucky's forgotten territory" since it can be reached only by a road from Tennessee. Its 12,000 acres contain some of the nation's richest soil, a gift from the Mississippi River.

TENNESSEE

The river road enters Tennessee at the small village of **Phillippy** and leads south past **Reelfoot Lake.** Though Reelfoot is the state's largest natural lake, it is relatively young. The 13,000-acre lake was formed during the winter of 1811–1812, when a series of powerful earthquakes shook the area and changed the course of the Mississippi so that it formed this large, shallow lake where a forest once stood. The forest stumps still remain underneath the water and have created a natural fish hatchery that is unsurpassed in the nation; almost sixty species of fish are found here. The lake is also noted as one of the best songbird areas in the country, and it is home to thousands of ducks and geese as well as a growing number of bald eagles. Daily eagle tours are conducted by park naturalists from mid-December through mid-March. The park visitors center (901–253–7756) on the lake's south shore has displays on the earthquake that formed the lake and its unique ecology.

From Phillippy travel south on Highway 78 for 35 miles to Dyersburg. The **Dyer County Courthouse** is the hub of Dyersburg's historic downtown. This classic columned building is on the National Register of Historic Places, and the surrounding square is the site of the town's annual Dogwood Festival and Dogwood Dash in April.

Dyersburg is also home to the **Dr. Walter E. David Wildlife Museum** (901–285–3200), on the campus of Dyersburg State Community College. The museum contains specimens of every kind of duck on the Mississippi Flyway and is open daily.

From Dyersburg follow Highway 51 south for 25 miles to Ripley, where an 8-mile detour east on Highway 19 will take you to the town of **Nutbush.** The village's claim to fame is that it was the girlhood home of singer Tina Turner—who was then known by the much less melodic name of Annie Mae Bullocks. Guided tours include a stop at the Nutbush Heritage Exhibit and Turner's birthplace and family church. A **Tina Turner Day Festival** is held in August. For information, call (901) 772–4265.

Another famous Tennessean grew up in **Henning,** a town located 5 miles south of Ripley. The **Alex Haley House and Museum** preserves the boyhood home of the Pulitzer Prize–winning author of the fictionalized chronicle *Roots,* including the front porch where Haley first heard stories about his ancestor Kunte Kinte. The home is furnished in the 1920s-style of Haley's childhood and features memorabilia from his life, family artifacts, audiotapes, and a small gift shop. The front lawn is the final resting place of this master storyteller. The state-owned historic site is at the corner of Haley Avenue and South Church Street and is open from 10:00 A.M. to 5:00 P.M., Tuesday through Saturday, and from 1:00 to 5:00 P.M. on Sunday. For information call (901) 738–2240.

For an interesting detour into Civil War history, from Henning head west on Highway 87 for 20 miles to **Fulton.** North of town is the **Fort Pillow State Historic Area,** the site of a garrison built in 1861 to help the Confederate forces control the Mississippi. The fort was captured by the Union in 1862 and recaptured by the South in 1864, when General Nathan Bedford Forrest killed many of the defenders and ignited charges of brutality in the northern press. The storm of controversy was matched by few other

Alex Haley's Roots

On the front porch of a house in the small town of Henning, the young Alex Haley heard family stories told by his grandmother and great-aunts. The tales began with Haley's ancestor Kunte Kinte, who was brought to America in 1767 from West Africa and sold into slavery. The stories continued through five generations of African-Americans struggling to gain independence and freedom in the New World.

Haley never forgot those stories, and as an adult he set off on a twelve-year journey that took him a half-million miles across three continents to research his family's history. He later wrote the best-seller *Roots*, a book that has been translated into over thirty languages. The miniseries it inspired was one of the most popular shows in television history. Although Haley's stories tell the history of one family, they helped ignite the rediscovery of an entire people's rich cultural heritage.

incidents during the war. The earthwork remains of the fort are preserved on the bluffs overlooking the river; an interpretive center (901–738–5581) explains the fort's history.

MEMPHIS

From Fulton head back to Highway 51 and then continue south for 45 miles to **Memphis**. Located on a cliff that rises 80 feet above the river, Memphis had been the site of French, Spanish, and American forts when Judge John Overton of Nashville, a close friend of President Andrew Jackson, planned its streets in 1819. The new city was named Memphis after the ancient Egyptian capital, and was laid out with wide, spacious streets, four public squares, and a promenade along the Mississippi. Its location was favorable on several counts: It was situated on the river but was high enough to escape flooding, and it was surrounded by the fertile and productive land of the Mississippi Delta.

Memphis soon became a rowdy, roaring river city and a gateway to the western frontier. During the Civil War its strategic location made it a primary target for northern forces. Because the city was captured early in the war, however, it escaped much of the destruction that befell many other southern cities. The city boomed during the war years, in fact, as it became a center for profiteering and contraband smuggling to both the Union and Confederate armies.

Then beginning in 1867, Memphis was ravaged by cholera and mosquito-borne yellow fever epidemics that killed thousands. Its citizens, angered by calls elsewhere in the state to burn the city down, resolved to make their city a model of cleanliness. Hundreds of miles of drainage ditches eliminated the breeding grounds of the deadly mosquito, and a new city began to emerge and grow, particularly after the 1890s, when Memphis became the center of the nation's largest hardwood market. Loggers swarmed in and out of Memphis, and steamboats loaded down with timber packed its harbor. Many elegant mansions were built with fortunes made in the lumber business and in Memphis' other major industry, the cotton trade.

Mud Island, on the riverfront, is the perfect place to begin your tour of the city. This fifty-two-acre river park and entertainment complex celebrates life on the river in all its forms and includes a spectacular "river walk" that is a five-block-long model of the Mississippi, built to scale, that traces its course through the continent. The eighteen-gallery **Mississippi River Museum** provides information on the natural and cultural history of the continent's greatest river through audiovisual productions, artifacts, and riverboat models. Here you can also board a full-scale replica of an 1870 riverboat and hear tales of river adventures told by life-size figures of Mark Twain, the legendary keelboatman Mike Fink, and others. Mud Island is located at 125 North Front Street and is open daily from April through late November (closed Mondays during the autumn months). The Mississippi River Museum is also open daily; admission is $6.00 for adults, $4.00 for children. For information call (901) 576-7241.

The Memphis Queen Line Riverboats dock near the museum at the foot of Monroe Street and offer a variety of sightseeing cruises on a fleet of five paddlewheelers. The boats operate from March through November; call (800) 221-6197 for information.

Next head to Memphis's most celebrated avenue: the **Beale Street Historic District.** Recognized worldwide as the birthplace of the blues, Beale Street is famous above all for its music clubs, but it also has an entertaining array of shops, restaurants, theaters, and parks. A visitors information center at 340 Beale Street is open daily (800-447-8278).

The **Beale Street Blues Museum** contains a wide variety of exhibits

Beale Street, the birthplace of America's first original music form, still pulses with some of the nation's best blues.

that celebrate the area's living musical heritage and includes many video programs and audiotapes of famous blues and gospel musicians. There are displays on such noted Beale Street figures as Louis Armstrong, B. B. King, and Muddy Waters as well as exhibits on slavery, cotton, and riverboats. The museum (901–527–6008) is at 329 Beale Street and is open daily.

Another Beale Street landmark is the **Center for Southern Folklore.** The private, nonprofit organization documents the people and traditions of the South. Located in the heart of the historic district, at 130 Beale Street, the center is known for its entertaining films and exhibits as well as books, recordings, and guided tours of Beale Street and the Memphis delta region. Its distinctive gift shop showcases southern folk art. The center is open daily year-round; call (901) 525–3655 for information.

Before leaving the Beale Street area, pay a visit to **A. Schwab's Dry Goods Store,** at 163 Beale Street. This historic general store has been owned and operated by the same family since 1876 and has three floors crammed with an astonishing variety of merchandise, including its own Beale Street Museum. Abram Schwab and his son Elliott offer everything from voodoo powders and magic potions to clerical collars and handcuffs. Schwab's motto

The Birthplace of the Blues

Beale Street, a fifteen-block avenue that stretches eastward from the Mississippi, became a haven of African-American prosperity from the 1890s to the 1920s. It was here that a young bandleader named W. C. Handy began writing music that took the spirituals and field chants that fellow blacks brought with them from the poverty and hardship of the delta cotton fields and shaped them into America's first original music form, the blues.

For decades aspiring musicians have flocked to Memphis to learn the blues at its source, including a young Mississippian who came to Beale Street in 1940 and soon developed a large following. He traded his name Riley for "The Beale Street Blues Boy," and today B. B. King is acclaimed as one of the masters of the genre. In the early 1950s another musician was profoundly influenced by the Beale Street sound—Elvis Presley, who also went on to make quite a name for himself.

W. C. Handy referred to this famous street with these words: "The seven wonders of the world I have seen, and many are the places I have been. Take my advice, folks, and see Beale Street first."

says it all: "If you can't find it at Schwab's, you're better off without it."

The city's role during the Civil Rights movement is commemorated at the **National Civil Rights Museum,** at 450 Mulberry Street. The museum is located on the site of the Lorraine Motel, where Dr. Martin Luther King, Jr., was assassinated in 1968. Opened in 1991, the museum offers a comprehensive overview of the struggle for civil rights from the mid-1800s to today through audiovisual and interactive exhibits, Civil Rights movement memorabilia, and scenes representing the various eras. The museum is open daily except Tuesday. Call (901) 521–9699 for information.

On a scenic spot overlooking the Mississippi, you'll find the **National Ornamental Metal Museum,** the only museum in the country dedicated to preserving the art of metalworking. Exhibits include displays of jewelry and architectural wrought iron plus a blacksmith shop, where you can see master artisans at work. Don't miss the pretty Victorian gazebo topped by a catfish weathervane on the museum grounds; it's a wonderful spot to watch the river flow by. The museum (901–774–6380), at 374 West California Avenue, is open Tuesday through Saturday, 10:00 A.M. to 5:00 P.M., and on Sunday from noon to 5:00 P.M.

The **Victorian Village Historic District** showcases some of the city's most beautiful mansions, many built from money that flowed into Memphis from the river trade. The three homes described below are open to the public; the rest are privately owned and can be enjoyed on a walking tour.

The **Mallory–Neely House,** at 652 Adams Avenue, reflects conspicuous consumption in all its glory. The twenty-five-room Italian villa–style mansion was built in the 1850s and contains original family antiques and furnishings, including exquisite stained-glass windows purchased at the 1893 Columbian Exposition in Chicago. The house (901–523–1484) is open Tuesday through Saturday, 10:00 A.M. to 4:00 P.M., and on Sunday from 1:00 to 4:00 P.M.

Just down the street is the 1836 **Magevney House,** a much more modest structure that is the oldest remaining home in Memphis. Although Eugene Magevney became quite wealthy and could have built a mansion, he was content in this simple clapboard home—though even this four-room house was considered large for the day. You'll find the house (901–526–4464) at 198 Adams Avenue. It's open Tuesday through Saturday, 10:00 A.M. to 4:00 P.M.

Another historic landmark is the **Woodruff–Fontaine House,** an 1870s French Victorian mansion at 680 Adams Avenue that houses exhibits of period textiles. The house has a collection of more than 2,000 articles of antique clothing that are displayed on a rotating basis, from delicate bridal gowns to sturdy sailor suits for little boys. The home has another claim to fame as well—the ghost of former owner Mollie Woodruff Henning is said to haunt one of the upstairs bedrooms where her first husband and two of her children died. The museum (901–526–1469) is open Monday through Saturday, 10:00 A.M. to 3:30 P.M., and on Sunday from 1:00 to 3:30 P.M.

The **Chucalissa Archeological Museum** provides insights into an even more distant past. On a bluff overlooking the Mississippi, archeologists have reconstructed an ancient Indian village that flourished here between A.D. 1100 and 1600. A group of thatched-roof huts stands atop the original earthworks built by the Indians, and a huge mound is topped by a chieftain's house. The original village was part of a network of Indian communities that once flourished along the banks of the Mississippi. The Spanish explorer De Soto spent several weeks in this area in 1541, replenishing his company's food supplies and constructing barges to cross the Mississippi.

A museum explains the culture and history of the Indians who once lived here, and Choctaw Indians frequently are on site to demonstrate traditional skills and talk to visitors. The museum (901–785–3160) is at 1987 Indian Village Drive and is open 9:00 A.M. to 5:00 P.M., Tuesday through Saturday, and from 1:00 to 5:00 P.M. on Sunday.

A good way to see the many historic attractions in Memphis is on board the **Main Street Trolley.** The line's antique trolley cars make regular rounds of many landmarks, including Mud Island, Beale Street, and the city's gleaming new pyramid, a multipurpose arena that rises thirty-two stories above the banks of the Mississippi. Call (901) 274-6282 for information.

There are a number of fine bed-and-breakfasts housed in historic structures in the Memphis area; call (901) 726–5920 to contact the city's bed-and-breakfast reservation service.

For fine dining in Memphis, try **Justine's,** a French restaurant housed in an 1843 French Colonial home listed on the National Register of Historic Places. Justine's (901–527–9973), at 919 Coward Place, is open 5:30 P.M. to midnight, Tuesday through Saturday. Prices are expensive. **The Pier** is

Hernando De Soto

The lure of gold drew Hernando De Soto on his monumental expedition to explore the North American continent. As one of the leaders of the Spanish conquest of the Incan empire, De Soto was already a wealthy man, but he desired still greater riches and power. In 1536 he returned to Spain, where he successfully petitioned the king for the right to explore and conquer the uncharted lands of North America.

Accompanied by several hundred men, De Soto searched for elusive treasures for three years, beginning on the west coast of Florida and wandering throughout the southern half of the continent. In 1541 he crossed the Mississippi somewhere south of Memphis and named the river *Rio del Spirito Santo,* meaning "river of the Holy Spirit."

De Soto never found the riches he sought, and encountered fierce opposition from many of the Indians his expedition encountered and tried to enslave. In 1542 he contracted a fever and died. His men weighted his body with stones and released it into the Mississippi—a fitting burial for the first European to see its mighty waters.

Antique trolley cars provide entertaining tours of Memphis landmarks.

another local favorite. The restaurant is housed in a turn-of-the-century warehouse overlooking the river on land once occupied by Confederate forces during their defense of Memphis. The Pier serves lunch Monday through Friday and dinner beginning at 5:00 P.M. daily; prices are moderate to expensive. You'll find the restaurant (901–526–7381) at 100 Wagner Place.

Finally, no description of Memphis would be complete without a reference to the famous **Peabody Hotel** (901–529–4000). The original Peabody opened its doors in 1869 during the turbulent days of Reconstruction, following the Civil War. The $60,000 hotel was one of the most opulent in the South, and hosted such notables as William Faulkner and Robert E. Lee. In 1925 the Peabody moved to its present location at 149 Union Avenue, and in the 1930s its famous duck parades began as a joke played by the hotel's general manager and some friends. The tradition has continued for more than sixty years. Each morning a 50-foot-long red carpet is unrolled, and a parade of ducks troops into the lobby. After a day spent splashing in the hotel's marble fountain, they make their way back to the elevator that takes them to their rooftop home. The ducks have helped make the Peabody world-famous, and even if you can't stay in this luxurious hotel, you can still enjoy the Peabody ducks.

The hotel is famous for another reason as well: According to author and historian David Cohn, the "Mississippi Delta begins in the lobby of the Peabody Hotel." From here southward the river road runs through the fertile region that has given birth to so much history, folklore, music, and culture.

FOR MORE INFORMATION
ABOUT KENTUCKY

Kentucky Office of Tourism (800) 225–TRIP, ext. 67

Kentucky State Parks (800) 255–PARK

Wickliffe (502) 335–3531

Hickman (502) 236–2902

FOR MORE INFORMATION
ABOUT TENNESSEE

Tennessee Department of Tourist Development (615) 741–2158

Tennessee State Parks (800) 421–6683

Reelfoot Lake Tourism Council (901) 885–0211

Memphis (800) 8–MEMPHIS

Arkansas

Blytheville
Osceola
Lepanto
Wilson

Marion
West Memphis

Marianna
Helena/West Helena

DeWitt

Dumas
Arkansas Post
Rohwer
McGehee
Arkansas City
Lake Village
Eudora

Mississippi River

N
W · E
S

Arkansas

n Arkansas the Mississippi passes through some of the richest and most productive agricultural land in the country. The fertile Arkansas portion of the Mississippi Delta produces bountiful harvests of soybeans, rice, cotton, and wheat. As in Tennessee and Kentucky, the river road runs primarily through rural countryside, past fields of ripening crops, pecan orchards with neat, straight rows, and forests and bayous of great natural beauty. The state's major river city is Helena, a town rich in Civil War history and lovely antebellum mansions.

Many travelers will be surprised to find that this part of the Mississippi Delta has hills. A unique geological formation called Crowley's Ridge runs for about 200 miles from southern Missouri to the Mississippi River at Helena, Arkansas. The tree-covered ridge is formed of loess, a highly erodible, fertile soil that was deposited by wind and water action over several million years. This scenic area has served as a recreational retreat for northeast Arkansas since the early 1800s and is named after Benjamin Crowley, a soldier during the War of 1812 who later founded the first settlement in this part of the state.

BLYTHEVILLE TO MARIANNA

The Mississippi River enters the state near **Blytheville,** 6 miles south of the Missouri state line. The town is home to the **Ritz Civic Center,** at 306 West Main Street, where local and touring stage productions are showcased in a renovated movie palace (501–762–1744). **Barfield Landing** is a county park that offers a lovely view of the river, and west of Blytheville is the **Big Lake National Wildlife Refuge,** one of the oldest refuges in the United States.

Follow Highway 61 south for 17 miles to **Osceola,** named for the Indian chief who fought against white settlers in Florida during the Seminole Wars of the 1830s. The bend of the Mississippi here is called Plum Point and was once the most feared stretch along the entire lower river. Many boats were wrecked by the bend's sandbars, unpredictable currents, and half-submerged trees and snags. Plum Point was also the site of one of the Civil War's few naval engagements, when seven Confederate steamers, converted into iron-nosed battering rams, sank two Union gunboats.

Continue on Highway 61 for 12 miles to **Wilson,** site of **Hampson Museum State Park.** The museum features a large collection of artifacts from the Nodena, a group of Native Americans who lived along the banks of the Mississippi here from A.D. 1350 to 1700. The Nodena were farmers who developed a civilization with elaborate art, far-reaching trade networks, and complex religious and political structures. The collection owes its existence to Dr. James K. Hampson, who along with his family meticulously excavated, studied, and inventoried the site in the 1930s. The museum (501–655–8622) is at the junction of Highway 61 and Lake Drive and is open 8:00 A.M. to 5:00 P.M., Tuesday through Saturday, and from 1:00 to 5:00 P.M. on Sunday.

Though the river road continues south from Wilson, you may want to take a 16-mile detour on Highway 14 west to **Lepanto,** where the **Le panto U.S.A. Museum** is housed in a historic bank building in the middle of this little delta town. Displays on early businesses, vintage photos, nineteenth-century fashions, and local history are featured. The museum (501–475–2222) is open noon to 4:00 P.M. on Saturday and 1:00 to 4:00 P.M. on Sunday from April through October.

Once you're back on Highway 61, continue south for 20 miles to Turrell and then head south again on Highway 77 for 12 miles to **Marion,** which hosts the **Esperanza Bonanza Festival** on the first weekend in May. Named after a fort that once stood in the area, the festival includes a Civil War battle reenactment, barbecue competition, crawfish bobbing contest, arts and crafts, and carnival rides. Call (501) 739–3071 for information.

Just south of Marion on Highway 77 is the sprawling city of **West Memphis,** located across the river from Memphis, Tennessee. The area is home to Southland Greyhound Park, the world's largest greyhound racing facility, and offers convenient access to all the attractions across the river.

Delta Farm Tours, though based in Memphis, offers guided tours of cotton plantations, catfish farms, cotton gins, and peanut farms on the Arkansas side of the river. Call (901) 527–6823 for information.

Each year on the third weekend in October, West Memphis hosts its **Livin' on the Levee Festival,** which celebrates the music, food, and culture of the delta region. Events include a carnival, live entertainment, a barbecue contest, a chili cook-off, and a catfish-cooking contest. Call (501) 732–7589 for information.

From West Memphis head west on Highway 70 for 12 miles and then south on Highway 79 for 36 miles to **Marianna.** The town was named after the daughter of its founder and is known as "the city beautiful." Dogwoods thrive along its streets and are so popular that Marianna hosts an annual dogwood competition. The **Marianna–Lee County Museum** occupies a house listed on the National Register and features Indian artifacts, pioneer exhibits, cotton displays, and memorabilia from the Civil War and World Wars I and II. The museum (501–295–2469) is at 67 West Main Street.

Mississippi Barges

One hundred and fifty years ago, steamboats crowded the Mississippi, but today towboats and barges dominate the river. Contrary to their name, towboats actually *push* their cargoes. Tows on the Upper Mississippi include a maximum of fifteen loaded barges, the equivalent of a 225-car train or more than 900 semitrailer trucks. On the wider channel of the lower river, loads of forty to forty-five barges are not uncommon.

The largest tonnage items on the river are petroleum products: gasoline, kerosene, fuel oil, and lubricating oil are shipped upriver from the oil fields of Texas and Louisiana. Huge shipments of coal also travel upstream, mainly from the coalfields of central and southern Illinois and western Kentucky. The principal product sent downriver is grain—primarily corn, wheat, oats, barley, and rye—which is loaded onto barges from riverside elevators. Most of the grain is headed to New Orleans, where it is loaded aboard ocean freighters and shipped overseas.

From Marianna you have a choice of two routes south. The first option runs south on Highway 1 for 15 miles and then east on Highway 49 for 7 miles to West Helena. The much lovelier route is the **St. Francis Scenic Byway,** which will give you a glimpse of the beautiful hardwood forests that once covered most of the region. The byway winds through the entire length of the 21,000-acre St. Francis National Forest, which encompasses cypress swamps, rolling pastures, and dense woods of yellow poplar, beech, oak, hickory, sassafras, and dogwood. Most of the forest is located along Crowley's Ridge, which rises more than 200 feet above the surrounding farmlands. The byway includes Arkansas Highway 44 and U.S. Forest Service Road 1900 and runs for about 21 miles between Marianna and Helena.

HELENA TO EUDORA

At **Helena** and West Helena, the river road returns to the Mississippi. West Helena sits atop Crowley's Ridge and is the more commercial and industrial of the two. Helena is a classic river town and occupies what Mark Twain described as "one of the prettiest situations on the Mississippi."

When Hernando de Soto crossed the Mississippi somewhere near Helena in 1541, he found a thriving native culture and large villages in the area. By the mid-1600s, however, up to 90 percent of the region's Indians had died, victims primarily of new diseases introduced by Europeans. The last survivors were forced onto a reservation farther west in 1833, the same year that Helena was incorporated as a town.

A single generation of land speculators, river traders, and cattle farmers transformed Helena into a thriving river port. Prior to the Civil War, the plantation system flourished in the Helena area, and many gracious plantation homes still stand today.

The city played an important role during the Civil War, when the Union army established a supply depot here. Confederate troops attacked the Union encampment in 1863, trying to regain the city and hamper the Union effort to seize Vicksburg. After a fierce battle they retreated, and the city remained in Union hands. The **Confederate Cemetery,** at 1801 Holly Street, contains a monument honoring those who died in the battle and the graves of some of the men who lost their lives here. The spot also affords a sweeping view of the Mississippi River.

Though Helena grew up along the riverbank, the Mississippi proved to be the nemesis of its downtown. Water Street, where much of the city's commercial activity was centered, eroded piece by piece into the river after the Civil War. Then in 1896, Congress appropriated money for riveting Helena's harbor, thereby checking the roving river. Willow mats were laid along its banks and weighed down with stone, and pieces of the mats can still be found today.

Helena has recently made a concerted effort to preserve and restore its many historic structures and is working to revitalize its riverfront with a number of projects. The **Delta Cultural Center** is the centerpiece of its efforts. Located in a restored 1903 railroad depot, the center has exhibits on the delta's first Native American inhabitants, the music of the delta, the steamboat and railroad eras, the Civil War, the diverse ethnic groups that settled the region, and the area's natural history. The center (501–338–8919) is at 95 Missouri Street and is open 10:00 A.M. to 5:00 P.M., Monday through Saturday, and 1:00 to 5:00 P.M. Sunday.

The 142-acre **Helena Reach River Park** is located adjacent to the center and includes an elevated boardwalk with a lovely view of the river. Another part of the revitalization project, the **Helena Marketplace,** can be found at 201 Cherry Street. A variety of crafts, antiques, and specialty foods are sold at the marketplace, which is also the site of a farmer's market and special events.

The **Phillips County Library and Museum** (501–338–3537) is an 1891 Second Empire–style structure at 623 Pecan Street that contains Civil War displays and other historical items. It's open 1:00 to 4:00 P.M., Monday through Saturday.

Elsewhere in town you'll find many restored antebellum and Victorian buildings. The Helena Tourism Commission (501–338–9831), at 226 Perry Street, publishes a guidebook to the town's most significant architecture. Take special note of Estevan Hall, an 1826 structure at 653 Biscoe Street that was occupied by the Union Army during the Civil War.

The **Edwardian Inn** is a Helena landmark that is considered one of the South's finest bed-and-breakfast inns. Built in 1904 by a local cotton broker and speculator, the home, at 317 Biscoe Street, has a beautiful circular porch, eight fireplaces, and richly detailed woodwork inside. Twelve guest rooms are offered, and the inn (501–338–9155) is also open for public tours from 10:00 A.M. to 6:00 P.M. daily.

The Edwardian Inn showcases Southern hospitality and style.

On the second weekend in October, Helena pays homage to its rich blues heritage with the **King Biscuit Blues Festival.** The event is named after the vintage radio program *King Biscuit Time,* a music show that began broadcasting from Helena in 1941. The program provided a forum for such blues legends as Sonny Boy Williamson and Robert Junior Lockwood. The festival includes live music, arts and crafts, and a barbecue cooking contest. For information call (501) 338–9144.

Though Highway 20 borders the Mississippi south of Helena, in order to cross the White River you need to go west on Highway 49 for 12 miles to Marvell and then take Highway 1 south. This route takes you through the 113,000-acre **White River National Wildlife Refuge,** the largest remaining tract of bottomland hardwoods in the state. An estimated 200 bears roam this primeval wilderness, making their dens in trees to avoid the floods that cover the area as many as six months out of the year.

Continue on Highway 1 for 33 miles to DeWitt and then head south on Highway 165. Six miles south of Gillett, take a 2-mile detour on Highway 169 to the **Arkansas Post National Monument.** The monument marks the location of one of the first permanent settlements in the Lower Mississippi River Valley. Henri de Tonti built a trading post here in 1686, and the settlement, named Arkansas Post, was designated as the territory's first capital in 1819. Three years later, however, the more centrally located settlement of Little Rock won the distinction of state capital, a twist of fate that led to the village's rapid decline. Though today no inhabitants remain, historians have identified the remains of at least ten different forts and settlements in the area. The monument's visitors center (510–548–2207) is open daily.

The nearby **Arkansas Post County Museum** includes a number of authentic structures from the delta region and an antique farm equipment exhibit. For information, call (501) 548–2207.

From Arkansas Post continue on Highway 165 for 15 miles to **Dumas,** home to the **Desha County Museum,** at 165 South Main Street. The site includes five restored buildings containing artifacts that re-create life in a typical south Arkansas farming community. The museum (501–382–4222) is open Tuesday, Thursday, and Sunday afternoons.

Dumas also hosts the **Ding Dong Days Festival,** named after the memorable country song that immortalized the town, "I'm a Ding Dong

Arkansas Post

I solated Arkansas Post is quiet today, but it has seen a considerable amount of history since 1682, when the French explorer Robert Cavelier, Sieur de La Salle, visited the region on his journey through the Mississippi River valley. La Salle hoped to found an inland empire that would extend from French Canada to the Gulf of Mexico and as part of that plan, he granted an extensive land and trading concession for the area to his trusted friend and lieutenant, Henri de Tonti. In 1686, de Tonti sent several men to build a trading post here near the confluence of the Arkansas and Mississippi rivers. The post later became the site of French and Spanish forts and trading stations, the scene of a skirmish in the wake of the Revolutionary War, a territorial capital, and a thriving river port.

Once the capital was moved to Little Rock in 1821, however, the town quickly declined. A fierce naval bombardment during the Civil War destroyed many of its buildings while the Arkansas River relentlessly eroded its land. Arkansas Post, once a thriving center for commerce, government, and transportation, faded into obscurity.

Daddy From Dumas." The celebration is held on the last weekend in April and includes parades, antique car shows, live music, a theater production, and barbecue.

From Dumas head south for 4 miles on Highway 65. A 17-mile detour east on Highway 138 and 2 miles south on Highway 1 will take you to **Rohwer,** the site of a Japanese internment camp during World War II. The **Rohwer Historic Marker** honors the former Rohwer internees as well as the 442d Japanese-American unit of the One Hundredth Battalion, which distinguished itself in World War II combat. The marker is a monument to courage in adversity.

Next continue south on Highway 1 for 11 miles to **McGehee,** a major railroad and agricultural center. You can see a sample of the town's railroad heritage in its city park, where an antique caboose is on display.

A 12-mile detour east on Highway 4 will take you to **Arkansas City,** a county seat that was once a busy steamboat port. The great flood of 1927 submerged the entire town, and the 650-mile levee built after the disaster is the longest in the United States. A few historic buildings remain in the town, including the **Desha County Courthouse,** which is one of the oldest in the state.

Return to Highway 65 and travel south for 20 miles to **Lake Village,** which sits on Lake Chicot, Arkansas' largest natural lake and the nation's largest oxbow lake. Twenty miles in length, the lake is part of the Mississippi Flyway and offers outstanding bird watching. On Lakeshore Drive the **Lindbergh Marker** notes the area where Charles Lindbergh made his first night flight in 1923.

From Lake Village continue south on Highway 65 for 17 miles to **Eudora,** the final town on the Arkansas portion of the Great River Road. Eudora is known as the state's catfish capital and hosts the **Arkansas Catfish Festival** on the second weekend in May. The celebration includes a catfish cook-off, catfish racing, a catfish eating contest, and a beauty pageant (for young women, not catfish). Call (501) 355–8443 for information.

The **Rubye and Henry Connerly Museum,** between South Main and Archer streets, houses local history displays in an old grocery store. The museum is open by appointment; call (501) 355–4633 for information.

The Main Street historic district in Eudora includes several Italianate structures listed on the National Register, including the 1901 **Dr. A. G. Anderson House,** which is the site of the town's chamber of commerce and visitors center. The house is at 185 South Main Street; call (501) 355–8443 for information.

FOR MORE INFORMATION

Arkansas Department of Parks and Tourism (800) – NATURAL

Blytheville (501) 762–2012

West Memphis (501) 732–7598

Helena (501) 338–9831

DeWitt (501) 946–3551

Lake Village (501) 265–5997

Eudora (501) 355–8443

Mississippi

he Mississippi River has given the state of Mississippi much more than simply its name. It has influenced the state's history and culture in countless ways, and it continues to be a powerful presence today.

The delta—which historian and writer David Cohn said "begins in the lobby of the Peabody Hotel in Memphis and ends on Catfish Row in Vicksburg"—is both a mood and a place in Mississippi. Its soil has nurtured rich veins of music and literature, including that distinctively American musical form, the blues.

A sense of history permeates the river towns in the state and can be felt in many antebellum landmarks. The plantation system flourished here before the Civil War, and many of the nation's wealthiest estates lined the Mississippi and its tributaries. The fertile land along the river banks assured abundant crops, and the waterways provided a convenient transportation system. Lucrative cotton—nicknamed "white gold"—was the major product, the foundation upon which the Old South was built.

The river also winds past landmarks that record the downfall of the Old South. Carefully preserved Civil War battlefields, most importantly the Vicksburg National Military Park, tell the story of a nation torn apart by civil war.

TUNICA TO VICKSBURG

The river enters Mississippi in DeSoto County, named for the Spanish explorer Hernando de Soto, who discovered the Mississippi River in 1541. From the Tennessee border follow Highway 61 south for 25 miles to

Tunica, the county seat of Tunica County. Casino gambling has helped revitalize the economically depressed area; there are eight gaming establishments in operation in Tunica County. For information about gambling call (601) 363–2865.

From Tunica continue south on Highway 61 for 20 miles to its intersection with Highway 49. Travel 2.3 miles west toward the river and you'll find a famed eatery named **Uncle Henry's Place.** Built in 1926, the restaurant was known as the Moon Lake Club in the 1930s and 1940s and appears in the works of both Tennessee Williams and William Faulkner. Long before the Tunica casinos were built, the club was known for its fine food and music and lively nightlife. Today the restaurant is famous for its seafood and Cajun and Creole dishes. It also operates a bed-and-breakfast establishment on its former casino floor. You'll find Uncle Henry's Place (601–337–2757) at 5860 Moon Lake Road.

Return to Highway 61 and head south for 15 miles to **Clarksdale.** There you'll find the **Delta Blues Museum,** which celebrates the unique music that was born on the Mississippi Delta. Blues greats such as W. C. Handy, Muddy Waters, Charlie Patton, and Robert Johnson once made their home in Clarksdale and surrounding Coahoma County, and the museum contains recordings, photographs, videotapes, books, and other memorabilia from their lives and those of many other blues musicians. The museum also provides a map of Clarksdale landmarks relating to the city's blues heritage, including several local "juke joints" and the former homes of Muddy Waters and Ike Turner. The museum shows how the blues evolved from the chants of slaves and field hands and describes their influence on American music. With their mournful wails and dryly humorous lyrics, the blues are sometimes described as a way of life as well as a musical form. The museum (601–624–4461) is housed in the Carnegie Public Library at 114 Delta Avenue and is open from 9:00 A.M. to 5:00 P.M., Monday through Friday, and from 10:00 A.M. to 5:00 P.M. on Saturday. The library also houses a collection of Native American artifacts.

Each August the Delta Blues Museum hosts the **Sunflower River Blues Festival,** when performers present the best in contemporary blues and gospel music. Call (601) 624–4461 for information.

From Clarksdale take Highway 322 west for 8 miles and then travel south on Highway 1 for 33 miles to Rosedale. There you'll find the **Great River Road State Park,** whose 800 acres include an observation tower that overlooks the Mississippi. Call (601) 759–6762 for information.

The Shrinking Mississippi

Throughout the Lower Mississippi, crescent-shaped lakes often lie next to the river. These are called oxbow lakes and are formed when a bend in the river becomes silted in and is cut off from the main channel. In effect, the river is continually trying to shorten its path to the sea by finding shortcuts that bypass wide bends.

Mark Twain had this opinion about the phenomenon:

In the space of one hundred and seventy-six years the lower Mississippi has shortened itself two hundred and forty-two miles. That is an average of a trifle over one mile and a third per year. Therefore, any calm person, who is not blind or idiotic, can see that in the Old Oölitic Silurian Period, just a million years ago next November, the Lower Mississippi River was upwards of one million three hundred thousand miles long, and stuck out over the Gulf of Mexico like a fishing rod. And by the same token any person can see that seven hundred and forty-two years from now the Lower Mississippi will be only a mile and three quarters long, and Cairo and New Orleans will have joined their streets together, and be plodding comfortably along under a single mayor and a mutual board of aldermen. There is something fascinating about science. One gets such wholesale returns of conjecture out of such a trifling investment of fact.

Mark Twain
Life on the Mississippi

From Rosedale continue on Highway 1 for 30 miles to **Winterville Mounds Historic Site,** just north of **Greenville.** The site preserves one of the largest Indian mound groups in the Mississippi Valley. A museum (601–334–4684) displays artifacts from the mounds and has exhibits on the culture of the people who built them. It is open Wednesday through Saturday.

Follow Highway 1 into **Greenville,** a busy river city that calls itself the "towboat capital of the world." Greenville is the center for commerce and culture on the delta. The **River Road Queen Welcome Center** is a good place to gather visitor information. The center is a replica of a nineteenth-century riverboat that was built for the Louisiana World Exposition. The center (601–332–2378) is located at the intersection of Highway 82 and Reed Road.

After getting oriented at the welcome center, pay a visit to the **Mississippi River Flood Museum,** which contains information on the 1927 flood, the largest and most devastating flood in the delta's history. The museum (601–378–3141) is in the Greenville chamber of commerce building at 915 Washington Avenue and is open from 8:00 A.M. to 5:00 P.M., Monday through Friday.

Travelers interested in the southern literary tradition should tour the **Greenville Writer's Exhibit** at the William Alexander Percy Memorial Library. This permanent exhibit honors the town's impressive literary heritage and includes memorabilia, photographs, and the original manuscripts of nearly fifty Greenville authors, including Civil War historian and novelist Shelby Foote, novelist Walker Percy, and poet Angela Jackson. The library (601–335–2331) is at 341 Main Street and is open Monday through Saturday.

Each year on the third Saturday in September, Greenville hosts the **Delta Blues Festival,** an outdoor celebration of the music of the region that includes performances by some of the world's best blues musicians as well as ethnic foods and arts and crafts. Call (601) 335–3523 for information.

For overnight accommodations in Greenville, try **Miss Lois' Victorian Inn.** The 1898 Victorian cottage–style bed-and-breakfast offers three guest rooms as well as a guest house. The inn (601–335–6000) is located at 331 South Washington Avenue.

From Greenville continue south on Highways 1 and 61 for 80 miles to the famed river city of **Vicksburg.** Located on the bluffs of the Mississippi, the city was founded in 1811 by the Reverend Newit Vick, a Methodist minister. When Mississippi seceded from the Union in 1861, the North immediately recognized the importance of gaining control of Vicksburg. One of the nation's largest and most sophisticated cities, Vicksburg dominated the Mississippi River and was a major port for the cotton trade. After a number of unsuccessful attempts to take the city by force, in 1863 Ulysses S. Grant and his troops laid siege to Vicksburg for forty-seven days.

Despite the city's heroism and tenacity, starvation broke the stalemate, and on July 4 Vicksburg surrendered. It took eighty-two years before the memories of the war had faded sufficiently to allow the city to celebrate Independence Day with the rest of the nation.

The Siege of Vicksburg

"Vicksburg is the key. . . . Let us get Vicksburg, and all that country is ours. The war can never be brought to a close until that key is in our pocket."

Abraham Lincoln's words indicated Vicksburg's enormous strategic importance during the Civil War. A captured Vicksburg would sever Texas, Arkansas, and Louisiana from the Confederacy and put the vital Mississippi River transportation corridor in Union hands.

General Ulysses S. Grant launched the Vicksburg campaign in the spring of 1863. After several attempts to take the city directly—and another attempt to bypass it by cutting a channel through the land opposite the city so that gunboats could travel the Mississippi beyond the range of Confederate guns—Vicksburg remained impregnable. In the words of one Confederate colonel: "I have to state that Mississippians don't know and refuse to learn how to surrender to an enemy."

Finally Grant decided that the only way the city could be taken was by siege. For forty-seven days and nights, Union troops shelled the city. Vicksburg citizens took shelter in caves dug into the hillsides and suffered through oppressive summer heat and inadequate water and food supplies as well as the constant rain of shells. Finally, on July 4, 1863, the city surrendered. When the Union soldiers entered the city, they found a starving population and barely a single window that had not been shattered by shells.

The campaign for Vicksburg is considered by many historians to be one of the most ingenious military actions in American history, and the fall of the city dealt a crushing blow to the Confederacy.

Memories of the Old South and the Civil War linger everywhere in Vicksburg. Its tree-shaded streets include many beautiful homes dating back to the days when "cotton was king," and a number of museums preserve its fascinating history. The city also boasts some of the country's finest bed-and-breakfasts, where guests can sample the antebellum life of the upper classes. (Most also offer tours for the general public for around $5.00.)

The best place to begin your tour of the city is at the **Vicksburg National Military Park,** considered by many to be the nation's best-preserved Civil War battlefield. Its 1,800 acres of rolling green lawns and wooded hills include many of the most significant sites of the Vicksburg campaign. The visitors center features exhibits and artifacts from the siege and shows an eighteen-minute film that recounts the military campaign. A 16-mile driving tour provides red markers that identify interpretive information relating to the Confederate army's role and blue markers that relate information on the Union forces. Nearly all of the twenty-eight states that sent soldiers to Vicksburg have erected monuments in the park, commemorating the valor of the troops on both sides of the conflict. The site also includes the Vicksburg National Cemetery, where nearly 17,000 Union soldiers are buried, of whom about 13,000 are unknown. (Many of the Confederate soldiers who died during the campaign are buried in the Vicksburg City Cemetery, which adjoins the park.)

The grounds also include the partially restored **U.S.S.** *Cairo,* an ironclad Union gunboat that sank during the war and was raised after one hundred years underwater. The nearby museum features displays of the boat's artifacts, which offer valuable information about the Civil War period.

Memories of tragedy and heroism linger at Vicksburg National Military Park.

Vicksburg National Military Park (601–636–0583) is located in the northeastern portion of the city; its entrance and visitors center are on Clay Street. The Cairo Museum is located in the park's northern section. Both museums are open from 9:00 A.M. to 5:00 P.M. daily.

After touring the park, pay a visit to the 1858 **Old Courthouse,** a structure considered to be the city's single most historic building. During the war the building's location on Vicksburg's highest hill made it a favorite target for Union shells—until all of the city's Union prisoners were transferred there, a ploy that saved the courthouse from destruction. It was here that the Confederate flag was lowered and the Union flag raised after the surrender of the city. Today the courthouse is a museum housing artifacts relating to the Civil War period, the native cultures of the area, and the steamboat era. Among its artifacts are the trophy antlers won in 1870 by the *Rob't E. Lee* when it beat the *Natchez* in the biggest steamboat race in history (see page 236 for more on this race). The Old Courthouse Museum (601–636–0741) is located at 1008 Cherry Street and is open from 8:30 A.M. to 4:30 P.M., Monday through Saturday, and from 1:30 to 4:30 P.M. on Sunday.

Next visit the **Gray and Blue Naval Museum,** which recounts the naval history of the Civil War. The museum includes the world's largest collection of Civil War gunboat models plus other artifacts, paintings, and reference materials relating to the war. The museum (601–638–6500) is located at 1823 Clay Street and is open from 9:00 A.M. to 5:00 P.M., Monday through Saturday, and from 1:00 to 5:00 P.M. on Sunday.

You can learn more about the human toll of the war at the old Strand Theater, in the city's downtown. The theater shows the film *Vanishing Glory,* which tells the story of the siege through the diaries and writings of the citizens and soldiers who lived through it. The multimedia presentation is shown daily on the hour, beginning at 10:00 A.M. The Strand Theater (601–634–1863) is located at 717 Clay Street.

More military history is on display at the **Toys and Soldiers Museum,** which includes Civil War artifacts, military uniforms, and a toy soldier collection that is one of the largest in the world. The privately owned museum is housed in an 1840s-era building that was once a grocery store. The site also includes a fine gift shop. The museum (601–638–1986), at 1100 Cherry Street, is open from 9:00 A.M. to 4:30 P.M., Monday through Saturday, and from 1:30 to 4:30 P.M. on Sunday.

Two other museums in Vicksburg, while not related to the Civil War period, give insight into its nineteenth-century past. Downtown you'll find the **Biedenharn Museum of Coca-Cola History and Memorabilia,** which preserves the site where Joseph Biedenharn, a young candy merchant, first bottled the popular soft drink in 1894 so that it could be shipped into rural areas. The museum (601–638–6514), at 1107 Washington Street, includes an authentically restored, turn-of-the-century candy store and soda fountain. It is open from 9:00 A.M. to 5:00 P.M., Monday through Saturday, and from 1:30 to 4:30 P.M. on Sunday.

Another museum with a historical theme is **Yesterday's Children Antique Doll and Toy Museum,** which is housed in an 1836 building and contains four rooms filled with more than a thousand toys dating from the 1880s. The museum (601–638–0650) is located at 1104 Washington Street and is open from 9:30 A.M. to 4:30 P.M., Monday through Saturday.

In addition to its museums, Vicksburg also shares its history in a dozen historic homes that are open year-round for tours. One of the oldest is the **Martha Vick House,** which was built for the unmarried daughter of the city's founder, Newit Vick. The 1830 Greek Revival home is furnished with eighteenth- and early nineteenth-century antiques and includes a large collection of French Impressionist paintings. The Vick House (601–638–7036) is located at 1300 Grove Street and is open from 9:00 A.M. to 5:00 P.M., Monday through Saturday, and from 2:00 to 5:00 P.M. on Sunday.

More antebellum history lives on in the **Duff Green Mansion,** an 1856 structure that is considered to be one of the finest examples of Palladian architecture in the state. Built by the prosperous merchant Duff Green for his bride, Mary, the home was hastily converted into a military hospital for both Union and Confederate soldiers during the siege of Vicksburg. The Confederate wounded were treated in the basement to protect them from the shelling, while Union soldiers were quartered on the roof. Mary Green gave birth to a son during the siege in one of the caves next to the mansion and appropriately named him Siege Green. The restored, 12,000-square-foot mansion is open for daily tours and also offers seven guest rooms. The Duff Green Mansion (800–992–0037) is at 1114 First East Street.

A block west of the Green mansion is **Anchuca,** an 1830 Greek Revival mansion furnished with period antiques and gas-lighted chandeliers. Its owners take pride in the fact that Jefferson Davis once addressed the townspeople of Vicksburg from the home's balcony. Anchuca (800–262–4822), at 1010 First East Street, is open for daily tours and also offers bed-and-breakfast accommodations.

The **McRaven Home** was once described by *National Geographic Magazine* as a "time capsule of the South." The mansion was constructed over several decades and illustrates three styles—1797 Frontier, 1836 Empire, and 1849 Greek Revival. Its furnishings include many original pieces as well as many Civil War artifacts. The owner of the house was killed in the garden by Union troops, and a live shell from Civil War days was removed from one of the house's walls by a bomb squad in the 1950s. Guided tours are offered daily and discuss the history of the home and city as well as the customs of the Old South. McRaven (601–636–1663) is located at 1445 Harrison Street.

The **Cedar Grove Estate** preserves more antebellum glory. The mansion was built around 1840 overlooking the Mississippi and is now one of the South's largest and loveliest historic inns. Its restored interior is furnished with beautiful antiques, and surrounding the home are four acres of gardens with fountains, gazebos, and courtyards. Daily tours are offered. In addition there are twenty luxurious guest rooms, and the home is also open daily for evening dining (prices are moderate to expensive). Cedar Grove (800–862–1300) is located at 2300 Washington Street.

Another home that should be on your tour list is the 1835 **Balfour House.** Considered to be one of the finest Greek Revival structures in the state, the mansion was the home of the noted Civil War diarist Emma Harrison Balfour, whose impressions of the siege of Vicksburg have proved invaluable to historians. Her home was a center for activity during the siege and was known as the "house of generals" because it was frequented by a number of Confederate military leaders. After the city's surrender, Balfour House became the headquarters for Union general James Birdseye McPherson's occupational forces. The award-winning restoration of the home in 1982 uncovered a cannonball and other Civil War artifacts. The Balfour House (800–294–7113) is located at Crawford Street and Hall's Ferry Road and is open for daily tours.

These and many more of Vicksburg's finest mansions are open for tours during the **Spring and Fall Pilgrimages,** held in March and October of each year. On Friday and Saturday evenings during the Spring Pilgrimage, the melodrama *Gold In The Hills* is performed at the Parkside Playhouse. For information call (800) 221–3536.

To experience the Mississippi itself and to learn more about how the river has influenced the city, book a **Mississippi River Adventure.** The hydro-jet boat tours depart from the city's waterfront at the foot of Clay

Spring Pilgrimage

Spring is Mississippi's loveliest season, bringing blooming azaleas and dogwoods, a brilliant palette of flowers, and the quintessentially southern tradition of the Spring Pilgrimage.

The pilgrimage tradition began in Natchez in 1932, when the mistresses of the city's magnificent antebellum mansions were preparing for a state convention of garden clubs. Shortly before the event a late frost blanketed the town and wiped out all the blooms. Instead of showing off their gardens, the women decided to open their homes to the out-of-town guests. The event was so successful that it became an annual event in Natchez, and eventually many other communities in the South followed their lead.

Today the pilgrimages offer a chance to step back into the romance of the Old South, with horse-drawn carriages delivering guests to mansions presided over by hostesses in hoop skirts. The proceeds from the events go in part to refurbish the homes, and many communities hold other activities in combination with the home tours, including theater performances, musical events, and historical reenactments. In short, there's no better time to play Scarlett O'Hara than during Spring Pilgrimage season.

Street for three 40-mile, narrated tours daily. Cruises are offered from March 1 through mid-November; tickets are $25 for adults and $15 for children. Call (800) 521–4363 for information.

Dockside gambling is also a popular attraction in Vicksburg. While the city's casinos don't cruise the Mississippi, they do offer good views of the river. For more information, call (800) 221–3536.

Vicksburg is also the site of the **Waterways Experiment Station,** the largest research facility operated by the U.S. Army Corps of Engineers. Inside are working scale models of many of the nation's rivers, dams, harbors, and tidal waterways. The sprawling, 673-acre station was established in response to the Mississippi River flood of 1927, one of the nation's most destructive natural disasters. Today it is one of the largest and most sophisticated research facilities of its kind in the world, with over 1,500 employees.

Visitors can tour its visitors center and enjoy the arboretum that surrounds the facility. The station's main entrance is located 2 miles south of Interstate 20 on Halls Ferry Road; guided tours are given from 10:00 A.M. to 2:00 P.M., Monday through Friday. Call (601) 634–2502 for information.

For dining with a historic theme, stop at **Tuminello's.** The restaurant is located on the site of a former marine hospital that was established in 1843 for the care of merchant seamen. After the hospital was demolished in 1892, Dominic Tuminello used many of its heavy timbers and bricks to construct a grocery, and in 1899 he opened a restaurant that catered to railroad workers. Today Tuminello's is known for its Italian and continental cuisine. The restaurant (601–634–0507) is located at 500 Speed Street and is open evenings from Tuesday through Sunday (prices are moderate to expensive).

The **New Orleans Cafe** is also housed in an antebellum structure, a building at 1100 Washington Street that once housed Freedman's Saving Bank, the first bank for blacks in the United States. The cafe (601–638–8182) is open from 11:00 A.M. to 10:00 P.M. daily, and the prices of its Creole cuisine are moderate.

A good time to visit Vicksburg is during **RiverFest,** held each year in mid-April. The event includes street dancing, live entertainment, and lots of good food. Then in May Civil War buffs converge on the city to stage a **Civil War Reenactment** of the Battle of Vicksburg. In July another reenactment is held, the **Assault on Vicksburg,** which includes living history demonstrations of how life was for Vicksburg citizens during the siege.

GRAND GULF TO WOODVILLE

From Vicksburg head south on Highway 61 for 20 miles and then go west on Grand Gulf Road for 8 miles to **Grand Gulf Military Park. Grand Gulf** was once a boom town and major river port and was named for a whirlpool formed where the Mississippi surged against the shore. That whirlpool proved the town's undoing in the late 1850s, when the Mississippi claimed the entire business section of the city. By the time the war began, Grand Gulf's population had dwindled to 150 people, but it was nevertheless an important Confederate stronghold because of its position on the river. After the Union victory at Port Gibson, Grand Gulf was abandoned by the

Confederates, and General Grant occupied the town and used it as a supply base for the inland phase of the Vicksburg campaign. When the troops left, they burned the town's remaining buildings.

Today Grand Gulf is a virtual ghost town, but the 400-acre military park preserves the Confederate fortifications and includes a museum filled with Civil War memorabilia and artifacts from Grand Gulf's history. The park's museum (601–437–5911) is open from 8:00 A.M. to 5:00 P.M., Monday through Saturday, and from 9:00 A.M. to 6:00 P.M. on Sunday. Also in the park is an observation tower that is a good place to view the wide waters of the Mississippi.

From Grand Gulf travel south to **Port Gibson,** one of Mississippi's oldest and most historic small cities. The town grew up in the 1700s around a boat landing for a plantation owned by Samuel Gibson on the south fork of the Bayou Pierre. During the Civil War the Union victory in the Battle of Port Gibson in 1863 was an important step in the campaign to capture Vicksburg. After Grant declared that the town "was too beautiful to burn," Port Gibson was spared the destruction that befell many other Southern cities.

Much of Port Gibson has been placed on the National Register of Historic Places, including a number of beautiful churches as well as historic mansions. The 1805 **Samuel Gibson House** is the oldest existing structure in Port Gibson and now houses the town's chamber of commerce and visitors information center. You'll find the Gibson House (601–437–4351) on Church Street, which is also Highway 61.

A number of mansions in the area offer overnight lodging and tours. One is **Oak Square,** Port Gibson's largest and most ornate mansion. Built around 1850, the Greek Revival home is filled with period furnishings and a collection of Civil War memorabilia. Its grounds include a courtyard, fountain, and gazebo, plus massive oak trees that give the house its name. The mansion (800–729–0240) is at 1207 Church Street.

Each March, Oak Square hosts the **1800s Spring Festival,** a living-history event that includes period music and dancing, a fashion show, and craft demonstrations. Call (601) 437–5421 for information.

Gibson's Landing is another Port Gibson landmark. The 1832 Federal-style home is famous for its spiral staircase, which extends for three stories. The house (601–437–3432) is located at Church and Coffee streets and offers bed-and-breakfast accommodations.

The above-mentioned houses and nearly a dozen more of Port Gibson's finest homes are open during the town's annual **Spring Pilgrimage,** held in March. Call (601) 437–4351 for information.

Just south of Port Gibson you'll find an interesting detour, the **Natchez Trace Parkway.** The Trace extends for over 400 miles from Natchez, Mississippi, to Nashville, Tennessee, and follows the route of an important frontier highway. No commercial traffic or advertising is allowed along the Trace, and the road winds through an unspoiled countryside of blooming shrubs, stately pines, towering oaks dripping with Spanish moss, and bayous of cypress trees. For more information call (800) 647–2290.

If you decide not to take the Natchez Trace, from Port Gibson take Highway 552 west for 12 miles to another antebellum showplace, the **Canemount Plantation,** an Italianate Revival mansion built in 1855. Canemount is a 6,000-acre working plantation offering bed-and-breakfast accommodations as well as guided tours. Call (800) 423–0684 for information.

The Devil's Backbone

The history of the Natchez Trace, which stretches from Natchez to Nashville, predates European settlement. The route was first "traced" by animals, then traveled by Indians, and finally trampled into a rough road by trappers and traders.

The trail had become a well-worn route by the end of the 1700s, when growing numbers of settlers and merchants began floating products and produce down the Mississippi River to be sold in either Natchez or New Orleans. Their primitive flatboats could not return upstream and so were dismantled and sold for lumber down south. The "Kaintucks"—the term for people who hailed from anyplace farther north than Natchez—then set off for home, taking the overland route along the Natchez Trace.

The long trip was not for the faint of heart. Bandits, unfriendly Indians, wild animals, and poisonous snakes roamed the wilderness, earning the Trace the nickname "the Devil's Backbone." Even as minor a mishap as a broken leg could spell death for a solitary traveler. Many people only made the journey with the protection of a post rider who knew the area.

During the early 1800s, the Natchez Trace was the busiest highway in the nation's southwest. Then came an astounding invention: steamboats that could travel *up* the Mississippi. Within a few years, the road that had nourished the frontier had nearly vanished.

Canemount is also the site of the haunting **Ruins of Windsor,** the remains of the largest and most spectacular mansion ever constructed in Mississippi. After the Battle of Port Gibson, the Union forces turned Windsor into a hospital. Though the 1860 mansion escaped destruction during the war, a fire in 1890 destroyed everything but twenty-three towering columns. The ruins served as a backdrop for scenes in the movie *Raintree County,* with Elizabeth Taylor and Montgomery Clift.

From Canemount continue on Highway 552 as it loops back to Highway 61 and head south for one mile to the town of **Lorman.** There you'll find the **Old Country Store,** which has been both a functioning general store and a tourist attraction for many years. The building was constructed in 1890, and most of its fixtures, furnishings, and display cabinets are original. The store includes a free museum with antique memorabilia, and visitors can buy everything from old-fashioned hoop cheese and sunbonnets to souvenirs and hardware. This place is a living remnant of southern history. You'll find the Old Country Store (601–437–3661) on Highway 61 in Lorman.

Two miles east of Lorman on Highway 552 is **Rosswood,** an 1857 Greek Revival mansion situated on a one-hundred–acre estate. Before the war Rosswood was a thriving cotton plantation with 1,250 acres and 105 slaves working its fields. Today Christmas trees grow here instead of cotton, but inside the house an antebellum atmosphere prevails. The wealthy doctor who built the home kept a detailed diary of its construction and the daily workings of the cotton plantation, and this journal is on display for visitors. The mansion offers bed-and-breakfast accommodations, and the owners, Colonel and Mrs. Walt Hylander, are happy to share the home's history on guided tours that are offered daily from March through December. For information call (800) 533–5889.

From Rosswood return to Highway 61 and head south for 9 miles to Fayette. Halfway between Fayette and the Natchez Trace Parkway, to the west, is the **Springfield Plantation.** Built between 1786 and 1791 during the time when the Spanish still controlled the area, Springfield was one of the first houses in the United States to have a full colonnade across its entire facade, a style that would later dominate plantation architecture. In 1791 Andrew Jackson was married to Rachel Robards in this home, which has retained most of its original interior. After more than two centuries, Springfield is still a working plantation and also offers daily tours. For information call (601) 786–3802.

From Springfield return to either the Natchez Trace Parkway or Highway 61 and head south for 17 miles to the town of **Washington.** There you'll find **Historic Jefferson College,** which was founded in 1802 and named in honor of President Thomas Jefferson. Before the Civil War the college played a major role in shaping the intellectual and cultural development of frontier Mississippi. After the war's end it became a preparatory school and later operated as a military academy until it closed its doors in 1964. Tradition has it that Aaron Burr was arraigned for treason in 1807 beneath what came to be known as the Burr Oaks. Since then the campus has been extensively restored by the Mississippi Department of Archives and History. Visitors can tour the buildings and peaceful grounds, including a nature trail that winds through the woods. Five films have been shot here, including John Wayne's *Horse Soldiers* and the television series *North and South.* The buildings of Historic Jefferson College (601–442–2901) are open from 9:00 A.M. to 5:00 P.M., Monday through Saturday, and from 1:00 to 5:00 P.M. on Sunday.

From Washington continue south on Highway 61 for 7 miles to lovely **Natchez,** one of the gems along the river. Natchez can make a good claim to being the single most historic city along the Mississippi. Founded in 1716, it is one of the oldest permanent settlements on the river, and the flags of five nations—France, England, Spain, the Confederate States, and the United States—have flown over it. The explorer La Salle pronounced its location on 200-foot bluffs overlooking the Mississippi as "the most desirable site on the river." Such well-known figures as Andrew Jackson, Jim Bowie, Jefferson Davis, Aaron Burr, and Mark Twain strolled its streets and were entertained in many of the antebellum homes that still stand today.

In 1716 the French established Fort Rosalie here on land inhabited by the Natchez Indians, for whom the city was later named. Settlers poured into the region, and Natchez became a jumping-off point for the frontier. The city later grew rich off the river trade and agriculture, particularly cotton. By the early 1800s Natchez was an affluent port, and prior to the Civil War, a good percentage of all the millionaires in the entire United States lived here. Steamboats crowded the docks, and the notorious Natchez-Under-the-Hill, the city's steamboat landing next to the river, was a rowdy center for gambling, drinking, and brothels.

Though the Civil War crippled Natchez's prosperity, the city was spared major destruction because it had no railroads and was of little strategic importance. No battles occurred here, and the city's opulent mansions were left intact, creating a time capsule of Old South grandeur. (According to local legend, some of the valuables buried by Natchez families to protect them from Union soldiers have never been recovered, and are still hidden beneath the formal gardens and manicured lawns of the town's mansions.)

More than 600 antebellum buildings stand in Natchez, the largest number to be found anywhere in the country. Over a dozen mansions are open for tours throughout the year, each one offering glimpses into a way of life long vanished. **The Natchez National Historic Park** includes three sites that highlight important aspects of the town's history. **Melrose** is a Greek Revival mansion completed around 1845 that was the urban estate of wealthy cotton planter John T. McMurran. It illustrates the life that revolved around the cotton trade—for those at the top of the economic ladder, that is. Melrose is open daily and is located at 1 Melrose–Montebello Parkway. The **William Johnson House** lends another perspective on antebellum life in Natchez. William Johnson was a prominent free African-American and the author of a diary that gives valuable insights into the history of the era. His home was built in 1841 and contains exhibits on Johnson's life and the history of African-Americans in Natchez. The house is at 210 State Street. The third site in the park is Fort Rosalie, which is in the process of being developed at its original 1716 location near 504 South Canal Street. The park's headquarters is at this address; for information about the three sites, call the office at (601) 442–7047.

The **Natchez Museum of Afro-American History and Culture,** at 307 Market Street, gives more insights into the contributions of blacks to Natchez life. The pre–Civil War plantation houses were built by African-Americans, and the cotton trade depended upon their labor; these facts are sometimes forgotten amid tours of the opulent mansions of the South. Although only one out of 12 whites who lived in Adams County was a slave owner, those who did own slaves often had large numbers—one wealthy planter owned more than 1,000. The Natchez Convention and Visitors Bureau (800–647–6724) publishes an informative brochure on the African-American experience in Natchez, and the museum's exhibits include hundreds of artifacts from both the free and slave communities. The museum (601–445–0728) is open from 1:00 to 5:00 P.M., Wednesday through Friday, and 11:00 A.M. to 4:00 P.M. on Saturday.

No visit to Natchez would be complete without sampling the hospitality at some of its many antebellum homes, each of which is a museum in its own right. The following are four of the best known, but there are many more that provide fascinating tours. For information about the homes that are open to the public, call (800) 647–6742. Admission prices average about $5.00.

Longwood is the largest octagonal house in the United States and a superb example of Orient-inspired architecture. Begun in the late 1850s, the home was left unfinished at the outbreak of the war. The tools used during its construction still remain where they were left by the northern craftsmen, who fled following Mississippi's secession from the Union. The northern sympathies of Longwood's owner, Dr. Haller Nutt, did not protect his extensive landholdings from being decimated by Union troops. Dr. Nutt raced to Vicksburg in a vain attempt to lodge a protest with General Grant but encountered bad weather and was forced to return home, where he soon contracted pneumonia and died. (His ghost and that of his wife, Julia, are said to still linger around the property.) Longwood remains unfinished to this day, but that only adds to its poignant charm. The home is on Lower Woodville Road and is open from 9:00 A.M. to 5:00 P.M.

The beautiful **Rosalie** is located on the Natchez bluff that overlooks the Mississippi and is named for the fort that once stood on the hill behind the house. During the war, the 1820 Georgian-style mansion served as the Union headquarters during the occupation of the town. The mansion, on South Broadway Street, is open daily from 9:00 A.M. to 5:00 P.M.

Magnolia Hall was the last great mansion to be completed in Natchez prior to the war and is one of the town's finest examples of Greek Revival architecture. The home includes a costume museum on its second floor and is open daily from 9:00 A.M. to 4:30 P.M. You'll find it at the corner of Pearl and Washington streets.

Yet another beautiful mansion is **Stanton Hall,** which occupies more than an entire city block and is surrounded by live oak trees more than a century old. Built in 1857, the museum is one of the most palatial residences of the pre–Civil War era and is furnished with many original items from the Stanton family. The home is located at the corner of High and Pearl streets and is open daily from 9:00 A.M. to 4:30 P.M.

These and more than twenty other historic homes are open for tours during the **Natchez Spring and Fall Pilgrimages** held in March and October each year. Guides in period dress escort visitors through the mansions, and a *Gone With the Wind* atmosphere prevails. While nearly two dozen Mississippi cities host annual pilgrimages, Natchez began the grand tradition in 1932 and has many of the loveliest homes in the South to tour.

There's no better time to see this enchanting small town. For information, call (800) 647–6742.

At any time of the year, you can tour Natchez in several charming ways. The **Natchez Trolley** runs throughout the downtown and the Under-the-Hill area from 11:00 A.M. to 11:00 P.M., Sunday through Thursday, and until midnight on weekends. Call (601) 442–5082 for information. The city also offers narrated **Carriage Tours** (800–647–6742), which begin at Canal and State streets daily and at the Natchez Eola Hotel in the evenings. Tickets are $8.00. Another way to tour the city is on an air-conditioned double-decker bus. The fifty-minute tours depart daily from Canal at State Street and cost $10 per person. Call (601) 445–9300 for information.

A number of restaurants in Natchez are housed in historic buildings, including the **Carnegie House Restaurant,** in Stanton Hall. Traditional southern dishes are served from 11:00 A.M. to 2:30 P.M. daily (and for dinner in the evening during the Spring and Fall Pilgrimages). Prices are moderate; call (601) 445–5151 for information.

The **Monmouth Plantation,** at 36 Melrose Avenue, offers elegant dining as well in a white-columned 1818 mansion situated amid twenty-six acres on the John A. Quitman Parkway. A prix-fixe dinner is served at 7:30 P.M., Tuesday through Saturday, and costs about $35 per person. Call (800) 828–4531 for information.

Overnight visitors to Natchez have a choice of more than thirty bed-and-breakfast establishments, many housed in historic mansions that will let you sample the life of the aristocracy of the Old South. For a brochure listing historic accommodations, call (800) 647–6724. Among the loveliest is the **Monmouth Plantation** listed above, which has been called one of the "top ten most romantic places in the United States" by USA Today and Glamour. For a panoramic view of the Mississippi, book a room at **Weymouth Hall** (601–445–2304), a Greek Revival mansion sitting on a bluff overlooking the river at 1 Cemetery Road. **Dunleith** is another of the town's landmarks. This 1856 mansion resembles a Greek temple with colonnaded galleries on all sides and is located in a forty-acre landscaped park. You'll find the home at 84 Homochitto Street; call (800) 443–2445 for information.

An even older era in Natchez history is preserved at the **Grand Village of the Natchez Indians.** The site was occupied from about A.D. 1200 to 1729, when Natchez Indians attacked Fort Rosalie and killed many of its French settlers. In retaliation the French killed many members of the tribe

Dunleith Mansion in Natchez gives guests a chance to sample antebellum life at its most opulent.

and sold others into slavery. The remaining Natchez Indians were absorbed by other tribes in the region, leading to the extinction of the tribe for whom the city is named. Today the site includes a museum and reconstructed mounds and dwellings. The village (601–446–6502), at 400 Jefferson Davis Boulevard, is open from 9:00 A.M. to 5:00 P.M., Monday through Saturday, and from 1:30 to 5:00 P.M. on Sunday.

Before leaving Natchez don't miss a visit to **Natchez–Under–the–Hill.** The area isn't nearly as rowdy as it once was, but it still has shops, bars, and restaurants plus the *Lady Luck Riverboat Casino* (800–722–5825), permanently docked on the river.

From Natchez travel south on Highway 61 for 34 miles to **Woodville,** your final stop on the Great River Road in Mississippi. There you'll find the **Rosemont Plantation,** the family home of Jefferson Davis. The home was built around 1810 by Samuel and Jane Davis and remained the Davis family home until 1895. The man who would become the president of the Confederacy grew up here and returned for visits throughout his life. Rosemont (601–888–6809) includes many of the family's original furnishings and portraits. It is located on Highway 24 just off Highway 61 and is open from 10:00 A.M. to 4:00 P.M., Monday through Saturday.

The Barbary Coast of the Mississippi

Steamboat landings were often rowdy places, but none had a more unsavory reputation than Natchez-Under-the-Hill. While the town's wealthy elite lived on the bluff above the river, the boat landing and warehouse area grew into a lawless domain of gaming halls, saloons, and brothels. The site was known as the "Barbary Coast of the Mississippi," with pirates taking the form of gamblers, thieves, and outlaws. Caverns in the bluff were used to hide contraband, and the Mississippi provided a convenient dumping ground for unfortunate victims of the more nefarious citizens of the settlement. Natchez-Under-the-Hill was a scandalous embarrassment to the citizens who lived above it and was denounced as the "worst hellhole on earth" by one evangelist of the day.

Over the years the Mississippi has reclaimed much of the landing and has reduced its original six streets to two. Scenes from the miniseries *North and South* and movie *Huck Finn* were filmed here, and much-subdued echoes of the landing's former boisterousness live on in its taverns, shops, and restaurants.

FOR MORE INFORMATION

Mississippi Division of Tourism Development (800) 647–2290

Mississippi Department of Natural Resources (601) 961–5255

Tunica (601) 363–2865

Clarksdale (800) 626–3764

Greenville (800) 467–3582

Vicksburg (800) 221–3536

Port Gibson (601) 437–4351

Natchez (800) 647–6724

Louisiana

In Louisiana the Mississippi River at last meets the Gulf of Mexico, 2,350 miles from its headwaters in northern Minnesota. What began as a clear wilderness stream is now a wide, muddy channel contained by levees and flood walls. Throughout much of the river's length, its depth has averaged about 10 feet, but at Baton Rouge it becomes dramatically deeper and faster. By the time it reaches the gulf it is so laden with sand, mud, and gravel that each day it deposits nearly 1½ million tons of sediment—enough to extend the delta an additional 6 miles each century.

The last state on the Great River Road is also one of the most fascinating. Louisiana has been governed under ten different flags and settled by many ethnic groups, creating a rich mixture of cultures and traditions. The state was christened *Louisiane* in 1682 by the explorer Sieur de La Salle in honor of the Sun King, Louis XIV, and is the only state that was once a French royal colony. Its years under Spanish rule also left their mark: Louisiana retains the Spanish colonial custom of calling its counties "parishes," which were originally church units set up by the Spanish provisional governor of Louisiana in 1669.

As the Great River Road follows the Mississippi's meandering path through the state, it also winds through a showcase of history. Before the Civil War a major portion of the nation's millionaires lived on plantations along the river, and many of their beautiful homes remain today. This is the Old South of the popular imagination, of white-columned mansions surrounded by huge live oak trees draped with Spanish moss.

At the end of the river road lies New Orleans: decadent, fascinating New Orleans, the port that grew rich off the steamboat trade and blossomed into a cosmopolitan city at a time when most of the nation's other settlements were rough and primitive. With its cornucopia of incredible food and music and its incomparable historical sites, New Orleans is a treasure lying at the end of the river road.

LAKE PROVIDENCE TO ST. FRANCISVILLE

The Mississippi enters Louisiana near **Lake Providence.** According to local legend this part of the river was frequented in the 1700s by pirates led by a Captain Bunch. If travelers made it safely past Bunch's Bend, they stopped and thanked Providence for sparing them. The name "Providence" stuck to both the oxbow lake that was once part of the Mississippi, and the town that grew up along its eastern end.

During the Civil War, Union engineers under the command of General Grant tried unsuccessfully to build a canal connecting Lake Providence and the Mississippi so that they could bypass the Confederate fortifications at Vicksburg by traveling on a network of bayous and rivers. Though the plan was eventually abandoned, for many years Grant's Canal remained as an open ditch in the town of Lake Providence, a perfect breeding ground for mosquitoes. In 1953 Louisiana senator Russell Long finally convinced the government to fill it in by arguing, "Since the Federal government dug it, it is only fitting that the Federal government should fill it up."

Twelve miles north of Lake Providence, on Highway 65, is the **Panola Pepper Corporation,** a family-owned business that produces a variety of hot sauces, seasonings, and gifts. The factory has a gift shop, and tours of its operations are available Monday through Friday, 9:00 A.M. to 5:00 P.M. Call (318) 559–1774 for information.

In Lake Providence itself visit the **Byerly House.** The turn-of-the-century home is one of the few remaining examples of Queen Anne–Revival architecture in the area, and now houses a visitors information and community center as well as the town's chamber of commerce. The Byerly House (318–559–5125) is located at 600 Lake Street and is open daily from 10:00 A.M. to 5:00 P.M.

Lake Providence Mosquitoes

A Mr. H. *furnished some minor details of fact concerning this region which I would have hesitated to believe had I not known him to be a steamboat mate. . . . He said that two of [the Lake Providence mosquitoes] could whip a dog, and that four of them could hold a man down; and except help come, they would kill him—"butcher him," as he expressed it. Referred in a sort of casual way— and yet significant way—to 'the fact that the life policy in its simplest form is unknown in Lake Providence—they take out a mosquito policy besides.' He told many remarkable things about those lawless insects. Among others, he said that he had seen them try to vote. Noticing that this statement seemed to be a good deal of a strain on us, he modified it a little: said he might have been mistaken, as to that particular, but knew he had seen them around the polls "canvassing."*

Mark Twain
Life on the Mississippi

From Lake Providence head south on Highway 65 for 10 miles to the village of **Transylvania**—which is difficult to miss because it sports the likeness of a bat on its water tower. **The Transylvania General Store** greets visitors with the sign WE'RE ALWAYS GLAD TO HAVE NEW BLOOD IN TOWN and sells a variety of vampire novelties.

Continue south on Highway 65 for 20 miles to **Tallulah,** supposedly named after a beautiful local woman who captured the heart of a construction engineer while he was helping to build the railroad through town. Each May the town hosts the **Bayou Festival,** when its courthouse square is a center for arts and crafts, food booths, parades, street dances, and a grandstand with live entertainment. A similar celebration is held in November for **Delta Cotton Day.** Call (318) 574–4537 for information.

From Tallulah continue south on Highway 65 past the Tensas River National Wildlife Refuge and the towns of Saint Joseph and Waterproof. The latter settlement got its name after being relocated four times because of floods and caving riverbanks. At last the town got a dry location on a high knoll and adopted its new name in triumph.

Seventy miles south of Tallulah is **Vidalia,** which lies just across the river from Natchez, Mississippi. The town was once a thriving steamboat port and the eastern end of the Texas Cattle Trail. One cattle driver called Vidalia "one of the toughest little towns in the world." Cowboys would take the payment they had received at the end of the cattle drives and spend it in the town's saloons, gambling houses, dance halls, and brothels. Later the town suffered through the Civil War, Reconstruction, fire, floods, and the economic ravages of the boll weevil. In 1940 the entire town was moved a mile back from the river and placed within a protective ring levee. Legend has it that the Bowie knife of frontier fame was first used here by Jim Bowie in a fight in 1827. Each October the **Jim Bowie Festival** commemorates the event with music, entertainment, arts and crafts, and good food. Call (318) 336–5206 for information.

For a hearty lunch or dinner, stop by the **Sandbar Restaurant,** which is housed in an 1820s home at the foot of the Vidalia–Natchez bridge; prices are moderate. The Sandbar Restaurant (318–336–5173) is open from 11:00 A.M. to 10:00 P.M. daily.

From Vidalia head south on Highways 131 and 15 for 60 miles. Near the town of Torras the Mississippi begins to flow through the center of Louisiana. Because the parishes that line the river tend to have strong local identities, much of the route from here south is organized by parish rather than by individual cities.

The town of Torras marks the northern border of Pointe Coupee Parish, which was settled in the early 1700s and maintains great pride in its French Creole heritage. Head south on Highway 1 for 25 miles to **New Roads,** which is located on the northern end of an oxbow lake named False River. The city is the commercial center of the parish, and in the early 1900s was a resort community for travelers from New Orleans who came to enjoy the beautiful waters of the lake.

Several of New Roads' nineteenth-century mansions now offer bed-and-breakfast accommodations, including the **Samson–Claiborne House.** The 1835 Creole cottage (for a definition of Creole, see sidebar on page 195) includes two suites with fireplaces and two additional bedrooms upstairs. The house (800–832–7412) is located at 401 Richey Street. **Mon Rêve** is an 1820 Creole plantation home constructed of cypress, brick, and bousillage (mud and moss), and has a gallery that overlooks False River. The home (800–324–2738) is located at 9825 False River Road. At the **Jubilee! Bed** and **Breakfast,** guests can enjoy a view of the Mississippi River from an 1840 Creole cottage. The Jubilee (504–638–8333) offers five guest rooms and is located at 11704 Pointe Coupee Road.

For refreshment visit the **Coffee House Creole Cafe,** which is housed in a former bank built in 1880. The menu features updated versions of time-honored Creole recipes, and prices are moderate. The cafe (504–628–7859) is open daily and is located at 124 West Main Street.

From New Roads travel south on Highway 1 for 6 miles to **Parlange,** a plantation home built in the 1750s by a French nobleman named Marquis de Ternant. Parlange is a classic example of the Louisiana Creole style of architecture, with wide balconies surrounding its exterior. During the war its owners were said to have saved the home from destruction by graciously entertaining the invading troops with the finest wines and foods. Parlange has remained in the same family for eight generations and contains many of its original furnishings. It is part of a working plantation that raises sugar-cane, corn, soybeans, cattle, and horses. Parlange (504–638–8410) is open daily for tours.

Next to the mansion is the **Pointe Coupee Parish Museum,** which is housed in an early eighteenth-century Creole cottage that was once part of the Parlange plantation. The house is furnished to reflect the modest lifestyle of many of Louisiana's early settlers and also houses a tourist information center and gift shop. The museum (504–638–9858) is located at 8348 False River Road (Highway 1) and is open Monday through Saturday.

Bed-and-breakfast accommodations are also available farther south on Highway 1 in the Greek Revival house **Mon Coeur,** which features massive white columns and a garden with gazebos, statuary, and hidden paths. The home (504–638–4334) offers four guest rooms and is located at 7739 False River Road.

On the east bank of the Mississippi, across the river from French-influenced Pointe Coupee Parish, is a region sometimes called English Louisiana, an area settled by people who traced their heritage to the British Isles. If you've chosen to travel on the east bank of the river, head south on Highway 61 through West Feliciana Parish to **St. Francisville.** The town actually began as a burial ground for Spanish monks who had established a church in the 1730s in Pointe Coupee Parish and needed a place to bury their dead that was safe from the area's periodic floods. The settlement that grew up around their graveyard took its name from St. Francis, the order's patron. Later in the eighteenth century, settlers from the Eastern Seaboard

Plantation Grandeur

Before the Civil War, it is estimated that two-thirds of all the millionaires in America lived along the Mississippi between Natchez and New Orleans—one indication of the enormous amounts of money that could be made on a well-managed plantation. An early lucrative crop was indigo, but later planters turned to the more labor-intensive sugarcane, tobacco, and cotton. The slavery system thus fueled the prosperity of the Old South and built the magnificent mansions that still line the river road today.

During the eighteenth century, homes were often built in the West Indies style, with wide galleries encircling their exterior. As planters grew wealthier, a Greek Revival style with imposing white columns became popular. Owners vied with each other to see who could erect the most ornate and beautiful homes, with much of the building itself done by skilled slave artisans. The interiors of the mansions were filled with the latest European furnishings, shipped upriver from New Orleans, and outside beautiful gardens bloomed. Homes were often built on the highest land available because of the frequent Mississippi floods, and in places where the floods were particularly common, living quarters were often located on the second floor.

The Civil War dealt a crushing blow to the plantation system. Many of the mansions were destroyed or severely damaged. After the war, their owners had to adapt to a world and economic system that had changed dramatically. Many families lost their magnificent estates, and most of those who managed to retain them never regained their former prosperity.

came here to start a new life in what was then West Florida. Many grew rich off the lucrative cotton trade and built beautiful plantation homes that still stand today in West Feliciana Parish.

St. Francisville is known both for its antebellum mansions and its connection to the great naturalist and painter, John James Audubon. Audubon had undertaken the enormous task of painting all the birds in North America and came to the wilderness of Louisiana as part of his quest. During the twenty-three months he spent in this area between 1821 and 1830, he painted eighty of his famous folios, drawing inspiration from the lush Tunica Hills around him.

Begin your tour of St. Francisville with a visit to the **West Feliciana Historical Museum,** which is housed in an 1895 store and recounts the nineteenth-century history of the town. There you can also receive directions for a walking tour of St. Francisville's landmarks, which include more than 140 buildings listed on the National Register of Historic Places. The museum (504–635–6330) is located on Ferdinand Street (Highway 1), and is open from 9:00 A.M. to 4:00 P.M., Monday through Saturday, and from 1:00 to 4:00 P.M. on Sunday.

On your walking tour of St. Francisville, be sure to note the lovely 1858 **Grace Episcopal Church,** constructed in Gothic style and surrounded by a picturesque cemetery and majestic oaks. Also in the downtown area is the **Wolf–Schlesinger House/St. Francisville Inn.** The house is an 1880 Victorian Gothic that now houses a restaurant and nine guest rooms. Restaurant prices are inexpensive to moderate. The inn (800–488–6502) is located at 5720 North Commerce Street.

After touring the historic downtown, take a driving tour of the area's many plantation homes. **Oakley House** is one of the most famous. John James Audubon came here in 1821 to tutor the daughter of its owners under an arrangement that also allowed him time to pursue his painting. The design of the house is simpler than that of many later plantation homes. Oakley House is built in the West Indies style, with front galleries enclosed by wooden louvered slats that allow the air to circulate while keeping out the sun and rain. Inside it is decorated with early nineteenth-century furnishings that reflect the period when Audubon lived there. The house is surrounded by the one-hundred-acre Audubon State Park, which gives visitors an idea of the landscape that helped inspire the painter's work. Oakley House (504–635–3739) is located on Highway 965 and is open daily.

From Oakley House drive to **Rosedown,** the grande dame of the many plantation homes in the area and a showcase of antebellum life at its most opulent. Rosedown was built in Louisiana-Georgian style in 1835 by a wealthy cotton planter, Daniel Turnbull, and his wife, Martha. The two traveled to Europe to purchase furnishings for their new residence, and were inspired there by the classic formal gardens they saw. The Turnbulls designed their own gardens to follow the seventeenth-century French style. Martha in particular was an avid gardener and kept a detailed diary of the garden's progress.

Through their efforts, Rosedown became an early proving ground for many exotic Oriental flora, including camellias and azaleas. Today the mansion has been restored to its original elegance, and its twenty-eight acres of landscaped gardens are breathtakingly beautiful. Rosedown (504–635–3332) is located at the junction of Highways 10 and 61 and is open for daily tours.

North of Rosedown you'll find **The Myrtles,** a plantation home nestled among live oaks, mimosas, azaleas, and the myrtle trees that give it its name. Built in 1796, The Myrtles has been called "America's most haunted house" because of the intriguing ghost stories associated with it. The house is supposedly built on an Indian burial ground, and during the two centuries since its construction, ten different murders have occurred within it—leading to a host of ghosts who are said to haunt the property. The home offers daily tours as well as "mystery tours" on Friday and Saturday evening. Its restaurant is open for lunch and dinner; prices are moderate to expensive. Overnight guests are also welcome. The Myrtles (504–635–6277) is located at 7747 Highway 61.

North of The Myrtles is **Butler Greenwood,** a 1790s plantation that has one of the area's finest original Victorian formal parlors. The home also includes extensive gardens and offers overnight accommodations for guests. Butler Greenwood (504–635–6312) is at 8345 Highway 61; tours are given daily.

More beautiful landscaping can be viewed at the **Afton Villa Gardens,** at the end of a mile-long alley of moss-draped oaks and huge azaleas. The Gothic mansion that once stood on the property burned in 1963, but the plantation's terraced gardens are tended to this day. The Afton Villa Gardens are located on Highway 61.

The **Cottage Plantation** is an early nineteenth-century home surrounded by its original outbuildings on 400 acres. One of the former slave quarters on the property was used in the filming of the television movie *The Autobiography of Miss Jane Pittman.* Daily tours are offered and overnight guests are welcome. The Cottage (504–635–3674) is at 10528 Cottage Lane.

The **Greenwood Plantation** should also be on your list. The original Greenwood Mansion was built in 1830 and survived the Civil War intact, only to be destroyed by a fire in 1960. Twenty years later the Greek Revival home was completely reconstructed, its plans based on hundreds of old photographs and interviews with people who had visited and lived there. Greenwood has been used as a location site for six movies, including the miniseries *North and South.* Greenwood (504–655–4475) is located at 6838 Highland Road and is open for daily tours.

A good time to visit the St. Francisville area is during its **Audubon Pilgrimage,** held each year on the third weekend in March. Tours of a number of historic homes and gardens are given, and evening entertainment is scheduled. Call (504) 635–6330 for information.

The Sounds of Steamboats

Two sounds are inextricably linked to steamboats: their distinctive whistles and the infectious melodies of their steam calliopes. During the nineteenth century, residents of river towns could often identify an approaching boat simply by its whistle, each of which was composed of one to five tubes that produced sounds ranging from melodic to shrill. While many a young boy's greatest ambition was to imitate the unearthly shriek of his favorite boat, other people were not so enamored of the sound. In 1885 officials in Paducah, Kentucky, even passed an ordinance that prohibited boats from blowing their whistles within a half-mile of the wharf.

Like the whistle, the sound of a calliope was generated by steam from the boat's engines, but its melodies were much easier on the ear. The instrument was patented in 1855 by Joshua Stoddard and was originally intended as a replacement for the bells in a nearby church tower. When parishioners objected to its less-than-holy sound, Stoddard's brother (who happened to be a steamboat captain) saw the instrument's potential. Many excursion boats and showboats installed calliopes to announce their arrival and attract customers.

It took a brave musician to play the early calliopes, for their brass keys were often very hot and each had to be pushed down with six to eight pounds of pressure. Musicians also had to be on guard for escaping steam and scalding water—hardly a conducive atmosphere for creating beautiful music.

PORT HUDSON TO DESTREHAN

From St. Francisville head south on Highway 61 for 10 miles to **Port Hudson,** the site of the **Port Hudson State Commemorative Area.** The 643-acre site marks the location of a forty-eight-day siege during the Civil War. Port Hudson was a strategic point because it was located high on the bluffs overlooking a bend in the river whose current forced boats to slow down considerably. After the surrender of New Orleans, the site was fortified and became the southern anchor of the Confederate hold on the Mississippi. Union troops laid siege to Port Hudson from May 23 to July 9, when word reached the Confederates that Vicksburg had fallen and that further resistance was useless. Today the site includes an interpretive center with displays of siege and battle artifacts, an audiovisual program, and a wooden boardwalk that leads to the Fort Desperate area, where the fiercest fighting took place. The Port Hudson State Commemorative Area (504–654–3775) is located on Highway 61 at 756 West Plains–Port Hudson Road and is open daily.

From Port Hudson continue on Highway 61 for 15 miles to **Baton Rouge,** a river city that became the state capital in 1845 after Louisiana's leaders decided to move the seat of government away from what they diplomatically termed the "distractions" of New Orleans. The city's French name supposedly refers to the red stick that once marked the boundary between two Indian tribes in the area, and its history is marked by a strong French influence, particularly from the French Acadians who settled in southern Louisiana in the mid-1700s. Later Baton Rouge became a major commercial center for the vast wealth of the plantation system, and within a short radius around the city are a large number of beautifully restored antebellum homes.

A good place to begin your tour of Baton Rouge is at the **Center for Political and Governmental History,** which is housed in the **Old State Capitol** that was completed in 1849 on a bluff overlooking the Mississippi. The Gothic Revival structure contains exhibits describing the state's colorful political history and includes rare film and archival material displayed in interactive exhibits. The center (504–342–0500) is located at 100 North Boulevard, at River Road, and is open from 10:00 A.M. to 4:00 P.M., Thursday through Saturday, and from noon to 4:00 P.M. on Sunday.

Next pay a visit to the structure that replaced the Old Capitol: the **Louisiana State Capitol,** which rises thirty-four stories and dominates the

Baton Rouge skyline. The Art Deco structure was built during the Depression at the urging of Louisiana's legendary governor, Huey Long, who vehemently disliked the former capitol building (perhaps because he was once impeached there). The new capitol was completed in 1932 and is the tallest state capitol in the United States. Its interior is graced by magnificent marble and bronze work, and a long series of steps commemorating the fifty states leads to its entrance. An observation deck on the twenty-seventh floor offers a panoramic view of the Mississippi and the grave of Huey Long, who was assassinated in 1935 in the building he worked so hard to build. The capitol includes a Louisiana Folklife exhibit that was part of the 1984 Louisiana World Exposition. The state capitol (504–342–7317) is located on State Capitol Drive, next to the river, and is open daily from 8:00 A.M. to 4:30 P.M.

On the grounds of the state capitol is the **Old Arsenal Museum,** a former powder magazine dating back to the early 1800s. The museum houses exhibits about the structure's history, and is open from 10:00 A.M. to 4:00 P.M., Monday through Saturday, and from 1:00 to 4:00 P.M. on Sunday. For information call (504) 342–0401.

Next pay a visit to **Magnolia Mound Plantation,** one of the oldest and most carefully restored plantation homes on the river. The French Creole–style home was built around 1791 on a ridge facing the Mississippi and has been restored to represent a working plantation of the period. Costumed interpreters guide visitors through the home and conduct open-hearth cooking demonstrations. The house is situated on sixteen acres of grounds that include an overseer's house and gardens. Magnolia Mound (504–343–4955) is located at 2161 Nicholson Drive and is open from 10:00 A.M. to 4:00 P.M., Tuesday through Saturday, and from 1:00 to 4:00 P.M. on Sunday.

Another Baton Rouge attraction, the **Rural Life Museum,** gives insight into the slave system that made plantations like Magnolia Mound possible. The five-acre, open-air museum is a complex of buildings operated by Louisiana State University that re-creates life on a nineteenth-century plantation. The emphasis is on the experiences of the "other half" of the plantation—the slaves and servants who are often overlooked on tours of antebellum mansions. This fascinating complex includes an overseer's house, slave cabins, blacksmith shop, open kettle sugar mill, plantation commissary, and African-American church, all filled with period artifacts and furnishings. The museum (504–765–2437) is located on Essen Lane, off Interstate 10, and is open from 8:30 A.M. to 4:00 P.M., Monday through Friday.

History of a later vintage is commemorated at the **U.S.S. *Kidd* and Nautical Center** in downtown Baton Rouge. The *Kidd* is a World War II destroyer that fought in nine major engagements, and is one of the most detailed ship exhibits in the world. The 369-foot vessel is berthed on the city's waterfront, and guided tours take visitors through its interior. The adjacent Nautical Center features model boats, a P-40 "Flying Tiger" aircraft, and other exhibits on naval history. The complex (504–342–1942) is located on Government Street at the levee and is open daily from 9:00 A.M. to 5:00 P.M.

A good way to tour the Mississippi in the Baton Rouge area is on board the ***Samuel Clemens Riverboat,*** a paddlewheeler that offers sightseeing excursions and dinner cruises. Call (504) 381–9606 for information.

The past few years have also seen the rebirth of another river attraction in Baton Rouge, riverboat gambling. Two boats operate along the waterfront. The ***Belle of Baton Rouge*** docks in Catfish Town, a historic area in the city's downtown that was once the waterfront warehouse district and is now a gaming and entertainment center. The 1,500-passenger boat is designed in nineteenth-century paddlewheeler style and cruises the river six times a day, seven days a week. Call (504) 344–8943 for information.

At the northern end of the downtown is the ***Casino Rouge*** paddlewheel riverboat, which, like the ***Belle of Baton Rouge,*** holds 1,500 passengers and cruises six times daily. In the terminal, across the street from the state capitol, is a cafe on a deck overlooking the river. Call (504) 922–9210 for information.

From Baton Rouge cross the Mississippi to **Port Allen,** the county seat of West Baton Rouge Parish. Port Allen is home to the **West Baton Rouge Museum,** which was built in 1882 as part of the courthouse for the parish. The museum describes the culture and history of the area and includes a slave cabin and an 1830 French Creole cottage. The museum (504–336–2422) is at 845 North Jefferson Avenue and is open from 10:00 A.M. to 4:30 P.M., Tuesday through Saturday.

For more information about the area, stop by the **West Baton Rouge Parish Tourist Center** (800–654–9701), at 2855 Interstate 10 Frontage Road. The center shows an audiovisual presentation on the history of the area. It's open from 9:00 A.M. to 5:00 P.M. daily.

From Port Allen head south on Highway 1 for 10 miles to **Plaquemine,** the gateway to Iberville Parish. The city was first settled in 1775 and is located where the Bayou Plaquemine meets the Mississippi. A lock at the mouth of the bayou was constructed between 1895 and 1909 and provided a shortcut into the interior of southwest Louisiana for six decades, the first opening to the west from the levee-encased Mississippi River. By 1909 the lock had become too small for barge traffic, and a new lock was built upriver in Port Allen.

Begin your tour of the city at the **Plaquemine Lock Museum,** a 1909 white brick building that also serves as the visitors information center for the city. The museum describes the history of the lock, whose designer was the chief engineer for the Panama Canal Locks, and includes a 40-foot observation tower that overlooks the Mississippi. The museum also distributes a walking tour brochure of Plaquemine's historic downtown, including the 1849 Greek Revival Old City Hall, across the street. The museum (800–233–3560) is open from 10:00 A.M. to 5:00 P.M., Monday through Friday.

From Plaquemine follow Highway 1 south for 18 miles to **Nottoway,** the largest plantation in the South. Beautiful Nottoway has been described as an American castle, a blend of the Italianate and Greek Revival styles that incorporated some of the most modern building innovations of the day, including indoor plumbing, gas lighting, and coal fireplaces. The home was built between 1849 and 1859 by a wealthy sugar planter, John Hampden Randolph, who had 7,000 acres in his domain. Nottoway was saved from total destruction during the Civil War by a Union gunboat officer who had once been a guest of the Randolph family. Among the mansion's fifty rooms is the spectacular, 65-foot-long Grand White Ballroom. Nottoway is open daily for guided tours and offers thirteen guest rooms. It also includes a restaurant that is open daily for lunch and dinner (prices are moderate to expensive). For information about Nottoway, call (504) 545–2730.

From Nottoway continue south on Highway 1 to Ascension Parish. The area was originally inhabited by the Houmas and Chetimatches Indian tribes and later became home to Spanish and German settlers as well as Acadians (later known as Cajuns) from the French colony of Nova Scotia. Sugarcane, cotton, indigo, timber, and tobacco brought wealth to the area and built many plantation homes that still stand today. The town of **Donaldsonville** lies on the west bank of the Mississippi and served as the capital of Louisiana from 1830 to 1831. Its historic district includes over 600 commercial and residential buildings dating from 1865 to 1933. (Because the city was burned during the Civil War, few buildings of earlier vintage remain.)

From Donaldsonville follow Highway 1 south, cross the Mississippi on the Sunshine Bridge, and follow the signs to **Burnside.** There the **Cajun**

Village preserves a collection of restored Acadian buildings that house a variety of specialty shops as well as the Ascension Parish Tourist Commission. The village (800–460–6815) is open daily.

Burnside is also the site of **The Cabin Restaurant,** which is housed in several slave cabins remaining from the old Monroe Plantation. The restaurant (504–473–3007) serves moderately priced Cajun and American food and is open daily. You'll find it at the corner of Highways 22 and 44.

Upriver from Burnside is the **Houmas House,** one of the South's most famous plantations. The Greek Revival mansion was built in 1840 on land that was once occupied by the Houmas Indians. At one time the home was the center of the state's largest sugar plantation, with 20,000 acres in cultivation. Irish immigrant John Burnside bought the Houmas House plantation in 1858 for $1 million and saved the mansion from destruction during the Civil War by warning the Union forces that it would create an international incident if the U.S. Army entered a home owned by a British citizen. The beautifully restored and furnished house has been featured in many periodicals and was the setting for the Bette Davis film *Hush, Hush, Sweet Charlotte.* Houmas House (504–473–7841) is located at 40136 Highway 942, Burnside, and offers daily tours.

Another of the South's elegant antebellum mansions is located downriver from Burnside on Highway 44. **Tezcuco** was one of the last plantation homes to be completed before the Civil War. Its name means "resting place," and its style is that of a Greek Revival raised cottage, with a broad stairway leading to a wide front gallery. Tezcuco has a fine collection of antique furnishings and is surrounded by huge live oaks, formal gardens, and brick paths. Its outbuildings include a Civil War museum, blacksmith shop, chapel, restaurant, and former slave quarters that have been remodeled into guest cottages. Guided tours are offered daily. Tezcuco Plantation (504–562–3929) is located at 3138 Highway 44, Burnside.

In addition to Donaldsonville and Burnside, Ascension Parish is home to the city of **Gonzales,** founded in 1887 by Tee Joe Gonzales. Each year on the first weekend in June the town holds its **Jambalaya Festival,** which celebrates the delicious Cajun-Creole dish made from a mixture of meat, rice, and seasonings. A world champion jambalaya recipe is designated each year. Other activities include the presentation of King and Queen Jambalaya, a carnival, art show, dancing, and live music. Call (504) 647–5779 for information.

The Voyage of the *New Orleans*

The voyage that marked the beginning of the steamboat era began in September of 1811 in Pittsburgh, Pennsylvania. The steamboat *New Orleans* carried Nicholas Roosevelt (a great-great uncle of Theodore Roosevelt) and his pregnant wife, Lydia, as well as their dog and twelve crew members and servants. The Roosevelts had previously scouted the route from Pittsburgh to New Orleans by flatboat and had returned to the East to build a boat based on a design by Robert Fulton. Though some thought it shameful that Roosevelt was taking his pregnant wife on such a dangerous journey, the intrepid Lydia had no such fears and described the upcoming trip as "jolly." She had, after all, spent her honeymoon on the flatboat journey—not a typical excursion for a well-to-do lady of that day.

The trip did have its hair-raising moments, however. The New Madrid earthquake and the birth of Lydia's baby both occurred during the voyage, and the boat also survived a fire on board and threats by Indians who feared that the noisy, smoking vessel had initiated the earth's tremors.

The Roosevelts arrived in New Orleans in late January of 1812, having given birth to both a new baby and a new era.

South of Ascension Parish lies St. James Parish. Each December the parish hosts the **Festival of the Bonfires,** when huge bonfires are lit on the levees in celebration of Christmas. Also included are music performances, a craft show, beauty pageant, Christmas parade, and wonderful Cajun food. Call (504) 869–9752 for information.

St. James Parish is home to one of the South's most photographed mansions, **Oak Alley Plantation.** Jacques Telesphore Roman, the brother of a Louisiana governor, built the Greek Revival home in 1836 on the site of a planter's cabin. The property's original owner had planted two rows of twenty-eight live oak trees on the path leading to his house, and those trees are now mighty sentinels that form the most dramatic "oak alley" in the

Mississippi Valley. Today the mansion operates as an inn and restaurant (prices are moderate to expensive), and daily tours are offered. The home also hosts a number of annual events: an arts and crafts festival in March, outdoor dinner theater performances, a Civil War reenactment in November, and a Christmas bonfire in December. Oak Alley (504–265–2151) is located at 3645 Highway 18 between St. James and Vacherie.

Another plantation in the area is the **Laura Plantation,** an 1805 home that is being restored to its original grandeur. Laura is one of the oldest and largest remaining plantation complexes along the river, with a dozen historic buildings that include two manor houses, slave quarters, and Creole cottages. The plantation has another claim to fame as well: It was here that the West African folktales of Compair Lapin, better known as Br'er Rabbit, were first recorded in the 1870s. The Laura Plantation (504–265–7690) is located at 2247 Highway 18 between St. James and Vacherie.

St. John the Baptist and St. Charles parishes are the final parishes north of New Orleans. Downriver from the town of Lutcher you'll find the **San Francisco Plantation,** which is one of the most unusual of all the plantation homes in Louisiana. The mansion was built in 1856 and is an eclectic blend of styles sometimes referred to as Steamboat Gothic—a tribute to the ornate steamboats much admired by the home's builder, Edmond Bozonier Marmillion. The main living quarters are on the second floor and include lovely painted ceiling frescoes. On the roof is an observatory, and large cisterns on each side provided the home with running water. Marmillion's son gave the mansion the name "San Frusquin," a phrase meaning "one's all," supposedly a reference to the huge amount of money spent building it. Later the frequently mispronounced name became San Francisco. The mansion (504–535–2341) is located on Highway 44 between Lutcher and Reserve and is open daily for tours.

The last of the great plantations on the river road between Baton Rouge and New Orleans is **Destrehan,** one of the oldest plantation homes left intact in the Lower Mississippi Valley. The home was built in the late 1780s in the West Indies style, and between 1830 and 1840 a major renovation added elements of Greek Revival. Two of the famous guests who are said to have stayed here were the pirate Jean Lafitte and the Duc d'Orléans, who later became king of France. Destrehan (504–764–9315) is located at 9999 River Road and offers daily tours.

NEW ORLEANS TO THE GULF OF MEXICO

Finally, the Great River Road arrives at legendary **New Orleans,** a place where—in the words of novelist Walker Percy—"the tourist is apt to see more nuns and naked women than he ever saw before." It's helpful to remember that in many ways the culture of New Orleans has more in common with a European city such as Paris than a Southern city like Vicksburg. Its ambiance and spirit reflect a cosmopolitan mixture of many ethnicities, especially French, Spanish, and African-American.

The city was founded by the French in 1718 and was named after Philippe, Duc d'Orléans, who at the time served as regent for the child-king Louis XV. Its early settlers managed to build a new colony despite frequent hurricanes, floods, attacks by Indians, and outbreaks of disease. The growing city became a Spanish colony in 1762 and then later passed into French hands once again. In 1803 Napoleon sold New Orleans to the United States as part of the Louisiana Purchase, and the city began to attract increasing numbers of American citizens, who at first were scorned by the Creoles, who were descended from the region's original French and Spanish settlers. Many of the new residents were African-American because of the city's proximity to the Caribbean and its status as a slave-trading port.

Although New Orleans's location near the mouth of the Mississippi had made it one of the continent's most important commercial centers from its earliest years, the development of the steamboat turned the city into a boomtown. Before steamboats, produce traveled mainly down the river by flatboat, but after 1812 steam-powered paddlewheelers hauled cargo up the river as well. Cotton and other bounty from the nation's interior arrived at New Orleans and were shipped to ports around the world. And every item imaginable left New Orleans for the settlements upstream: fine furniture, French wines, imported delicacies, the latest fashions, plus less tangible things such as news, culture, and artistic trends. Hundreds of steamboats crowded the New Orleans riverfront, making the city one of the busiest ports in the world.

Today New Orleans preserves much of its distinctive history and culture. The city is a fitting place to complete a journey on the Great River Road, for here in the "Big Easy" many of the ethnic and historical influences that are part of the Mississippi's story come together in one fascinating tapestry.

Begin your tour of New Orleans in its famous **French Quarter,** an area of ninety square blocks that is the city's major tourist attraction. The quarter is also known as the *Vieux Carré,* meaning "old square," and is the site of the original colony of Nouvelle Orléans that was founded on high ground tucked into a bend of the Mississippi. Though fires in 1788 and 1794 destroyed most of the settlement's original structures, the quarter is filled with beautiful late eighteenth- and early nineteenth-century buildings, many rebuilt by the Spanish in their native country's architectural style. Most are two- and three-story structures with balconies lined with elaborate ironwork. Secluded courtyards are hidden in the interiors of many blocks. The narrow streets of the quarter are filled with activity day and night, from sophisticated entertainment clubs to genteel antique shops and wonderful restaurants.

Much of the action in the French Quarter is centered on **Jackson Square.** Once a parade ground for soldiers (as well as the site of public executions), the square today is a public park where artists display their work and musicians, fortune tellers, jugglers, mimes, and magicians entertain strolling visitors. The square also includes the city's most photographed landmark, a statue of Andrew Jackson. The 14-foot, 15-ton bronze statue commemorates

Colorful Bourbon Street is a legendary French Quarter attraction.

the hero of the 1815 Battle of New Orleans, when General Jackson and his Tennessee Volunteers joined forces with local citizens to defeat the British.

Since the French Quarter lines the Mississippi, this is a good spot for river viewing. Directly across from Jackson Square is the **Moon Walk** (named after former mayor Moon Landrieu). The walk is a great place to view the busy boat and barge traffic on the Mississippi.

Away from the river, on the other side of the square, is **St. Louis Cathedral,** the country's oldest active cathedral. A church has occupied this site since 1727; the present structure was completed in 1851. The cathedral is the principal church of the Roman Catholic Archdiocese of New Orleans and is open daily for religious services and tours.

Surrounding the square are several historic properties owned and operated by the Louisiana State Museum. The **Cabildo** is the 1799 building that once housed the Spanish colonial government and is where the Louisiana Purchase was formalized in 1803. The Cabildo was badly damaged by a fire in 1988 and re-opened in 1994 after a $6.5 million restoration effort, one of the largest and most complex preservation projects of its kind ever undertaken. Today it is a premier educational resource and visitor attraction, housing exhibits that tell Louisiana's history from colonial days through the nineteenth century.

Another building owned by the Louisiana State Museum is the **Presbytère,** at 751 Chartres Street, which was originally built to house the priests who served the cathedral. Later it was used as a courthouse, and today it features changing exhibits on the state's history.

The third museum property on the square is the **1850 House,** which is furnished with items that illustrate middle-class life during the most prosperous time in the city's history. The house was built by Baroness Pontalba, who helped revitalize Jackson Square during the nineteenth century. The Cabildo, Presbytère, and 1850 House are all open from 10:00 A.M. to 5:00 P.M., Wednesday through Sunday. Call (504) 568–6968 for information.

From the Jackson Square area stroll along the river to the **French Market,** where you'll find stores, restaurants, and a farmers' market overflowing with fresh produce. The Jean Lafitte National Historic Park operates a **Folklife and Visitors Center** in this area at 916–918 North Peters Street. Free tours of the French Quarter and other historic districts of the city are given. There are also programs on New Orleans history and culture and Louisiana crafts, music, and cooking. The center (504) 589–2636 is open daily from 9:00 A.M. to 5:00 P.M.

In the same area you'll find another property in the Louisiana State Museum system, the **Old U.S. Mint.** The mint was built in 1835 and during the Civil War produced the Confederate currency. It served as a prison after the city was occupied by Union troops, and after the war it became a mint again. In the 1970s the mint was taken over by the state and renovated into a museum. Today it houses two major collections: the **Mardi Gras Exhibit** and the **New Orleans Jazz Collection.** The history behind New Orleans's most famous festival is recounted through floats, tableaus of carnival balls, costumes from various eras, and other memorabilia. The Jazz Collection tells the story of the city's rich musical heritage through murals, vintage photographs, and audio- and videotapes of jazz performances. The Old U.S. Mint (504–568–6968), at 400 Esplanade Street, is open from 10:00 A.M. to 5:00 P.M., Wednesday through Sunday.

Mardi Gras

No New Orleans event draws more attention than Mardi Gras, the wild and raucous revelry known worldwide. *Mardi Gras* is French for "Fat Tuesday," which is the final day of the carnival held before the penitential season of Lent begins on Ash Wednesday. Costumed balls for Mardi Gras were held in New Orleans as early as 1740, but the festival's roots are actually much older, a blend of Christian and pagan influences that originated in southern Europe.

During carnival season, New Orleans throws a gigantic party that includes more than fifty parades. The event has no official sponsor or supervising organization. Instead, individual activities are organized by nonprofit clubs called "krewes," many of which are named after mythological figures such as Eros or Hermes. Krewes stage parades, parties, balls, and other carnival activities. Each krewe works independently, and many do their work in secret, without revealing the themes of their parades until the night of the event. Krewe members ride on grandiose floats and toss souvenirs to the crowds, and some invite celebrities to officiate at their events. It all adds up to what New Orleanians proudly describe as the greatest free show on earth.

An excellent place to learn more about the history of the city is the **Historic New Orleans Collection,** which is housed within a complex of buildings in the French Quarter. The 1792 Merieult House features displays of rare materials from the collection's holdings, including transfer documents from the Louisiana Purchase, antique maps of the city, and other research materials. The Williams Residence is a townhouse dating from the late 1800s that was owned by the collection's founders, General and Mrs. L. Kemper Williams, and is furnished in 1940s style. A third area, the Gallery, showcases changing exhibits on local history. The Historic New Orleans Collection (504–523–4662) is located at 533 Royal Street, and is open for tours from Tuesday through Saturday.

The French Quarter is also home to the **New Orleans Pharmacy Museum,** which describes itself as the finest pharmacy museum in the United States. The museum is housed in a structure built in 1823 by Louis J. Dufilho, Jr., America's first licensed pharmacist. A botanical garden in the building's walled courtyard supplied medicinal herbs for Dufilho's practice and today flourishes once again. The museum explores the history of nineteenth-century Louisiana and the role played by its pharmacists. The collection includes handmade antique apothecary jars containing medicines of the day and voodoo powders and potions, plus medical equipment, ladies' cosmetics, and other artifacts. The museum also houses a soda fountain with a rare Italian black-and-rose marble counter made in 1855. The Pharmacy Museum (504–565–8027) is at 514 Chartres Street and is open from 10:00 A.M. to 5:00 P.M., Tuesday through Sunday.

The **New Orleans Historic Voodoo Museum** offers insights into a fascinating part of the city's history. Voodoo was brought to New Orleans by African slaves and had considerable influence on the city during the eighteenth and nineteenth centuries. The museum recounts the religion's history through many authentic artifacts and sells charms, potions, and other items. The Voodoo Museum (800–677–7479), at 724 Dumaine Street, is open daily from 10:00 A.M. to dusk.

The French Quarter is filled with historically significant homes, several of which are open to the public. The **Gallier House Museum** is an elegant 1857 home built by James Gallier, Jr., one of the city's most innovative architects. The house has been restored to its original nineteenth-century style. A tour includes short presentations on architectural craftsmanship. The museum (504–523–6722) is at 1118–32 Royal Street and is open from 10:00 A.M. to 4:30 P.M., Monday through Saturday.

Another historically significant home is the **Beauregard–Keyes House.** The 1826 Greek Revival was home to the Confederate general Pierre G. T. Beauregard after the Civil War. In 1944 it became the winter residence of the writer Frances Parkinson Keyes, who wrote many of her novels while living there, including *Dinner at Antoine's* and *Blue Camellia.* The Beauregard–Keyes House (504–523–7257), at 1113 Chartres Street, is open from 10:00 A.M. to 3:00 P.M., Monday through Saturday.

Another fine restoration in the French Quarter is the **Hermann–Grima Historic House,** an 1831 mansion with authentically restored interiors and courtyards. The home depicts the lifestyle of a prosperous Creole family before the Civil War, and on Thursdays from October through May interpreters prepare meals and demonstrate cooking techniques used from 1830 to 1860. The Hermann–Grima House (504–525–5661) is at 820 St. Louis Street and is open from 10:00 A.M. to 4:00 P.M., Monday through Saturday.

A pleasant way to get around the French Quarter is on the **Riverfront Streetcars.** The vintage streetcars are painted red with gold trim and are affectionately known as the Ladies in Red. The trolley line connects the various attractions along the riverfront.

After touring the French Quarter, take a ride on the **St. Charles Avenue Streetcar** to view the stately mansions of the **Garden District.** After New Orleans became part of the United States, Americans flocked to the city to share in its growing riches. Snubbed by the French Quarter Creoles, many of the wealthy newcomers built lavish homes upriver in a region that came to be known as the Garden District because of its lovely landscaping (in contrast to the cloistered courtyards of the quarter, which were not visible from the street). While the homes are not open to the public, the streetcar travels past many lovely mansions.

Another popular—if macabre—attraction in New Orleans is the **Cities of the Dead.** Because New Orleans is below sea level, burying its dead has posed great problems for generations of residents. The solution has been to build above-ground cemeteries, many of which are filled with elaborate tombs and mausoleums. New Orleans cemeteries have become legendary for their beauty and the colorful stories associated with them, and they are often included on tours of the city. Call (504–566–5011) for information.

Civil War buffs won't want to miss the **Memorial Hall Confederate Museum,** which opened in 1891 and is the state's oldest museum. The building was originally constructed as a meeting place for Confederate veterans to reflect on their Civil War experiences and to house and protect their relics. Today it contains one of the nation's largest collections of Civil War artifacts, with over one hundred battle flags, a large array of uniforms and swords, and personal items of such famous figures as Jefferson Davis and Robert E. Lee. Memorial Hall (504–523–4522) is located at 929 Camp Street and is open from 10:00 A.M. to 4:00 P.M., Monday through Saturday.

Several other historic homes offer more insights into the city's past. The **Pitot House Museum** is the only plantation home in New Orleans open to the public on a regular basis. The house was built around 1799 and in 1810 became the residence of James Pitot, the first mayor of the newly incorporated city of New Orleans. Today the West Indies–style structure is furnished with antiques from the early 1800s and captures the flavor of life in the city during that period. The museum (504–482–0312), at 1440 Moss Street, is open from 10:00 A.M. to 3:00 P.M., Wednesday through Saturday.

One of the city's most beautiful properties is the **Longue Vue House and Gardens,** an urban estate that was the home of philanthropists Edgar Bloom Stern, a New Orleans businessman and cotton broker, and his wife, Edith, an heir of the Sears Company. The Greek Revival mansion is surrounded by eight acres of gardens, which include a lovely Spanish courtyard inspired by the Alhambra gardens in Spain. The house is now a decorative arts museum with changing exhibits in its galleries. Longue Vue (504–488–5488) is at 7 Bamboo Road and is open from 10:00 A.M. to 4:30 P.M., Monday through Saturday, and from 1:00 to 5:00 P.M. on Sunday.

A number of riverboats operate in the New Orleans area and offer visitors a chance to cruise the Mississippi in grand style. The *Natchez* is one of the nation's few remaining steamboats, a sternwheeler that offers daily sightseeing cruises as well as a dinner and jazz evening cruise. The boat departs from the wharf next to the Jax Brewery, near Jackson Square; call (800) 233–BOAT for information.

The *Cotton Blossom* departs daily from the wharf next to the Jax Brewery for a three-hour cruise that combines information on the history and culture of New Orleans with an ecological presentation by the Louisiana Nature and Science Center. Call (504) 586–8777 for information.

The *Cajun Queen Riverboat* (800–445–4109) and *Creole Queen Paddlewheeler* (800–445–4109) depart daily from the Poydras Street Wharf, next to the French Quarter's Aquarium of the Americas, and offer a variety of cruise options. New Orleans has also recently approved riverboat gambling. The *Queen of New Orleans,* a re-creation of a turn-of-the-century paddlewheeler, offers casino gambling on daily cruises. Call (800) 587–5825 for information.

Creoles and Cajuns

Two words that you'll often hear in Louisiana are *Creole* and *Cajun*. While their contemporary definitions have blurred, originally they referred to two distinct ethnic groups. Creole was used to describe someone who was a descendent of an early French or Spanish settler. During the eighteenth century, the Creoles dominated the cultural and social life of the city. Many clung to the French language and traditions and socialized mainly with other Creoles, disdaining American ways. Though the original Creoles eventually became outnumbered and marginalized, the term *Creole* is often used today to describe something that is indigenous to the region.

The Cajuns were also of French descent. Their ancestors had immigrated to the settlement of New Acadia in Nova Scotia, and were driven from there by the British in 1765. Thousands of refugees found a new home in Louisiana, where the term *Acadian* became *Cajun*. While Creoles were sophisticated city dwellers, the Cajuns lived along the bayous and swamps of southern Louisiana. The French-speaking Cajuns were clannish and isolated, and they developed their own unique customs, foods, and music, plus an accent that can be traced to the provincial French spoken in the Acadians' ancestral home in Brittany.

The city is also the home port of the **Delta Queen Steamboat Company.** For over one hundred years the company has been offering paddlewheeler cruises on the nation's inland waterways and is the only cruise line on the Mississippi to offer overnight excursions. The company operates three steamboats: the **Delta Queen, Mississippi Queen,** and the newly launched **American Queen.** Each is truly a floating palace, with brilliant red paddlewheels, tall black smokestacks, and wide decks that are perfect places to watch the river flow by. In addition to delicious food and entertainment, each boat also has on board a "riverlorian," an expert on river lore and history. These boats offer an unparalleled opportunity to experience the romance of the Mississippi and the adventure of the steamboat era. Year-round cruises ranging from three to fourteen nights are offered on the Mississippi, Ohio, Tennessee, Cumberland, and Arkansas rivers. For more information, call (800) 543–1949.

On the Delta Queen *and* Mississippi Queen, *the romance of the steamboat era lives again.*

Visitors to New Orleans can choose from a wealth of dining options. It's difficult to get a bad meal in the city and very easy to find an exceptional one. The French Quarter in particular is filled with excellent restaurants housed in historic properties. Two restaurants that have achieved well-deserved fame are **Brennan's** (504–525–9711), at 417 Royal Street, and **Arnaud's** (504–523–5433), at 813 Bienville Street. Arnaud's is especially known for its Sunday Brunch and Jazz. Both restaurants fall into the expensive category but are worth every penny.

The Delta Queen Steamboat Company

During the lean years that followed the end of the steamboat era, the Greene Line—which later became the Delta Queen Steamboat Company—was largely responsible for keeping river cruising alive. Gordon C. Greene founded the line in 1890, and along with his wife, Mary, operated a fleet of steamboats on the Ohio and Mississippi rivers.

In time the business passed into the capable hands of their son, Tom, who in 1946 purchased the *Delta Queen*. The boat had begun her career in 1927 as an overnight steamer traveling on the West Coast between Sacramento and San Francisco, and during World War II she had served as a Navy ferry boat. Greene had the big boat crated like a piano and towed down the West Coast, through the Panama Canal, and up the Gulf of Mexico to the Mississippi River. There she was completely refurbished and launched once again as a passenger vessel.

Cruises on the *Delta Queen* were so popular that in 1976 the company—now known as the Delta Queen Steamboat Company—launched the *Mississippi Queen,* the largest and grandest steamboat ever built. In 1995 an even larger and more elaborate steamboat was launched, the *American Queen,* with six decks, decorated in grand Victorian style, that house 420 passengers.

For accommodations try **Le Richelieu,** an intimate hotel that offers eighty-six individually decorated rooms. Parts of the building date back to 1845. Call (800) 535–9653 for reservations. The **Soniat House** is a seventeen-room, 1830 Creole townhouse that's been designated a Historic Hotel of America by the National Trust. Each room is furnished with antiques, and the hotel has a beautiful, secluded courtyard. You'll find the Soniat House (800–544–8808) at 1133 Chartres Street.

Along with Mardi Gras, New Orleans's calendar is full of events celebrating its multiethnic roots, food, music, and distinctive traditions. During the **French Quarter Festival** in April, the *Vieux Carré* celebrates its unique heritage. The event coincides with the **Spring Fiesta,** which includes tours of many of the city's historic private homes, courtyards, and plantations. In late April and early May, the city's rich musical traditions are put onstage for the **New Orleans Jazz and Heritage Festival.** Over 4,000 musicians, cooks, and craftspeople assemble in New Orleans for a ten-day festival held at the fair grounds and throughout the city. For information about any of these events, call (504) 566–5068.

Though New Orleans is often considered to be the end of the river road, travelers can continue to follow the Mississippi as it makes its way through the huge delta to the Gulf of Mexico. From New Orleans head south on Highway 23 to Plaquemines, Louisiana's southernmost parish, which extends as a finger of land into the gulf. Plaquemines Parish (not to be confused with the town of Plaquemine, farther north) is a center for commercial and recreational fishing and is also among the world's leaders in oil and natural gas production.

Sixty-five miles south of New Orleans you'll find **Old Fort Jackson,** which was built between 1822 and 1832 under the recommendation of General Andrew Jackson. The fort was built near the site of even older earthen and timber fortifications that dated back to the mid-1700s. Named after General Jackson, the fort was readied in 1846 for service during the Mexican War, but its defenses were not needed. During the Civil War the Confederacy seized control of the fort to help protect New Orleans. The fort withstood an 1862 attack by the Union forces under the command of Flag Officer David Farragut, only to surrender later because of a mutiny among its men. Farragut was then able to travel up the Mississippi River and capture New Orleans, a significant turning point in the war. Today the restored fort includes camping facilities and a museum with information on the fortification's history. The museum (504–657–7083) is open daily from 9:00 A.M. to 4:00 P.M.

From Fort Jackson continue south on Highway 23 for 7 miles to **Venice,** named after another city surrounded by water. On a site near here in 1682, Robert Cavelier, Sieur de La Salle, claimed the entire Mississippi Valley for France. At the time King Louis XIV was unimpressed: "I am convinced, like you, that the discovery of the Sieur de La Salle is very useless," he wrote to one of his advisers.

South of Venice the river enters a maze of islands formed from topsoil carried thousands of miles by the restless river. Here, at last, the mighty Mississippi dissolves into the embrace of the sea.

FOR MORE INFORMATION

Louisiana Office of Tourism (800) 33GUMBO

Louisiana Office of State Parks (504) 342–8111

Lake Providence (318) 559–5125

Tallulah (318) 574–4537

Vidalia (318) 336–5206

Pointe Coupee Parish/New Roads (504) 638–9858

West Feliciana Parish/St. Francisville (504) 635–6330

Baton Rouge (800) LA–ROUGE

West Baton Rouge Parish/Port Allen (800) 654–9701

Iberville Parish/Plaquemine (504) 687–3560

Ascension Parish (504) 675–6550

St. James Parish (504) 869–9752

New Orleans (504) 566–5011

Plaquemines Parish (504) 392–6690

THE GREAT
TRIBUTARIES

The Missouri and Ohio Rivers

Missouri River

Liberty

Kansas City

Lexington

Independence

Arrow
Rock

Glasgow

Boonville

Jefferson
City

Hermann

Defiance

St. Charles

St. Louis

Washington

Missouri

N

W   E

S

THE
Missouri River

From St. Louis to Kansas City

he Missouri River is the longest tributary of the Mississippi, extending for 2,315 miles from the Rocky Mountains in Montana to St. Louis, Missouri. A good case can
be made, in fact, that the Missouri is the main upper channel
of the Mississippi. It exceeds the length of the Upper Mississippi by almost
1,600 miles and drains a far larger area. Because European explorers discovered the Upper Mississippi first, however, the Missouri has to be content as
a tributary of the mighty river rather than its source.

During the steamboat era, the Missouri played a vital role in the opening of the American frontier. The river was navigable from St. Louis to the
western Montana outpost of Fort Benton, and steamboats were an econom-
ical way of transporting supplies and passengers to remote settlements.

Those who lived along the banks of the "Big Muddy" said that the river
was "too thick to drink and too thin to plow." The Missouri was even more
treacherous than the Mississippi. Its channel was more shallow, its strong currents shifted more frequently, and snags, sandbars, and floods took a heavy toll
on boats. In addition, the river's muddy water was particularly hard on steamboat engines. During the nineteenth century, more than 400 steamboats sank
along the Missouri, and Missouri River pilots said scornfully that managing a
boat on the Mississippi was child's play next to doing so on the Big Muddy.

The tour outlined in this chapter takes you from St. Louis to Kansas City
along 375 miles of the meandering Missouri. The route follows the path of

westward settlement and winds through beautiful, rural countryside dotted with historic settlements.

ST. CHARLES TO HERMANN

Begin your tour along the Missouri with a visit to the historic community of **St. Charles,** the oldest city on the river. Founded by French Canadians in 1769, St. Charles was known as *Les Petites Côtes* ("the little hills") because of its location on low bluffs along the river. As the embarkation point for travelers heading west, the settlement grew into a thriving river port. Lewis and Clark wintered here in 1804 prior to embarking on their exploration of the Louisiana Purchase, and St. Charles served as Missouri's first state capital from 1821 to 1826.

Historic South Main Street is the oldest and largest historic district along the Missouri River and illustrates the city's evolution from a frontier trading post. A variety of architectural styles are visible, including French Colonial, Federal, and a blend of French and German influences. The brick streets are lined with dozens of shops and restaurants, and the Tourism Center (800–366–2427), at 230 South Main Street, provides information on self-guided tours.

The **Lewis and Clark Center,** at 701 Riverside Drive, presents exhibits relating to the famous expedition that passed through here, an epic journey that lasted over two years and covered more than 8,000 miles. The center includes a hands-on museum and a period trading post. It's open daily from 10:30 A.M. to 4:30 P.M. Call (314) 947–3199 for information.

You'll find **Missouri's First State Capitol** at 200–216 South Main Street. The complex of buildings contains fully restored legislative chambers, an interpretive center, two private residences, the governor's office, and a restored mercantile establishment. The site (314–946–9282) is open from 10:00 A.M. to 4:00 P.M., Monday through Saturday, and from noon to 6:00 P.M. on Sunday.

The *Goldenrod Showboat,* a National Historic Landmark built in 1909, recalls the days when showboats brought entertainment to settlements lining the nation's rivers. Live professional theater is offered year-round, including Broadway, off-Broadway, and children's theater productions. During Labor Day weekend the showboat hosts a **Ragtime Festival,** a celebration of ragtime and jazz music. The boat is docked at 1000 Riverside Drive, on the Missouri River. Call (314) 946–2020 for information.

Next to the *Goldenrod* is the **Casino St. Charles** riverboat, which features three decks of casino gambling. The boat (800–325–7777) docks at the St. Charles Riverfront Station.

Another way to see the city is on board the **St. Charles Trolley,** which provides transportation between visitor attractions and parking locations for a small fee. The trolley (800–366–2427) runs daily from June through September and on weekends during the rest of the year, except for January, February, and March.

St. Charles hosts more than a dozen annual festivals, several of which celebrate its rich history. The **Lewis and Clark Rendezvous** is held on the riverfront during the third weekend in May and includes trader and military encampments, parades with fife and drum corps, and nineteenth-century crafts and demonstrations. **Riverfest** is a traditional Independence Day celebration complete with fireworks from barges on the Missouri River. In mid-August the **Fête Des Petites Côtes** re-creates a nineteenth-century atmosphere with craft demonstrations, live entertainment, and food booths. A **Civil War Reenactment** is held in September. For information about any of these events, call the St. Charles Convention and Visitors Bureau at (800) 366–2427.

The city is home to a number of bed-and-breakfasts housed in historic properties, including the **Boone's Lick Trail Inn,** at 1000 South Main Street, in the historic district. The 1840 home is listed on the National Register and offers five guest rooms. For information, call (800) 366–2427.

From St. Charles you can choose to explore the rest of the Missouri River Valley by car, or you can hike or bike the **Katy Trail State Park,** a rail-trail that runs along the route of the old Missouri-Kansas-Texas Railroad as it follows the river. When completed, the trail will run for 200 miles from St. Charles to Sedalia. The 38-mile portion from Frontier Park, in St. Charles, to Marthasville was one of the first sections to be completed and offers a wonderful way to see the countryside. For a map and information, call the Missouri Department of Natural Resources at (800) 334–6946.

From St. Charles take Highway 94 west for 20 miles to **Defiance,** the site of the **Daniel Boone Home,** a four-story, Georgian-style structure built between 1803 and 1810 that was home to the remarkable frontiersman for more than twenty years. The trailblazer, Indian fighter, scout, trapper, surveyor, Virginia state legislator, and judge came to Missouri in 1799, when the territory was just opening up to white settlement. His long journey from Kentucky in a dugout canoe took him down the Ohio, up the Mississippi to the Missouri, and then to this beautiful spot where the Femme Osage River joins the Missouri. Boone supervised the construction of this home and lived here until his death in 1820 at the age of 86. The house contains many items from the Boone family and other pieces of early Americana. The grounds include a chapel, schoolhouse, woodshop, and kitchen house—the nucleus of a living history village that will grow up around the home in years to come. The home (314–987–2221) is located at 1868 Highway F and is open daily from March through November and on weekends only during the winter.

For an overnight stay in Defiance, try the **Country Porch Bed and**

Missouri's Rhineland

The 100-mile portion of the Missouri River that stretches from Defiance to Jefferson City is known as Missouri's Rhineland, a tribute to its strong German heritage, scenic hills, and tidy villages lined with brick homes.

The region is also the heart of one of the Midwest's premier wine-producing areas. The German immigrants who began to settle here in the 1830s brought with them an extensive knowledge of viniculture. They found that the region was well-suited for the growing of grapes, with well-drained soil and bluffs that protected the grapes from frost.

During the second half of the nineteenth century, Missouri was the nation's second-largest producer of wines. It even helped save the French wine industry after it had been devastated by a pest called phylloxera during the 1880s. An estimated ten million pest-resistant root stocks were shipped from Missouri to France, and Hermann Jaeger, the Missouri vintner who had helped find the cure for the plague, was awarded the Cross of the French Legion of Honor by the grateful French.

Though Prohibition and the Depression destroyed Missouri's wine industry, during the past few decades the vineyards have experienced a rebirth. Missouri wines are once again winning national and international recognition.

Breakfast, at 15 Walnut Springs Drive. The 1856 Victorian home (314–987–2546) offers three guest rooms.

From Defiance continue west on Highway 94 for 15 miles to Dutzow, then travel south on Highway 47 for 4 miles to **Washington.** This town had its beginnings in the 1820s as a ferry landing on the southern bank of the Missouri River. Among its earliest settlers were followers of Daniel Boone, and later during the 1830s many German immigrants began settling in the area, giving the town a German flavor that it retains to this day.

The **Washington Historical Society Museum,** at 314 West Main Street, has exhibits on local history and the town's growth as a steamboat port. The museum (314–239–2715) is open from 1:00 to 4:00 P.M. on Saturday and Sunday, April through December.

The **Missouri Meerschaum Company** preserves another part of Washington's heritage. Established in 1869, the company is the world's largest manufacturer of corncob pipes. Legend has it that a local farmer whittled a pipe out of a corncob and liked it so much that he asked woodworker Henry Tibbe to try turning some on his lathe. The farmer was well pleased, and Tibbe began selling some of the new pipes in his shop. Soon the pipes became so popular that Tibbe was selling them nationwide. Today's pipes are made from a special hybrid corn that produces big, thick cobs. The company (314–239–2109) is located at 400 West Front Street and has a visitor room that is open Monday through Friday.

The **Washington Brewery Bar and Restaurant,** at 108 Busch Street, is an 1854 structure that once housed a brewery owned by John B. Busch, Sr., brother of Adolphus Busch, who founded the Anheuser–Busch Brewery in St. Louis. The restored building has retained much of its nineteenth-century flavor and is open daily for lunch and dinner; prices are moderate. Call (314) 239–9113 for information.

Mense's Landing, LTD is another restaurant housed in an historic structure. Built in the 1850s as a hotel and restaurant, the Landing is located at 300 West Front Street, on the riverfront, and serves lunch and dinner daily. Prices are moderate; call (314) 239–4359 for information.

Three historic buildings overlooking the river offer overnight lodging. The **Schwegmann House** was built in the 1860s by John Schwegmann, who made his fortune from a riverfront flour mill. The stately home (800–949–2262), at 438 West Front Street, has ten guest rooms. The **Weirick–Hoelscher Estate,** at 716 West Main Street, was built in 1879 and has three guest rooms. Call (800) 791–4469 for information. The **Washington**

House (314–239–2417), at 3 Lafayette Street, is an old 1837 inn with three rooms for guests.

From Washington continue on Highway 100 for 27 miles to **Hermann,** the center of a thriving winery and tourism area. The town was founded in 1836 by the German Settlement Society of Philadelphia, whose members were concerned about the loss of their native customs and language among their countrymen in America. Their new colony was meant to be a "second fatherland" that would preserve German heritage and traditions. A site was chosen here on the steep hills that line the Missouri River because it reminded the immigrants of the Rhine River region in Germany, and the colony quickly attracted a variety of professionals, artisans, and laborers. Though the young settlement was plagued by internal dissension in its early years, it has remained a center for German heritage and traditions—a little bit of Germany in the Midwest.

The **Deutschheim State Historic Site,** at 109 West Second Street, includes two historic homes and a museum celebrating German handcrafts. The Pommer–Gentner House was built in 1840 and is one of the town's oldest homes. The German Neoclassical structure was owned by two families who were original members of the German Settlement Society. The Strehly House was home to Hermann's first German-language press and later became a winery and tavern. Its interior is furnished in an 1860s to 1880s middle-class style. Both homes feature period gardens. Deutschheim (314–486–2200) is open from 10:00 A.M. to 4:00 P.M. daily.

The **Historic Hermann Museum,** at the corner of Fourth and Schiller streets, offers more insights into local history. The building, an old schoolhouse, was constructed in 1871 and was used as an elementary school until 1955. It now houses a variety of craft and historical exhibits, including steamboat era displays in its River Room. The museum also has maps that outline walking tours through Hermann's historic districts. The museum (314–486–2017) is open from 10:00 A.M. to 4:00 P.M. daily, from April to November.

Overlooking the Missouri River at 232 Wharf Street is the **White House Hotel,** a museum and bed-and-breakfast establishment. At the time it was built in 1868, it was one of the most luxurious hotels in the region and accommodated such dignitaries as William Jennings Bryan, who reportedly said, "It took the town of Hermann to put me in the White House." Visitors can tour thirty rooms of period furniture and the hotel's doll and mineral museums and then sample homemade breads and goodies in its country kitchen. The hotel (314–486–3200) is open for tours from May through October from 1:00 to 5:00 P.M.

Many of the wineries in the Hermann area have a long history that dates back to the early days of the colony. Among the oldest is the **Stone Hill Winery,** which began making wine in 1847 and by the turn of the century was the third largest winery in the world. During Prohibition Stone Hill survived by using its enormous cellars to grow mushrooms. Wine production began again in 1965 under the ownership of the Held family, and in 1989 Stone Hill became the first Missouri winery to be awarded a gold medal in a national wine competition. The entire winery (which is the largest in Missouri) has been declared a national historic district, and visitors are welcome to tour its buildings and sample its wines. The **Vintage 1847 Restaurant** is located beside the winery in what was once a barn and carriage house and is considered one of the state's finest restaurants. Prices are moderate to expensive. Stone Hill Winery (314–486–2129) and Vintage 1847 Restaurant (314–486–3479) are located on the Stone Hill Highway.

Contact the Visitor Information Center (314–486–2744) at 306 Market Street for more information about other area wineries. The center also has information on the more than twenty bed-and-breakfasts in Hermann, many of which are housed in historic buildings.

A good time to visit Hermann is during one of its annual festivals. **Maifest** in May and **Octoberfest** (in October, naturally) celebrate the town's German heritage with food, music, dancing, and winery and museum tours. Another fun event is the **Great Stone Hill Grape Stomp** in August, when visitors have the chance to make wine the old-fashioned way. For information on Hermann festivals, call (314) 486–2744.

JEFFERSON CITY TO LEXINGTON

From Hermann continue west on Highways 100 and 50 for 60 miles to the Missouri state capital, **Jefferson City.** The selection of the capital involved considerable politicking on the part of Missouri's early citizens. The federal government agreed to donate land for the capital, provided that it be "within 40 miles from the mouth of the Osage River and located on the Missouri River." Leading citizens lobbied for various sites, and the present location

was chosen in part because it had been less involved in the frenzy of specu-
lation. The city was established here in 1821 on the banks of the Missouri
and was named after Thomas Jefferson. Many of the new settlers were from
Virginia and had known Jefferson, who was said to be highly pleased with
the honor bestowed upon him.

Many of Jefferson City's historical attractions are located in the riverfront
area that gave birth to the fledgling capital in the 1820s and 1830s. Begin
your tour with a visit to the **Missouri State Capitol,** on Capitol Avenue.
The previous building was destroyed by fire in 1911 and this impressive,
Renaissance-style structure covering three acres was constructed in its place.
The first floor includes a museum with displays on state history, and on the
third floor, Thomas Hart Benton's famous mural *A Social History of the State
of Missouri* is painted on the walls of the House lounge in the west wing. On

Divided Loyalties

Following the attack on Fort Sumter that began the Civil War, Missouri—which contained key sections of both the Mississippi and
Missouri rivers—became a vital link in the strategies of both the
North and South. Though its economic interests were closely tied to the
North, Missouri had been admitted to the Union as a slave state, and its
loyalties were deeply divided. Many settlers traced their roots to southern states and southern sentiment was particularly strong in the rich
slaveholding counties that lined the Missouri River.

Missouri's governor, Claiborne Fox Jackson, called openly for secession from the Union, and the state legislature became the political arena
in which tensions came to a head. Although a state convention voted to
remain with the Union, Jackson issued a call for a state militia to support the Confederacy. He personally led the militia in an engagement
against Union troops at Boonville on June 17, 1861.

A month later the state convention met again and removed Jackson
and other pro-South leaders from office. The two camps continued to
battle for control of Missouri, however. Renegade guerrilla groups also
raided the state and caused great suffering among its citizens. The bit-
terness caused by the war lingered for many years.

the northeast side of the Capitol you'll find the All Missouri Veterans Memorial, with a limestone colonnade, terraced waterfall, reflecting pool, and eight black marble posts. Guided tours of the capitol are offered daily; phone (314) 751–4127 for information.

Across the street from the Capitol is the **Jefferson Landing State Historic Site,** which includes three buildings dating back to the glory days of the city's river trade. The **Lohman Building** is a three-story structure built in the mid-1830s, making it the oldest remaining building in Jefferson City. Between 1850 and 1870 the building housed an inn, store, and warehouse operated by German immigrant Charles Lohman. Today it houses a museum (314–751–3475) with displays on area history and a visitors center. The Lohman Building is open daily from 8:30 A.M. to 4:30 P.M. The neighboring **Union Hotel** was built in the 1850s and now houses an art gallery that's open daily.

Next to the Union Hotel is the **Governor's Residence,** an 1871 Renaissance Revival mansion that serves as the official home of Missouri's governor. Tours of its first floor are given each Tuesday and Thursday, except during August and December. For information, call (314) 751–2800. After touring the mansion, stroll through the Governor's Garden, which began as a W.P.A. project during the 1930s.

Across the street from the mansion is the **Cole County Historical Museum,** housed in a row house built in 1871 by the former Missouri governor B. Gratz Brown. Historical exhibits include a display of inaugural ball gowns worn by governors' wives. The museum (314–635–1850) is open Tuesday from 10:30 A.M. to 3:30 P.M., and Wednesday through Saturday, noon to 3:30 P.M.

From Jefferson City head north on Highways 179 and 98 for 48 miles to **Boonville,** the oldest town in central Missouri. The city is located in the heart of an area known as Boon's Lick, which is named for a large salt lick worked by Daniel Boone's sons Nathan and Daniel Morgan beginning in 1805. At the time salt was a valuable commodity and a key ingredient for food preservation, and the salt lick attracted many settlers to the region.

Boonville's position on the Missouri River also fueled its settlement, and a prosperous river trade gradually developed. Located at a point where the Ozark uplands meet the western prairies, the town was a natural outfitting center for overland routes west. With the outbreak of the Civil War, Boonville's strategic location made it a coveted outpost for both the Union and Confederacy, and two battles were fought here in June and September of 1861.

The **Old Cooper County Jail and Hanging Barn,** at 614 East Morgan Street, preserves local history in a structure built by slave labor in 1848. The barn was the site of one of the last public hangings in Missouri, in 1930. The jail and barn (816–882–7977) are open daily.

Thespian Hall was built in 1857 and is the oldest surviving theater west of the Allegheny Mountains. Each year it hosts numerous events, including the **Missouri River Festival of the Arts** in August, which attracts nationally known performance groups. For information, call (816) 882–7977.

Another historic structure is **Roslyn Heights,** an 1895 Queen Anne mansion furnished with period furniture that serves as the state headquarters for the Daughters of the American Revolution. The mansion (816–882–5320) is open Thursday and Sunday, 2:00 to 4:00 P.M.

Several bed-and-breakfasts offer accommodations in historic structures. The **Morgan Street Repose,** at 611 Morgan Street, is an 1869 Victorian home with two guest suites; call (800) 248–5061 for information. The 1840s **River City Inn,** at 311 East Spring Street, has five rooms; call (816) 882–5465 for information. The **Lady Goldenrod Inn** (816–882–5764), at 629 East Spring Street, is a 1900 Queen Anne home on the National Register that offers four guest rooms.

Boonville celebrates its history each June with **Boonville Heritage Days,** which include an antiques carnival, beer and wine garden, arts and crafts, street dances, and living-history demonstrations. Call (816) 882–2721 for information.

Before leaving Boonville, pay a visit to **Harley Park,** overlooking the river. The park was established in 1887 and contains four Hopewell Indian burial mounds dating from 100 B.C. to A.D. 500.

Just across the river from Boonville is the **Rivercene Bed and Breakfast,** a fifteen-room mansion built by the riverboat baron Captain Joseph Kinney in 1864. Kinney had come to Boonville in 1844 and worked for twelve years in a variety of jobs to save up enough money to pursue his first love of steamboating. His fleet eventually grew to include twenty-one boats that carried passengers and freight from Montana to New Orleans. He began building Rivercene in 1864, using materials he had collected from around the world, including Italian marble for its nine fireplaces. The mansion's design was so admired that the state of Missouri later duplicated it for the governor's residence in Jefferson City. Today Rivercene still stands on the banks of the Missouri, though the house was once called Kinney's Folly because the locals were certain a river flood would eventually destroy it. Innkeepers Jody and

The Wise Use of Rivers

The flood of 1993, which did great damage along both the Mississippi and Missouri rivers, helped stimulate a nationwide debate on the proper management of America's rivers. For over a century, the U.S. Army Corps of Engineers has been responsible for controlling the Mississippi and the Missouri, building dams and locks to maintain channels deep enough for barge transportation, and constructing levees to protect the lands that border the rivers. The 1993 flood was a sobering reminder that such measures can be counterproductive: In many areas the destruction would have been much less serious if the water could have seeped slowly through a network of wetlands instead of being confined to a channel.

The loss of wetlands along these rivers is troubling for other reasons as well. Wetlands restore water quality and remove pollutants from the air and are among the earth's most productive landscapes. In North America three-quarters of the native bird species depend upon wetlands for feeding, nesting, or resting, and two-thirds of the commercial fish and shellfish that are harvested require wetlands for part or all of their life cycle. As marshes, swamps, and floodplains are drained, many species of fish and wildlife suffer.

The struggle between the nation's agricultural, commercial, recreational, and environmental interests is likely to continue. There are no easy solutions for managing the awesome power of the Mississippi and Missouri.

Ron Lenz offer daily tours from 1:00 to 6:00 P.M. You'll find Rivercene at 127 County Road 463; call (800) 531–0862 for information.

From Rivercene you have a choice of two routes. The more direct one continues north on Highway 87 for 20 miles to Glasgow. For an interesting detour, head back across the river and drive north on Highway 41 for 12 miles to the charming village of **Arrow Rock.** Founded in 1829, Arrow Rock was once a busy steamboat port and the home of two Missouri governors and the artist John Caleb Bingham. It was here that the Santa Fe Trail crossed the Missouri River. A ferry here also contributed to Arrow Rock's growth into an important trading center.

The town preserves its history with a number of attractions. Each summer visiting artists present nineteenth-century crafts that include weaving and pottery making along the downtown's wooden boardwalk, which is lined with a number of antiques and specialty shops. **Historic walking tours** are another way to sample the town's past. The tour includes visits to the 1837 George Caleb Bingham House and the 1844 Sites Gun Shop as well as several other sites. The tour takes about ninety minutes and is offered several times daily from June through August and on weekends in April, May, September, and October. Call (816) 837–3231 for information. The tour departs from the Friends Information Center on Main Street and is sponsored by the Missouri Department of Natural Resources.

One of the stops on the tour is the **Old Arrow Rock Tavern,** at 302 Main Street, a structure built in 1834 that is one of the oldest restaurants west of the Mississippi. It serves country-style lunches and dinners Wednesday through Saturday and brunch on Sunday. Prices are moderate to expensive, and reservations are required for the evening meal (phone 816–837–3200).

Another eating establishment located in an historic building is the **Evergreen Restaurant,** located one block north of Main Street on Highway 41. Housed in a restored 1840s-era home, the restaurant serves lunch and dinner (call 816–837–3251 for hours). Prices are moderate to expensive.

Half a dozen bed-and-breakfasts offer overnight accommodations in Arrow Rock, including **Miss Nelle's Bed and Breakfast** (800–795–2797), which was built in 1853 and is located on Main Street. For other listings, call the Friends of Arrow Rock Information Office at (816) 837–3231.

From Arrow Rock take County Roads AC and P north for 12 miles, then head east on Highway 240 for 5 miles to the bridge that will take you into **Glasgow.** The city was founded in 1836 and became a prosperous shipping and trading center with a typical Southern economy based on hemp and tobacco cultivated by slaves. The Civil War split the town into two factions, and in 1864 a bloody battle was fought here between the Union forces who occupied the town and Confederate troops looking for supplies. After heavy fighting the outnumbered Union soldiers surrendered, but only after burning City Hall and all the munitions stored within.

Prosperity returned after the war ended, and large mansions, lavish hotels, and bathing spas were constructed. The Glasgow Homes Tour Committee (816–338–2377) publishes a guide to more than fifty historic sites, including many antebellum mansions.

The **Glasgow Community Museum,** at 402 Commerce Street, is located in an 1861 Gothic Revival structure that once housed a church. Its upper floor contains period church furnishings and in its basement are displays of local memorabilia. The museum (816–338–2377) is open from 3:00 to 5:00 P.M., Tuesday, Thursday, Saturday, and Sunday from May 15 to October 15.

From Glasgow continue west on Highways 240 and 65 for 65 miles to **Lexington.** Founded in 1822 by settlers from Lexington, Kentucky, the town became a booming farming community and river outpost. Traders, fur trappers, and suppliers brought brisk business to the community, which for a few years was the westernmost settlement outfitting wagon trains for the Santa Fe and Oregon trails. The town was a major port on the Missouri, with factories and docks lining the riverbanks and a thriving steamboat industry. The shipping firm of Russell, Majors, and Waddell had their headquarters here. They were the founders of the famous Pony Express as well as outfitters for Mexican and California traders and western U.S. Army posts.

The Battle of the Hemp Bales

Lexington became an important military post early in the Civil War. The Union colonel James Mulligan was ordered to hold the strategic Missouri River port at all costs in order to keep the Confederate forces north of the Missouri from joining the Missouri State Guard under General Sterling Price's command.

In 1861 Price surrounded the Union forces stationed in Lexington. Mulligan's forces withstood Price's advances for three days, until Price devised an ingenious plan. He ordered his men to soak hemp bales awaiting shipment on the wharf below and place them at the base of the hill occupied by the Union soldiers. With three Confederates behind each bale, the Rebel army used the bales as movable breastworks as they advanced. When Price's men were within one hundred yards of the Union entrenchments, the white flag finally appeared, and the Confederates took 3,000 prisoners. Thus the Missouri River helped carry the day for the Confederate Army.

As operators of overland wagon trains across the Great Plains, the company employed as many as 4,000 men and owned 3,500 wagons, 1,000 mules, and 40,000 oxen.

During the Civil War, Lexington was strategically important because it was a busy river port, and it was the site of one of the largest battles in the Western Campaign. After the war Lexington became a coal mining and educational center; today it's part of the state's most productive apple-growing region.

Lexington today is filled with many historic structures, including over one hundred antebellum homes. Its Civil War history lives on at several sites. The **Battle of Lexington State Historic Site,** located on an extension off Highway 13, includes remnants of the Union breastworks and trenches. Also on site is the **Anderson House,** built in 1853 by Oliver Anderson and used as a hospital during the battle. Bloodstains and bullet holes still remain, and the home is furnished in Civil War–era style. Anderson House (816–259–4654) is open from 10:00 A.M. to 4:00 P.M., Monday through Saturday, and from noon to 4:30 P.M. on Sunday.

The oldest courthouse still in use in Missouri stands on the square in downtown Lexington. A cannonball that hit the 1849 building during the Battle of Lexington remains embedded in one of its front columns.

Every three years in September, the Missouri Department of Natural Resources sponsors a **Reenactment of the Battle of Lexington,** with re-creations of the Union and Missouri guard camps. Call (800) 334–6946 for information.

The **Lexington Historical Museum** is housed in an 1846 structure that once served as a church. It features steamboat artifacts, a Pony Express collection, and extensive exhibits on the Battle of Lexington as well as other displays on the town's history. The museum (816–259–6313) is at 112 South Thirteenth Street and is open daily, May to September, from 1:00 to 4:30 P.M.

The **1830s Log House Museum** was once a tavern overlooking the riverfront and is the oldest wooden structure remaining in Lexington. Furnished with pre–Civil War artifacts, it includes displays on pioneer cooking, quilt making, and frontier tools and has an herb garden. The museum (816–259–4711) is at the corner of Broadway and Main streets, and is open from 11:00 A.M. to 4:00 P.M., Wednesday through Saturday, with additional hours from 1:00 to 4:00 P.M. on Sunday, May through September.

For overnight accommodations, visit **Linwood Lawn,** a plantation home built in 1850 by William Limerick. The twenty-six-room showplace offers six guest rooms. You'll find it off State Road on the outskirts of Lexington; call (816) 259–4290 for information.

FORT OSAGE TO KANSAS CITY

From Lexington travel west on Highway 24 for 20 miles to Buckner and then follow the signs north to Sibley, site of **Fort Osage.** The fort overlooks the Missouri River and was built in 1808 under the direction of William Clark, co-commander of the Lewis and Clark expedition of 1804. Reconstructed in the 1940s, the fort operates as a living history site taking visitors back to the days when it was a center for the fur trade and one of the first military outposts in the Louisiana Purchase. The fort is open from 9:00 A.M. to 4:30 P.M., Wednesday through Sunday, from April 15 to November 15, and on weekends during the rest of the year. For more information, call (816) 795–8200, ext. 260.

While you're touring Fort Osage, take note of the Santa Fe Trail markings that are still visible here. The thousands of wagons that passed through on their way west have left permanent marks on the prairie—wide depressions in the earth whose grass is usually greener in spring and shorter in the summer than the surrounding grass.

From Fort Osage return to Highway 24 and continue west for 5 miles to **Independence,** once one of the West's most important cities. Independence became a town in 1827, when settlers chose a site near an Indian gathering place named Big Spring as their new county seat. By the 1840s the town had grown into a prosperous supply depot, providing services and goods for pioneers headed out on the Santa Fe, Oregon, and California trails that converged here. Travelers of the day reported that in the spring there would be at least 10,000 oxen grazing in the fields outside of town, waiting to haul wagons west. More than 250,000 immigrants traveled the trails between 1842 and 1870, making this westward movement the largest peacetime migration in history.

Among the early pioneers to the area was the Mormon prophet Joseph Smith, Jr., who led his followers into town in 1831. Smith selected a plot of land not far from the present-day town square to be the site of a new temple. Before it could be built, however, a hostile community ran his followers out of Independence. The group fled to Nauvoo, Illinois (see page 83), where Smith was killed in 1844. Although some of Smith's followers left Illinois for Utah, another contingent returned to the area and formed the Reorganized Church of Jesus Christ of Latter-Day Saints, which was led by Smith's son. Smith's great-grandson is now president of the denomination, which has its headquarters in Independence.

Beginning in the 1850s the town felt the rumblings that preceded the Civil War. A significant number of townspeople had loyalties to the South, though Missouri remained part of the Union. Many Independence citizens closed their businesses and joined the rebel ranks.

In 1862 Confederate soldiers drove the Union forces from the town in an engagement known as the First Battle of Independence. In 1864 the Second Battle of Independence was fought as part of the larger Westport Campaign. (Call the Independence Tourism Office at 800–748–7323 for a brochure that outlines the battle sites.)

After the war Jesse James's gang of outlaws also left its mark on Independence. They were blamed for two holdups in the area, in 1879 and 1881. The gang's reputation for leaving citizens alone while robbing banks and railroad companies—and their earlier role as Confederate guerrillas—made them folk heroes to many of the county's residents. After Jesse's death in St. Joseph, Missouri, his brother Frank James surrendered to the governor of Missouri and was taken to the old Jackson County Jail and held until his trial in Gallatin, Missouri. He was acquitted of all charges, lived the rest of his life in the area, and was buried in a quiet cemetery in the northern part of Hill Park, at Twenty-third Street and Maywood.

Independence has many sites that relate to its colorful nineteenth-century history. Begin your visit with a stop at the **National Frontier Trails Center.** Located near a spring where settlers filled their water barrels before heading west, the center describes the westward expansion that changed the face of the nation and made Independence the "Queen City of the Trails." Period artifacts, diaries, a full-scale pioneer wagon, and a film tell about the arduous journeys endured by the travelers. The museum (816–325–7575) is located at 318 West Pacific Street. It's open from 9:00 A.M. to 4:30 P.M., Monday through Saturday, and 12:30 to 4:30 P.M., Sunday, from April through October, and on weekends the rest of the year.

The **Bingham–Waggoner Estate** was built in 1855 alongside the Santa Fe Trail and has been restored as a testament to the prosperity found in early Independence. Situated on a nineteen-acre estate, the three-story house was once home to the Missouri artist John Caleb Bingham. The house (816–461–3491) is at 313 West Pacific Street and is open from April through October. Its hours are 10:00 A.M. to 4:00 P.M., Monday through Saturday, and 1:00 to 4:00 P.M. on Sunday.

The spectacular **Vaile Mansion** gives more insights into the era. Built in 1881 by local entrepreneur Harvey Vaile, the ornate mansion is one of

The Vaile Mansion was one of the nation's most opulent homes when it was built in 1881.

the finest examples of Victorian architecture in the United States. The flamboyant Vaile built his dream home for the princely sum of $150,000 and furnished it with the latest in conveniences and decor, including marble fireplaces, hand-stenciled ceilings, running water, and a speaker tube communications system. You'll find the mansion at 1500 North Liberty Street. It is open from April through October, 10:00 A.M. to 4:00 P.M., Monday through Saturday, and 1:00 to 4:00 P.M. on Sunday. Call (816) 325–7430 for information.

You can get a glimpse of frontier-style justice at the **1859 Jail, Marshal's Home, and Museum,** a complex of buildings at the corner of Truman Road and Main Street. Frank James was one of the prisoners once held in the jail, and the Federal-style house was home to a succession of county marshals and their families until the early 1930s. Both have been restored and feature period furnishings. The museum houses a new interactive exhibit and displays on Jackson County history. You'll find the complex, which also includes an 1860s schoolhouse, at 217 North Main Street. Its hours are from 10:00 A.M. to 4:00 P.M., Monday through Saturday, and from 1:00 to 4:00 P.M. on Sunday. Phone (816) 252–1892 for information.

The **Mormon Visitors Center** gives more information about the role Mormons played in the early history of Independence. Artifacts, exhibits, and artwork document the heritage and beliefs of the denomination. The center (816–836–3466) is located at 937 West Walnut Street and is open daily from 9:00 A.M. to 9:00 P.M.

Before leaving Independence, don't miss two more landmarks of a more recent era. The **Truman Library and Museum** explores the public and private lives of Independence's most famous native son, Harry S Truman. Included are exhibits on the history of the Truman administration and the nature and history of the American presidency plus a full-scale reproduction of the Oval Office in 1948. Harry S and Bess Truman's graves are in the library's courtyard. The library and museum are located on Highway 24 at Delaware Street and are open from 9:00 A.M. to 5:00 P.M. daily. Phone (816) 833–1400 for information.

After visiting the library, pay a visit to the **Truman Home,** at 219 North Delaware Street. It was built by Bess Truman's grandfather in 1885 and was home to the Trumans from the time of their marriage until their deaths. Known as the Summer White House from 1945 to 1953, the Victorian house is a time capsule that takes visitors back to the years when the plain-speaking, spirited president lived here. The home (816–254–9929) is open from 9:00 A.M. to 5:00 P.M. daily (closed Monday from Labor Day to Memorial Day). Tickets may be purchased at the Truman Home Ticket and Information Center, at the corner of Main Street and Truman Road.

Independence hosts a number of festivals each year, including the **Queen City Rendezvous** on Memorial Day weekend, when mountain men, Indians, and traders recreate life during the mid-1800s. On Labor Day weekend the **Santa-Cali-Gon** commemorates the three westward trails with a carnival, large arts and crafts sale, and three entertainment stages. For information call (800) 836–7111.

Missouri Water

Here was a thing which had not changed; a score of years had not affected this water's mulatto complexion in the least; a score of centuries would succeed no better, perhaps. It comes out of the turbulent, bank-caving Missouri, and every tumblerful of it holds nearly an acre of land in solution. I got this fact from the bishop of the diocese. If you will let your glass stand half an hour, you can separate the land from the water as easy as Genesis; and then you will find them both good: the one good to eat, the other good to drink. The land is very nourishing; the water is thoroughly wholesome. The one appeases hunger; the other, thirst. But the natives do not take them separately, but together, as nature mixed them. When they find an inch of mud in the bottom of a glass, they stir it up, and then take the draught as they would gruel. It is difficult for a stranger to get used to this batter, but once used to it he will prefer it to water.

Mark Twain
Life on the Mississippi

From Independence head north on Highway 291 for 7 miles to **Liberty,** a town that was settled around 1819 and which, like Independence, flourished during the 1830s and 1840s as a trading post and outfitting center for pioneers heading west.

The **Jesse James Bank Museum,** at 103 North Water Street, preserves the site of the first successful daytime bank robbery in the United States, the place where Frank, Jesse, and the rest of the James Gang came calling in 1866. The bank includes its original 1858 vault and safe and other banking and James family artifacts. The museum (816–781–4458) is open from 9:00 A.M. to 4:00 P.M., Monday through Saturday, and from noon to 4:00 P.M. on Sunday.

Liberty is also the site of the **Liberty Jail Historic Site,** where the Mormon prophet Joseph Smith spent more than four months during the winter of 1838–1839. The jail now houses a visitors center with exhibits on Smith and the Church of Jesus Christ of Latter-Day Saints. The jail (816–781–3188) is at 216 North Main and is open daily from 9:00 A.M. to 9:00 P.M.

The **Clay County Historical Museum** gives more information on regional history. Located in an 1877 drugstore on Liberty's town square, the

221

museum still has the drugstore's original walnut cabinetry, stained glass, and medicines and a doctor's office from around 1915. Victorian-era rooms are also featured. The museum (816–792–1849) is located at 14 North Main Street and is open from 1:00 to 4:00 P.M., Tuesday through Saturday.

From Liberty head southwest on Interstate 35 for 10 miles to the **Kansas City** metropolitan area, the final stop along your Missouri River tour. The city stands on land once occupied by the Kansa, Osage, Otoe, and Missouri Indian tribes. In 1804 Lewis and Clark camped here briefly on their expedition to explore the western territories, followed by Zebulon Pike in 1806. In 1821 François Chouteau, a Frenchman in the service of the American Fur Company, established a trading post here on the banks of the Missouri to take advantage of the growing fur trade with local Indian tribes.

Twelve years later the town of Westport was founded as a supply station for travelers bound west on the California, Oregon, and Santa Fe trails. Kansas City itself grew up along the riverfront at a natural levee on the Missouri that became a steamboat landing. The warehouses, stores, and saloons that sprang up around the landing soon rivaled the neighboring town of Westport, which was absorbed by Kansas City in 1897.

The city prospered as a supplier for the westward expansion. Though the area saw several fierce battles during the Civil War, it rebounded after the conflict ended, when the growth of the railroads brought even greater wealth to the city. Later it became a major center for stockyards, cattle trading, and the grain market, earning a reputation as the "queen of the cow towns," with luxurious gambling houses and rowdy saloons. Lavish homes and commercial establishments were built with the money that flowed into the city, and hundreds of new immigrants arrived each day.

A good place to begin your tour of the city is at the **Kansas City Museum,** at 3218 Gladstone Boulevard. The museum is housed in the 1939 R. A. Long Mansion and contains displays on the westward migration, pioneer life, and Kansas City's early years as a steamboat port. There is also an impressive collection of Native American artifacts and a re-creation of an 1821 trading post. The museum (816–483–8300) is open from 9:30 A.M. to 4:30 P.M., Tuesday through Saturday, and from noon to 4:30 P.M. on Sunday.

Missouri Town 1855 is a living history village where craftsmen and interpreters portray the life of the region's early settlers. Its thirty-five buildings represent a typical western Missouri village of the 1850s, and its grounds include period field and garden crops and rare livestock breeds. Missouri Town (816–795–8200, ext. 260) is located on the east side of Lake Jacomo in the town of Blue Springs, and is open from 9:00 A.M. to 4:30 P.M., Wednesday through Sunday, from April 15 to November 15 and on weekends during the rest of the year.

Kansas City's steamboat era lives on at the *Arabia* **Steamboat Museum,** at 400 Grand Avenue. When the *Arabia* sank in the treacherous waters of the Missouri in 1856, she carried 130 passengers and 200 tons of cargo, which enticed treasure hunters for more than a century. Her excavation in 1988 uncovered a time capsule of remarkably well-preserved frontier supplies, including china, jewelry, hardware, and food. A full-scale replica of the boat's 171-foot deck features a 28-foot working paddlewheel and the original engines, oilers, and hull section. A theater presentation shows scenes of the excavation from 1988 to 1989 and a working preservation lab allows visitors to see how artifacts are prepared for display. The museum (816–471–4030) is open from 10:00 A.M. to 6:00 P.M., Monday through Saturday, and from noon to 5:00 P.M. on Sunday.

The 1856 **Alexander Majors House** was home to one of the founders of the Pony Express and the owner of the largest freight company to serve the westward expansion. Visitors can tour Majors's nine-room home and see a working blacksmith shop. The house (816–333–5556) is located at 8201

Artifacts at the Arabia *Steamboat Museum provide a window into frontier life.*

State Line Road and is open from 1:00 to 4:00 P.M., Thursday through Sunday, from April through December.

The **John Wornall House Museum** preserves the 1858 Greek Revival home of one of Kansas City's earliest settlers. The farmhouse was also used as a field hospital for both the Union and Confederate armies during the Battle of Westport in 1864. Interpreters re-create the daily life of prosperous farm families before the Civil War with cooking demonstrations and special events. There are also extensive herb and perennial gardens. The house (816–444–1858) is at Sixty-first Terrace and Wornall Road and is open from 10:00 A.M. to 4:00 P.M., Tuesday through Saturday, and from 1:00 to 4:00 P.M. on Sunday.

After a long day of sightseeing, board the **Missouri River Queen** for a tour of the city by water. The 600-passenger paddlewheeler offers a variety of sightseeing, dinner, and luncheon cruises that dock at 1 River City Drive. Call (800) 373–0027 for schedule and ticket information. Riverboat gambling is also a popular attraction in Kansas City. The **Argosy Riverboat Casino** docks in Riverside, Missouri, near the junction of I-635 and Highway 9. Call (800) 270–7711 for information. Harrah's **North Star** docks in North Kansas City near the junction of Highway 210 and Chouteau Trafficway. Call (800) HARRAHS for information.

To tour Kansas City itself, step on board the **Kansas City Trolley.** The bright red cars run a continuous circuit through the city's main corridor each day from March through December. Call (816) 221–3399 for information.

In the heart of Kansas City's downtown historic district, the 1888 **Hotel Savoy** (816–842–3575) offers lodging in twenty-two suites decorated in opulent Victorian style. The adjoining **Savoy Grill** (816–842–3890) has been serving fine food since 1903 and is known for the hand-painted murals that line its walls. The grill was a favorite hangout for Harry Truman when he was in town. It's open from 11:00 A.M. to 11:00 P.M. daily; prices are moderate to expensive. You'll find the establishments at Ninth and Central streets.

Another Kansas City landmark is **Southmoreland on the Plaza,** a 1913 Colonial Revival inn located in the city's Country Club Plaza area. The hotel's twelve rooms are named for Kansas City notables and are decorated in the era and personality of their namesakes. The Southmoreland has won many awards and is considered one of the nation's top bed-and-breakfast inns. You'll find it at 116 East Forty-sixth Street; call (816) 531–7979 for reservations.

For a hearty meal head to the **Majestic Steakhouse,** housed in a 1910 downtown building that was once a hunting and fishing club. The steakhouse has a giant mural depicting famous people who spent time in Kansas City, and it also features live jazz. Prices are moderate to expensive. The steakhouse (816–471–8484) is at 931 Broadway and is open for lunch Monday through Friday and for dinner daily.

FOR MORE INFORMATION ON THE MISSOURI RIVER

Missouri Department of Tourism (314) 751–4133

Missouri Department of Natural Resources (800) 334–6946

St. Charles (800) 366–2427

Washington (314) 239–2715

Hermann (314) 486–2744

Jefferson City (800) 769–4183

Boonville (816) 882–2721

Arrow Rock (816) 837–3231

Glasgow (816) 338–2562

Lexington (816) 259–4711

Independence (800) 748–7323

Kansas City (800) 767–7700

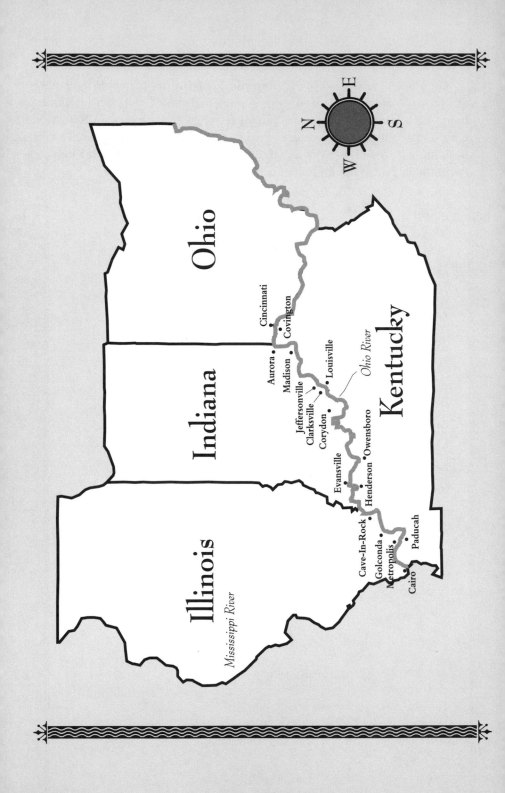

THE
Ohio River

From Cairo to Cincinnati

he Ohio River is the Mississippi's second longest tributary, extending for 981 miles from Pittsburgh, Pennsylvania, to Cairo, Illinois. The Iroquois Indians who lived along the river's banks called it *Ohio,* a word meaning "shining" or "beautiful." During the eighteenth century the river served as the main artery of European exploration and settlement, with settlers floating down its current on makeshift rafts and flatboats in search of new lands and opportunities.

During the steamboat era hundreds of paddlewheelers traveled on the Ohio, hauling raw materials, agricultural produce, and industrial products as well as passengers. The upper Ohio Valley became one of the busiest industrial regions in the United States, producing much of the coal, steel, iron, and oil that fueled the nation's growing economy.

Devastating floods have periodically wreaked havoc along the Ohio Valley and led many towns to turn their backs on their waterfronts. Now many of those towns and cities are rediscovering the river as a source of cultural identity and recreation. Cincinnati, Ohio, and Louisville, Kentucky, have been particularly successful in transforming their riverfronts into dynamic public spaces.

The following chapter describes a tour along the southern portion of the Ohio, beginning in Cairo and heading upriver to Cincinnati. This stretch of river is less industrialized than the northern portion and winds through regions of great natural beauty with many lovely small towns and historic attractions.

ILLINOIS

If you've chosen to travel on the northern bank of the Ohio, from Cairo go north on Highway 51 for 8 miles to **Mound City.** At the intersection of Highways 51 and 37 you'll find the **Mound City National Cemetery,** which includes nearly 3,000 graves of unknown Union soldiers who died during the Civil War—and one grave designated "Confederate Spy." During the war Mound City was the site of a naval hospital that treated wounded soldiers from the battles of Shiloh, Belmont, and Fort Donelson, among others. The Navy's first hospital ship, the U.S.S. *Red Rover,* transported the wounded along the Ohio and Mississippi rivers to Mound City, and many never left again.

From Mound City head north on Highway 37 for 4 miles. The route takes you past the turnoff to **America,** a small collection of houses that once had aspirations to be the nation's capital. After the British burned Washington, D.C., during the War of 1812, the founders of the town of America hoped to have their settlement designated as the new capital because of its location in the center of the country and its strategic site near the confluence of the Ohio and Mississippi rivers. Unfortunately the shifting currents of the Ohio River and outbreaks of malaria and yellow fever—as well as the equally unstable currents of national politics—dashed the settlement's grand plan by the 1840s. All that remains today of the town's hopes are a few houses and its grandiose name.

Continue to follow the river road for 30 miles as it winds through Grand Chain, Hillerman, and Joppa to **Metropolis.** The town's name should be familiar to comic book fans as the home of America's favorite man of steel, Superman. A 15-foot statue of the caped hero was erected in front of the town's courthouse in 1993, and each year on the second weekend in June Metropolis stages a **Superman Celebration** in his honor. (Even the local newspaper, the *Metropolis Planet,* pays homage to Superman.)

At any time of year you can visit the town's **Super-Museum,** which contains sixty years of Superman memorabilia, including original movie props, comic books, early radio premiums, and rare Superman toys. The museum (618–524–5518) is on the courthouse square and is open daily from 9:00 A.M. to 9:00 P.M.

Metropolis is also the site of **Fort Massac State Park,** the oldest state park in Illinois. The 1,450-acre park includes a replica of a fort overlooking the Ohio River built here in 1794. In 1805, Vice President Aaron Burr and General James Wilkinson met here to draw up plans to conquer Mexico and the Southwest. Author Edward Everett Hale later described the plot in his novel *The Man Without a Country*. Each year on the third weekend in October, the **Fort Massac Encampment** recreates the spirit of the late 1700s, and other living history weekends are held throughout the year. The park's museum displays many of the artifacts excavated from the site as well as recreations of historical clothing and implements. Fort Massac (618–524–4712) is located on the east side of Metropolis at 1308 East Fifth Street.

Before leaving Metropolis you might want to try your luck on board the *Players Riverboat Casino,* a replica of a nineteenth-century riverboat that roams the Ohio River on five daily cruises from its home base on the city's riverfront. The boat offers three decks of Las Vegas–style casino gambling, and its landing has two restaurants. For information call (800) 935–7700.

From Metropolis take Highway 45 east for 5 miles to Brookport and then follow the river road for 10 miles to New Liberty. The **Shawnee Hills on the Ohio Scenic Byway** begins north of New Liberty and winds for 70 miles through the Shawnee National Forest. The forest covers over 250,000 acres in southern Illinois and includes thick woods, winding canyons, scenic waterfalls, unusual rock formations, and beautiful vistas along the river. For information call (800) 342–3100.

Between New Liberty and Bay City is the Smithland Locks and Dam, one of the largest navigational locks of its kind in the nation. The **Smithland Pool** was created by the dam in 1980, when the water level of the river was raised by 15 feet, inundating lowland areas and creating a 23,000-acre fishery known for its fine bluegill, crappie, largemouth bass and channel catfish.

From Bay City continue on the byway north for 10 miles to **Golconda.** The town was originally named Sarahsville after a woman who operated a ferry across the Ohio River in the 1700s. Golconda became a town in 1816, two years before Illinois was granted statehood, and the entire town has been placed on the National Register of Historic Places. Later in the nineteenth century, the area was part of the infamous Trail of Tears traveled by the Cherokee Indians, who were forced to leave their homes in the Southeast for Oklahoma. During the winter of 1838–1839, many of the Cherokees were stranded in this part of southern Illinois by harsh weather. With little food and no shelter, as many as 2,500 are believed to have died here.

The **Pope County Historical Society Museum,** on Main Street, has exhibits on local history and offers visitors information about Golconda and the surrounding area. The museum (618–683–3050) is open from 2:00 to 4:00 P.M., Saturday and Sunday.

A historic landmark in town is the 1894 **Mansion of Golconda,** built by John Gilbert, a banker and steamboat owner who also served as mayor of Golconda. The mansion operates a restaurant that is open for lunch and dinner (prices are moderate to expensive), and a bed-and-breakfast with three guest rooms. You'll find the mansion on Columbus Street; call (618) 683–4400 for information.

The **Silk Stocking Bed and Breakfast** also offers overnight accommodations. The 1850s home is located on Columbus Street and has five guest rooms. Call (618) 683–2231 for information.

From Golconda take Highway 146 for 17 miles to **Elizabethtown,** settled in the early 1800s and named after the wife of James McFarlan, who operated a ferry on the Ohio. In 1812 McFarlan built a sturdy house with 2-foot-thick walls, which his son later converted into a hotel for travelers. The Old Rose Hotel is now owned by the state and is in the process of being renovated into a tourist information center.

Another Elizabethtown landmark is the **River Rose Inn.** Built in 1914 by the banker Ed Wall, a great-grandson of James McFarlan, the inn overlooks the Ohio River and offers five guest rooms furnished with antiques. You'll find the inn (618–287–8811) at 1 Main Street.

From Elizabethtown continue on Highway 146 for 10 miles and follow the signs to **Cave-In-Rock State Park.** The park is located on the banks of the Ohio and is named for the 55-foot-wide cave that was carved out of the surrounding limestone rock by water many thousands of years ago. The cave—which extends for 200 feet into the bluff—was discovered in 1729 by a French explorer and was a curiosity frequently mentioned by later travelers in their journals and diaries. After the Revolutionary War the cave became a lair for outlaws, bandits, and river pirates who preyed on people traveling on the river. By the mid-1830s the encroachment of civilization and the growth of local commerce drove out the pirates and the cave began to serve as temporary shelter for pioneers on their way west. Throughout the nineteenth century the cave was an important landmark on maps that guided travelers. More recently it served as backdrop for the Jimmy Stewart movie *How the West Was Won.* Today the cave is part of a 200-acre park with heavily wooded hills and rugged bluffs along the river. For information call (618) 289–4325.

Each year on the Fourth of July, the neighboring village of Cave-In-Rock helps host the **Davy Crockett Ohio River Flatboat Fest.** Flatboats, canoes, sailboats, kayaks, and other craft begin at Cave-In-Rock and race 25 miles downriver to Golconda. The communities along the way host such attractions as frog and toad jumping contests, turtle races, a flea market, live music, and food stands. Call (618) 997–3919 or 672–4396 for information.

From Cave-In-Rock head north on Highway 1 for 20 miles and east on Highway 13 for 8 miles to Old Shawneetown, the final Illinois town on the Ohio River. There you'll find the Shawneetown Bank, an institution that during the days when Illinois was still a territory once refused a loan of $10,000 to Chicago to finance development. Chicago did quite well for itself despite the refusal, while Old Shawneetown drowses in the quiet along the Ohio River.

Flatboats and Keelboats

It's difficult to fully appreciate what a miraculous invention the steamboat was without knowing something about the crafts it replaced, the flatboat and keelboat. Flatboats were essentially floating rafts that could move downstream only and were usually dismantled at the end of their journeys and sold as lumber. Keelboats were similar to flatboats, but they were manned by a crew of men who either poled the boat back upstream or pulled it along from the shore with ropes—a feat that required almost superhuman strength. The keelboat crews were said to be "half horse, half alligator, and a little touch of snapping turtle." Though the keelboat and flatboat could carry substantial loads of cargo and passengers, they were hard to maneuver and were vulnerable to snags and floating debris. Their biggest disadvantage, however, was the fact that they could travel only downstream with any degree of ease.

Thus when people heard of a new kind of boat that could travel upstream as easily as down, the very idea seemed ridiculous. When the steamboat *New Orleans* passed through Cincinnati in 1811, the city's mayor bid its owners farewell with these words: "We see you for the last time. Your boat may go down the river, but as to coming up, the very idea is absurd."

KENTUCKY

If you've chosen to follow the Ohio River along the Kentucky bank, begin your journey at **Wickliffe,** just downriver from Cairo, Illinois. Travel east on Highway 60 for 28 miles to **Paducah,** a city located at the confluence of the Ohio and Tennessee rivers that once had a reputation as one of the wildest cities on the Ohio. The region was originally home to the Chickasaw Indians, who sold the area to President Andrew Jackson in 1818. The region, in fact, is still sometimes referred to as the Purchase Area. The city takes pride in two homegrown celebrities: Vice President Alben W. Barkley, who served under Harry Truman, and the humorist and author Irvin S. Cobb. Cobb once said of the town, "Here in Paducah, one encounters, I claim, an agreeable blend of Western kindliness and Northern enterprise, superimposed upon a Southern background. Here, I claim, more chickens are fried, more hot biscuits are eaten, more cornpone is consumed, and more genuine hospitality is offered than in any town of like in the commonwealth."

A good place to get information about Paducah and its attractions is at the **Whitehaven Tourist Welcome Center.** The graceful mansion with a Corinthian-columned front porch dates back to 1860 and is now a state welcome center for the area. Whitehaven (502–554–2077) is located at exit 7 off Interstate 24 and is open twenty-four hours daily. Tours of the mansion are given from 1:00 to 4:00 P.M.

Paducah's historic downtown lines the river and is listed on the National Register of Historic Places. Its focal point is the 1905 **Market House.** A local 1877 drugstore has been meticulously reconstructed inside the Market House, which also includes a museum, art gallery, and community theater. You'll also find information about river history, an exhibit of rare musical instruments, and memorabilia and mementos of Alben Barkley and Irvin S. Cobb. The museum (502–443–7759) is located on Old Market House Square and is open from noon to 4:00 P.M., Tuesday through Saturday, and from 1:00 to 5:00 P.M. on Sunday.

Downtown Paducah is also home to the impressive **Museum of the American Quilter's Society,** which displays hundreds of antique and contemporary quilts in three galleries—ample proof that quilting is an art form as well as a craft. The building also houses a gift shop with many Kentucky handcrafts as well as quilt-related items. Each April the museum sponsors the **American Quilter's Society National Quilt Show,** which is held in conjunction with the city's Dogwood Festival. Awards and prizes are given in many different categories, and the show draws thousands of quilting enthusiasts from around the country. The museum (502–442–8856) is at 215 Jefferson Street and is open from 10:00 A.M. to 5:00 P.M., Tuesday through Saturday, and from 1:00 to 5:00 P.M. on Sunday.

For more information about Vice President Barkley, visit the **Alben W. Barkley Museum,** which is housed in the 1852 residence of the boat captain William Smedley. Inside you'll find information on the life of Barkley as well as riverboat and Kentucky artifacts. The museum (502–554–9690), at 533 Madison Street, is open from 1:00 to 4:00 P.M. on Saturday and Sunday.

A good time to visit Paducah is during its **Summer Festival,** a ten-day celebration held in late July. The festival includes a variety of entertainment on the riverfront and an 80-mile circle tour of the Ohio, Cumberland, and Tennessee rivers by a flotilla of private boats. Call (502) 443–8783 for information.

From Paducah continue east on Highway 60 for 90 miles to **Henderson,** a river town founded in the late 1700s. During the 1937 flood that devastated most of the river towns along the Ohio Valley, Henderson remained high and dry and later adopted the motto, "Henderson: On the river but never in it."

Henderson takes great pride in its most famous former resident: John James Audubon, the great painter and naturalist. Audubon came to Henderson in 1810 with his wife, Lucy, and infant son and lived here for nine years, participating in a variety of business ventures that eventually ended in failure. During his time in Henderson, Audubon came up with the idea of painting likenesses of every bird in North America and then reproducing his paintings in books. Much of his time in Kentucky was spent studying and sketching birds—which perhaps explains his lack of business success. Audubon later traveled around the country following his dream, and his work eventually helped change the consciousness of the young nation. At a time when most Americans took the country's abundant natural resources for granted, he helped ignite an appreciation for nature and an interest in studying its creatures.

The **John James Audubon Museum and Nature Center** is dedicated to the life and work of the famous naturalist. The heart of its holdings is a collection acquired by the L. S. Tyler family, who were descendants of Audubon. The museum houses the world's largest collection of Audubon material, including letters, journals, paintings, prints, and clothing. Four galleries tell the story of Audubon's life and legacy. The museum itself is a reproduction of a French Norman inn, a style chosen because of the painter's French heritage and because its design allows holes in its masonry for nesting birds.

The adjoining nature center includes an observation room with binocular-equipped windows that look out on a garden of native plants and a woodland pond. Other exhibits describe bird locomotion, behavior, feeding, and habitat. The center and museum (502–827–1893) are in the John James Audubon State Park, on Highway 41 on the north side of Henderson. The site is open daily from 10:00 A.M. to 5:00 P.M.

A good time to visit Henderson is during its **W. C. Handy Blues and Barbecue Festival.** The musician known as the Father of the Blues once lived in Henderson, and the festival celebrates his work with great blues performances and delicious barbecue. The event begins the second Sunday in June; call (502) 826–3128 for information.

From Henderson continue east on Highway 60 for 30 miles to **Owensboro,** Kentucky's third largest city. During the steamboat era, Owensboro was an important river port. Today it's known for its barbecue (the city boasts of being the barbecue capital of the world) and its status as the headquarters of the International Bluegrass Music Association (IBMA). Each year the city hosts several riverfront music festivals, including the **IBMA Bluegrass Fan-Fest** in September. Call (502) 684–9025 for information.

At any time of year, you can visit the city's **Bluegrass Music Museum and Hall of Fame,** which is housed in the RiverPark Center, a performing arts facility on the banks of the Ohio. The museum tells the history of bluegrass music through vintage audiotapes, films, photographs, and interactive displays. You'll find it at 207 East Second Street; call (502) 684–9025 for hours.

The **Owensboro Area Museum of Science and History** is a good place to learn more about the history of the area. The museum (502–683–0296) is at 2829 South Griffith Avenue and is open from 8:30 A.M. to 4:30 P.M., Monday through Friday, and from 1:00 to 4:00 P.M. on Saturday and Sunday.

From Owensboro continue east on Highway 60 for 78 miles until it intersects with Highway 31W north of Radcliff. There you'll find the legendary **Fort Knox,** the repository for most of the nation's gold reserves. You can see the vault (from the outside only, for obvious reasons) from Highway 31W or Bullion Boulevard, which leads into the fort.

Fort Knox is also the site of the **Patton Museum of Cavalry and Armor.** The museum is one of the largest in the U.S. Army system and is named after General George S. Patton, Jr. Inside are many personal items used by Patton as well as displays of American and foreign fighting vehicles, uniforms, and weapons. The museum (502–624–3812), on Fayette Avenue near the Chaffee Avenue entrance to Fort Knox, is open daily.

From Fort Knox head north on Highway 60/31W for 25 miles to **Louisville,** Kentucky's largest city. Louisville was founded in 1778 by General George Rogers Clark as a base from which to harass the British during the Revolutionary War, and is located at the Falls of the Ohio, a stretch of rapids that formed a natural barrier to river travel.

The only falls on the river, the rapids rush over a 350-million-year-old fossil reef that extends across the riverbed. Its drop of 26 feet over the course of 3 miles made the river impassable until the construction of a canal in 1830. Today the McAlpine Locks and Dam System is the busiest canal in the world. More tonnage passes through here than the Panama Canal and the St. Lawrence Strait combined. A major interpretive center for the Falls of the Ohio is located across the river in Clarksville, Indiana (see page 247).

Louisville has worked hard to develop its riverfront area. A centerpiece of its efforts is the **Louisville Falls Fountain,** the world's largest floating fountain, which sprays water 350 feet into the air to form a fleur-de-lis, the city's symbol. The fountain floats on the Ohio River at the end of Fourth Street and is clearly visible from the city's Waterfront Park.

The best place to view the Ohio River in Louisville is from on board the *Belle of Louisville.* The steampowered paddlewheeler, commissioned in 1914, is the oldest operating steamboat in the nation and one of only a hand-

The beloved Belle of Louisville *is one of only a handful of steam-powered boats still in operation.*

ful of steampowered boats that still offer cruises. The *Belle* was purchased in 1962 by the city of Louisville and Jefferson County, which joined forces to renovate this National Historic Landmark. The *Belle* (502–574–2355) docks at the wharf at 401 West River Road and offers a variety of cruises from Memorial Day through Labor Day.

During the Kentucky Derby Festival in May (see page 237), the *Belle of Louisville* participates in the **Great Steamboat Race** with the legendary *Delta Queen*. The boats have competed in an annual race for more than thirty years. Call (800) 928–FEST for information.

Another way to see the river is on board the ***Star of Louisville,*** a modern boat that offers brunch, lunch, dinner, and moonlight cruises year-round, accompanied with music and entertainment. The *Star of Louisville* (502–589–7827) docks at 151 West River Road.

Steamboat Races

"In the 'flush times' of steamboating, a race between two notoriously fleet steamers was an event of vast importance," wrote Mark Twain. "The date was set for it several weeks in advance, and from that time forward, the whole Mississippi Valley was in a state of consuming excitement."

At one time or another, most steamboat captains participated in races with other boats, often for no other reason than sheer pride. Engineers would stuff the boats' fireboxes with fuel, adding oil, pitch, or even pork fat to make the fire burn hotter. Often they'd also put an anvil or some other weight on the boiler's safety valve to increase the pressure inside the engine—which also, of course, increased the chances of a dangerous explosion. The victorious boat would earn the right to display the traditional trophy of a steamboat race, a set of antlers. A traveler needing to reach his destination in a hurry would always choose a boat that possessed such a trophy.

The most famous race of the steamboat era occurred between the *Rob't E. Lee* and the *Natchez,* which raced between New Orleans and St. Louis in 1870. The *Lee* (whose river nickname was Hoppin' Bob) won the race with a time of three days, eighteen hours, and fourteen minutes—a record that still stands today.

Louisville is best known, of course, as the site of the **Kentucky Derby.** The nation's most prestigious horse race is held on the first Saturday in May each year. The **Kentucky Derby Festival** is held during the two weeks that precede the race and is one of the nation's largest civic celebrations. The festival includes a wide range of events held throughout the community. Call (800) 928–FEST for information.

If you can't be in Louisville for the "greatest two minutes in sports"—as the locals modestly refer to the derby—the next best thing is to tour the **Kentucky Derby Museum.** The facility's three floors provide an entertaining introduction to the art and science of thoroughbred horse racing. A 360-degree, multimedia presentation gives visitors a sense of what it's like to be in the center of the action. Other exhibits allow you to weigh in on a jockey scale, climb on a horse in a real starting gate, and trace a racehorse's pedigree. Weather permitting, visitors to the museum are also taken on guided tours of the adjoining Churchill Downs, the oldest continuously operated racetrack in the United States and a National Historic Landmark. The museum (502–637–7097) is at 704 Central Avenue and is open daily from 9:00 A.M. to 5:00 P.M.

For information on the city's river history, visit the **Portland Museum,** which includes a terrain model of the Falls of the Ohio with dioramas and lifelike mannequins. The museum (502–776–7678), at 2308 Portland Avenue, is open from 10:00 A.M. to 4:30 P.M., Monday through Saturday.

For a glimpse into the city's nineteenth-century past visit **Old Louisville,** a historic district located along Third and Fourth streets that includes many splendid nineteenth-century homes. The **Filson Club Historical Society,** an association that was founded in 1884, is located in a turn-of-the-century Old Louisville mansion. The club maintains a museum and library of Kentucky history and genealogy with over 50,000 books, maps, and pictures. The museum (502–635–5083) is located at 1310 South Third Street and is open from 9:00 A.M. to 5:00 P.M., Monday through Friday, and from 9:00 A.M. to noon on Saturday.

Another landmark in Old Louisville is the **National Society Headquarters of the Sons of the American Revolution Historical Museum,** which contains exhibits on American history from the colonial period and the Revolutionary War. The museum (502–589–1776), at 1000 South Fourth Street, is open from 9:30 A.M. to 4:30 P.M., Monday through Friday.

The **Conrad–Caldwell House** is also located in Old Louisville. The 1895 mansion is built in the Richardsonian-Romanesque style with a hand-carved stone exterior and period furnishings. Located at 1402 St. James Court, the house (502–636–5023) is open from 1:00 to 5:00 P.M., Sunday through Wednesday.

You can learn more about the city's history at the **Locust Grove Historic Home,** a 1790 Georgian-style plantation house that was the last home of General George Rogers Clark, the Revolutionary War hero who founded the city of Louisville. Locust Grove is restored to reflect the period from 1790 to 1822, and on its fifty-five acres of grounds are gardens and servants quarters. The house (502–897–9845) is at 561 Blankenbaker Lane and is open from 10:00 A.M. to 4:30 P.M., Monday through Saturday, and from 1:30 to 4:30 P.M. on Sunday.

Another landmark is the **Farmington Historic Home,** a Federal-style house built in 1810 from a plan designed by Thomas Jefferson. The interior is restored with nineteenth-century furnishings; fourteen acres of grounds include a period garden, a working blacksmith shop, and a fieldstone barn. The Farmington Home (502–452–9920), at 3033 Bardstown Road, is open from 10:00 A.M. to 4:30 P.M., Monday through Saturday, and from 1:30 to 4:30 P.M. on Sunday.

Victorian life in downtown Louisville is preserved at the 1868 **Brennan House,** an Italianate home that was occupied by the Brennan family for eighty-five years. Today the restored home includes many of the family's original furnishings, art, and memorabilia. Located at 631 South Fifth Street, the Brennan House (502–540–5145) is open from March through December, Tuesday through Saturday, from 10:00 A.M. to 4:30 P.M.

Riverside, the Farnsley–Moremen Landing, is an antebellum home and farmstead located on the banks of the Ohio. Adjoining the home is a visitors center with information about the house and its former residents. Riverside (502–935–6809) is located at Moorman and Lower River roads and is open from 10:00 A.M. to 4:30 P.M., Wednesday through Saturday, and from 1:00 to 4:30 P.M. on Sunday.

The **Thomas Edison House** is an 1850s cottage where the famous inventor lived from 1866 to 1867 while employed by the Western Union Company. The house includes models of Edison's early inventions and other memorabilia from his life. You'll find the home (502–585–5247) at 729–31 East Washington Street. It is open from 10:00 A.M. to 2:00 P.M., Tuesday, Wednesday, Thursday, and Saturday.

A good way to tour Louisville is on board the **Toonerville II Trolley,** which offers free rides throughout the city's downtown. The trolley is named after the Toonerville Trolley cartoon strip, which was drawn by the Louisville native Fontaine Fox and appeared in over 200 newspapers for forty years. Call (502) 585–1234 for information.

A favorite restaurant in Louisville is the **Captain's Quarters,** a former tavern dating back to the 1840s located at the spot where Harrod's Creek meets the Ohio. The restaurant serves lunch and dinner daily; prices are moderate to expensive. Captain's Quarters (502–228–1651) is at 5700 Harrod's Creek Road in Harrod's Creek (follow River Road north about 15 miles from downtown Louisville).

For overnight accommodations try the **Old Louisville Inn,** which was built in 1901 as a private home in the Old Louisville section of the city. Today it's an intimate hotel with eleven richly decorated rooms. You'll find the Old Louisville Inn (502–635–1574) at 1359 South Third Street. Another local landmark is the downtown **Seelbach Hotel.** The Seelbach is Louisville's grand hotel, a 1905 showplace whose lobby features murals depicting events from Kentucky history. It's at 500 Fourth Avenue; call (502) 585–3200 for reservations.

From Louisville take Highway 42 for 55 miles as it winds northward to the river town of **Carrollton,** which sits at the confluence of the Kentucky and Ohio rivers. Carrollton has been an active trading center since the 1830s, and its twenty-five-block historic district preserves over 300 buildings and offers many lovely views of the two rivers that meet here.

The **Old Carroll County Jail and Museum** is a good place to begin your tour. The 1880 stone building includes restored cells and local history displays as well as a visitors information center. Located on Courthouse Square in downtown Carrollton, the museum (800–325–4290) is open from 9:00 A.M. to 4:30 P.M., Monday through Friday.

Another historic structure in town is the 1790 **Masterson House,** which claims to be the oldest two-story brick house on the Ohio River between Pittsburgh and Cairo. The house (800–325–4290) is on Highway 42 and Highland Avenue and is open Sunday afternoons from Memorial Day through Labor Day.

Carrollton is also the site of the General Butler State Resort Park, which is named for William Orlando Butler, a hero of the War of 1812. Inside the park you'll find the **Butler–Turpin House,** an 1859 home built by General Butler's nephew, which has been restored with period furnishings and contains many family heirlooms. The house (800–325–0078) is at the Eleventh Street entrance to the park and is open for daily tours from 2:00 to 4:00 P.M.

Each July Carrollton presents **The Point In Time—Where Two Rivers Meet,** an outdoor performance that tells the story of the region through music and firsthand accounts of the people who have lived here. The performances are held at Point Park Pavilion, on Second and Main streets; call (800) 325–4290 for information.

Overnight guests to the Carrollton area can stay at the **Carrollton Inn,** an 1882 structure that offers eight guest rooms as well as a restaurant. The inn (502–732–6905) is located at 218 Main Street.

From Carrollton travel east on Highway 42 for 7 miles to the small village of Ghent, where the **Ghent House** offers overnight accommodations overlooking the Ohio River. This 1833 home is at 411 Main Street; call (502) 347–5807 for information.

From Ghent continue on Highway 42 for 10 miles to the charming river town of **Warsaw.** The town has over one hundred buildings listed on the National Register of Historic Places, including the 1837 **Gallatin County**

The Mistress of the Mississippi

Faced with intense competition from the railroads after the Civil War, steamboat owners built increasingly opulent boats to lure passengers back to the river. The *J. M. White* was launched in 1878 and soon became the acknowledged Mistress of the Mississippi. It took the Howard Shipyards in Jeffersonville, Indiana, nearly a year to complete the 320-foot long vessel, and its 12-foot wheel frequently required the efforts of two men to turn it.

Though not the largest boat on the river, the *J. M. White* set standards for luxury unequaled for a century. Inside and out the boat was a marvel of extravagance, with parquet floors and brightly patterned carpets, hand-carved moldings, stained-glass windows, intricate gingerbread trimming, and decorative "feathers" on top of its twin chimneys that were 8 feet tall. Passengers dined in the main cabin off of hand-painted china underneath huge chandeliers, and outside on the decks a spittoon was placed every 6 feet for the convenience of male passengers.

The *J. M. White* ruled the Mississippi for eight years, until a fire in 1886 took just fifteen minutes to destroy it.

Courthouse and the 1843 **Hawkins–Kirby House** (tours by appointment; call 606–567–5900).

From Warsaw take Highways 42 and 338 for 25 miles to **Rabbit Hash,** a town with perhaps the oddest name of any settlement along the Mississippi River system. There are several stories that claim to explain how the town got its unusual name; one of the more likely candidates dates back to 1816, when a flood on the Ohio River drove many animals—including a host of rabbits—into the surrounding hills. When a traveler who was passing through the town inquired about what there was to eat, one resident told him, "Plenty of rabbit hash." The center of this quaint little town is the **Rabbit Hash General Store,** which has been in business since 1831.

From Rabbit Hash go east on Highway 536 for 12 miles to Interstate 75 and then north for 5 miles to the greater Cincinnati metropolitan area. On your way to the river, stop in **Fort Mitchell** at the Oldenberg Brewery. Oldenberg is one the nation's most honored microbreweries and is home to the **American Museum of Brewing History and Arts.** The museum has a huge collection of memorabilia and information about the American brewing industry. The Oldenberg Brewery (606–341–2804) also includes a brew-pub and a beer garden. You'll find it at the Buttermilk Pike exit off Interstate 75.

Continue on Interstate 75 to the river city of **Covington,** which lines the southern bank of the Ohio, across the river from Cincinnati. One of Covington's major attractions is near the 1866 Roebling Suspension Bridge (which served as a prototype for the Brooklyn Bridge): **Covington Landing** is the largest floating restaurant and entertainment complex on the nation's inland waterways. The centerpiece of the landing is the *Spirit of America,* a boat modeled after the famous *J. M. White.* The sidewheeler has four large decks with several restaurants and entertainment areas. Another attraction on the landing is a floating theater that shows the twenty-five-minute film *The Wilderness Adventure,* which recounts the early days of settlement in Kentucky, Ohio, and Indiana. The landing also includes The Wharf. Modeled after a nineteenth-century warehouse, it contains a variety of shops and restaurants, all with lovely views of the river and the skyline of Cincinnati. Covington Landing (606–491–3100) is at the foot of Madison Avenue.

On the east side of the landing is another Covington landmark, the *Mike Fink.* The boat is a National Historic Landmark that now operates as a seafood restaurant (prices are moderate to expensive). Call (606) 261–4212 for information.

On the west side of the landing you'll find **BB Riverboats,** a fleet of vessels that includes the paddlewheelers *Becky Thatcher* and *Mark Twain*. The company offers a variety of sightseeing, dining, and theme cruises, including two- and four-day cruises to other Ohio River towns. For information call (606) 261–8500.

Another cruise operation, **Queen City Riverboats,** is based upriver in Dayton, Kentucky. The *Spirit of Cincinnati* and *Queen City Clipper* offer sightseeing and dinner cruises. Queen City Riverboats (606–292–8687) is located off Route 8, at 303 O'Fallon Street in Dayton.

Covington has several historic districts, including **MainStrasse Village,** a revitalized German neighborhood filled with shops and restaurants housed in renovated buildings. Listen to the chimes from the village's 100-foot Carroll Chimes Bell Tower, whose animated figures enact the tale of the Pied Piper, and then stop in at the **Northern Kentucky Visitor Center,** at 605 Philadelphia Street, for information and a multimedia show on the area. MainStrasse Village is located at exit 192 off Interstate 75/71; call (800) STAY–NKY for information.

Covington's German heritage endures in MainStrasse Village.

Along the river you'll find the **Riverside Drive–Licking River Historic Area,** a thirteen-block neighborhood that includes many nineteenth-century homes. The area's river walk includes seven bronze statues of famous figures from the region's history, including naturalist John James Audubon and riverboat captain Mary Greene. You'll find the neighborhood between Riverside Drive and Eighth Street in Covington.

For more information about Covington history, visit the **Behringer–Crawford Museum,** which is housed in a mid-1800s mansion in Covington's scenic Devou Park. The museum features exhibits on northern Kentucky's cultural and natural history, including displays on life on the Ohio River, nineteenth-century home life, and the Civil War. The museum (606–491–4003), in Devou Park off Western Avenue, is open from

Captain Mary Greene

During the nineteenth century river boating was essentially a man's business, with one notable exception: Captain Mary Greene. With her husband, Gordon C. Greene, she operated a steamboat line that dominated river traffic for many years and continues to live on today as the Delta Queen Steamboat Company (see page 197).

Mary hailed from near Marietta, Ohio, and married Gordon in 1890. The two newlyweds lived on board their first boat, the *H. K. Bedford*, and often stood watch together in the pilot house. By 1895 Mary had learned enough to be granted both her pilot's license and master's credentials, which enabled her to become a riverboat captain in her own right—the only woman on the Ohio River to join that exalted fraternity. Within a year she was in command of her own boat and even beat her husband by an hour in a steamboat race from Pittsburgh to Cincinnati.

After Gordon's death in 1927, Mary and her two sons took over the company and were able to keep it afloat during the hard years of the Depression. They prospered by offering overnight cruises along the nation's inland waterways, and in 1946 they purchased the famed *Delta Queen* that has become a beloved symbol of the grand tradition of steamboating.

10:00 A.M. to 5:00 P.M., Tuesday through Saturday, and from 1:00 to 5:00 P.M. on Sunday.

One of the premier historical mansions in Covington is **Mimosa Mansion,** an Italianate home built between 1853 and 1855, which was later remodeled in the Colonial Revival style. Its twenty-two rooms are furnished in grand Victorian fashion and include the home's original gas and electric lighting systems. The Mimosa Mansion (606–261–9000) is located at 412 East Second Street and is open from 1:00 to 6:00 P.M. on Saturday and Sunday.

There are a number of bed-and-breakfasts in the Covington area, including several in historic properties. The 1815 **Carneal House Inn** was one of the first brick homes to be built in northern Kentucky and is an outstanding example of Federal architecture. Among its guests were Andrew Jackson and Henry Clay. The house is said to be haunted by the ghost of a girl who killed herself during a ball at the mansion in 1825. The Carneal House Inn (606–431–6130) is located at 405 East Second Street in the Riverside Historic District. Another B & B in the same area is the **Amos Shinkle Townhouse,** an 1850s structure that includes a carriage house with horse stalls converted into sleeping quarters. You'll find the Amos Shinkle (606–431–2118) at 215 Garrard Street.

INDIANA

The first major city along Indiana's portion of the Ohio River is **Evansville,** named after the territorial legislator General Robert M. Evans. During the Civil War Evansville was a stop on the Underground Railroad that helped slaves escape to freedom. The city also became a focal point for German immigration. Many Germans were drawn by construction jobs on the Wabash and Erie Canal, which ended here. By World War I more than half the city's population was German.

A good place to learn more about the history of the area is at the **Evansville Museum of Arts and Science,** a facility located on the banks of the Ohio that includes exhibits on history, art, anthropology, and science. A highlight is "Rivertown U.S.A.," a re-creation of a turn-of-the-century street that visitors can stroll along to get a feel for the history of the area. The museum (812–425–2406) is at 411 S.E. Riverside Drive and is open from 10:00 A.M. to 5:00 P.M., Tuesday through Saturday, and from noon to 5:00 P.M. on Sunday.

Another landmark in Evansville is the **Historic Reitz Home,** in the heart of the city's downtown historic district. The French Second Empire home was built in 1871 by the lumber baron John Augustus Reitz and filled with elegant furnishings. Today it's restored to its original opulence and shows how nineteenth-century life was lived in this river city. The Reitz Home (812–426–1871) is at 224 Southeast First Street and is open from 1:00 to 4:00 P.M., Wednesday through Sunday, February through mid-December.

History of an earlier vintage is preserved at the **Angel Mounds State Historic Site.** The mounds are located on the banks of the Ohio and are part of one of the best preserved prehistoric Indian settlements in the United States. Mississippian Indians occupied this site from A.D. 900 to 1600 and built eleven earthen mounds as platforms for elevated buildings. The settlement included several thousand people and served as an important trade, political, and religious center. For reasons unknown to archeologists, the settlement was abandoned before European explorers came to the area. Today the site includes reconstructed houses, a temple, and a portion of a stockade wall, as well as an interpretive center that explains the culture and artifacts of the Indians who lived here. Angel Mounds (812–853–3956) is located east of Evansville, at 8215 Pollack Avenue, and is open mid-March through December from 9:00 A.M. to 5:00 P.M., Tuesday through Saturday, and from 1:00 to 5:00 P.M. on Sunday.

From Evansville head east on Highway 66 for 6 miles to **Newburgh,** a town that was once a busy river port. You can find a number of historic buildings converted into restaurants and shops in its downtown. Call (800) 636–9489 for information.

Continue east on Highway 66 for 90 miles as it follows the bends in the Ohio through scenic, rolling countryside. At Sulphur head east on Highway 62 for 20 miles to **Corydon.** While Corydon isn't a river town, it does have a number of historic landmarks associated with its status as Indiana's first state capital. On Capitol Avenue you'll find the **Indiana State Capitol Building,** the town's foremost landmark. Built of rough limestone, the building was completed in 1816 and served as the center of Indiana government until the capital was moved to Indianapolis in 1825. Nearby you'll find **Governor Hendricks Headquarters,** a Federal-style brick house that was used by William Hendricks during his tenure as governor from 1822 to 1825. Both sites are open from 9:00 A.M. to 5:00 P.M., Tuesday through Saturday, and from 1:00 to 5:00 P.M. on Sunday. Call (812) 738–4890 for information.

More history is on display at the **Posey House,** a large brick home built in 1817 that now houses a museum operated by the Daughters of the American Revolution. Call (812) 738–2553 for hours and information.

Another attraction in the area is the **Corydon 1883 Scenic Railroad,** which offers a ninety-minute ride through the lovely countryside of southern Indiana. The depot is located at Walnut and Water streets. Call (812) 738–8000 for information.

Overnight guests to Corydon can stay at the **Kinter House Inn,** which offers bed-and-breakfast accommodations in an 1873 restored inn. Its fifteen guest rooms are furnished with Victorian and country antiques. Daily tours are offered. The inn (812–738–2020) is located on Capitol Avenue and Chestnut Street.

Just south of Corydon on Business Route 135 another piece of history is commemorated: the **Battle of Corydon Memorial Park** marks the site where the Harrison County Home Guard fought a group of Confederate raiders in one of the few Civil War battles fought on northern soil. Markers describe the battle and list the casualties on both sides, and a log cabin gives visitors a glimpse into life during this period. The park is open daily from 8:00 A.M. until dark.

From Corydon head south on Highway 135 for 10 miles to **Squire Boone Caverns and Village.** The site takes its name from Squire Boone, the younger brother of the famous Daniel Boone. Squire was a notable pioneer in his own right and discovered these caverns with his brother in 1790. In the early 1800s he moved here with his family and built a gristmill at the mouth of the spring that flows from the caverns. Today visitors can tour the caverns and stroll through the pioneer village above ground, which includes log cabins and the original mill. Hayrides, craft demonstrations, a bakery, and a petting zoo are part of the attractions. The village (812–732–4381) is open daily from 10:00 A.M. to 6:00 P.M., Memorial Day through August 20, and on weekends through Labor Day.

From Squire Boone Caverns and Village you have a choice of two routes: Either follow Highway 135 back to Corydon and then take Highway 62 for 15 miles to New Albany, or else take a more scenic route by traveling south on Highway 135 for 4 miles and then heading east along the river on Highways 11 and 111 for 40 miles.

At **New Albany** you'll enter the Indiana side of the Louisville (Kentucky) metropolitan area. The **Culbertson State Historic Site** preserves the 1867 home of William S. Culbertson, once considered to be the wealthiest man in Indiana. His three-story, Second Empire mansion includes twenty-five rooms filled with opulent furnishings and exquisite architectural details, such as hand-painted ceilings and a carved rosewood staircase. The Culbertson House (812–944–9600) is at 914 East Main Street and is open from 9:00 A.M. to 5:00 P.M., Tuesday through Saturday, and from 1:00 to 5:00 P.M. on Sunday.

The **Floyd County Museum** in New Albany is known for its Yenawine Exhibit, an animated folk art diorama carved by Merle Yenawine. Its scenes are based on memories of Yenawine's turn-of-the-century childhood in Floyd County and include 475 moving objects powered by electric motors. You'll find the quirky exhibit (along with other information on Floyd County's history) at 201 East Spring Street. The museum (812–944–7336) is open September through July from 10:00 A.M. to 4:00 P.M., Tuesday through Saturday.

From New Albany travel east to **Clarksville,** site of the **Falls of the Ohio Interpretive Center.** This spot should be on everyone's tour of the Ohio River valley, for it preserves a wide range of information relating to the geology, wildlife, history, archeology, botany, and ecology of the river. The center overlooks the site of the only naturally occurring obstruction and rapids on the Ohio River, a crossroads for both natural and cultural history. The river was dammed and its channel diverted in 1830, exposing a 350-million-year-old, 220-acre fossil bed with over 600 fossil species, 400 of which were first described here. The bed is like a miniature Grand Canyon, and visitors are welcome to explore its wonders on their own or on a guided tour. Inside the center, you can take a walk through time as the geological, historical, and cultural evolution of the area is described through exhibits, photographs, videotapes, Native American artifacts, and lifesize models of the creatures embedded in the fossil beds. The center (812–280–9970) is at 201 West Riverside Drive and is open daily from 9:00 A.M. to 5:00 P.M.

From the Falls of the Ohio head east on Market Street to the city of **Jeffersonville,** which was laid out in 1802 according to a plan for an "ideal city" designed by Thomas Jefferson. Its location on the Ohio helped make Jeffersonville an important commercial and manufacturing center. In 1819 the country's first large steamboat, the *United States,* was built here, and the city eventually became one of the nation's foremost steamboat-building centers.

Boatbuilders for the Nation

The son of a poor weaver who brought his family to America from England, James Howard fell in love with steamboats as a young boy in Cincinnati. Possessed of a keen and quick mind, he apprenticed himself to a steamboat builder to learn the trade. In 1834 Howard came to Jeffersonville to build his first steamboat, the *Hyperion*. Within a few decades the Howard Shipyards became one of the premier boatbuilding operations of the steamboat era and the largest inland shipyard in the United States.

The Howard Shipyards were owned and operated by three generations of the Howard family, who built many of the nineteenth century's most legendary vessels, including the *J. M. White*, the era's most luxurious steamboat, the *Robert E. Lee II,* and the *City of Louisville,* which still holds the speed record on the Ohio River.

During World War II, the U.S. Navy purchased the Howard Shipyards to build boats for the war effort. Then in 1948 the shipyards were bought by Jeffersonville Boat and Machine Company, which later became Jeffboat. The company has carried on the Howard tradition by constructing hundreds of vessels, including the *Mississippi Queen* and Opryland's *General Jackson.*

Don't miss a visit to the **Howard Steamboat Museum** while you're in the area. The museum is housed in a Richardsonian Romanesque mansion built in 1893 for the Howard steamboat-building family. Constructed by the same craftsmen who worked in the shipyards, the mansion contains many details also found in the steamboats of the day, including a grand staircase, decorative woodwork, stained glass, and a very efficient use of space. Today the house has been converted into a museum with a fascinating array of steamboat models, tools, documents, photos, and drawings as well as personal items and furnishings from the Howard family. The museum is one of the best places in the country to get a feel for the steamboat era. The Howard Steamboat Museum (812–283–3728), at 1101 East Market Street, is open from 10:00 A.M. to 3:00 P.M., Tuesday through Saturday, and from 1:00 to 3:00 P.M. on Sunday.

The Howard Steamboat Museum is filled with artifacts and displays that bring the steamboat era to life.

For a sweet treat before leaving Jeffersonville, stop by **Schimpff's Confectionery,** in the city's downtown historic district, where the Schimpff family has been making candy since 1891. The building has its original tin ceiling, a soda fountain, and antique memorabilia. The confectionery (812–283–8367) is located at 347 Spring Street.

From Jeffersonville head north on Highway 62 for 40 miles to **Madison,** a lovely river town that thrived in the early nineteenth century as a center of commerce and a supply town for pioneers traveling to the Northwest Territory. Most of its downtown commercial buildings were constructed before the Civil War, with new cast-iron fronts and Italianate ornamentation added during a period of prosperity in the 1870s. The town has been called the nineteenth-century Williamsburg of America and has 133 blocks listed on the National Register of Historic Places.

A good place to begin your tour of Madison is at its **Visitor Center,** which shows a ten-minute presentation on "Madison, A Storybook City" and distributes walking tour brochures of its historic neighborhoods. The center (800–559–2956) is located at 301 East Main Street and is open daily.

During the 1840s Madison became a major railroad center for the Ohio Valley. The **Madison Railroad Station and County History Museum** is an 1895 structure that preserves the rail and local history of the area. The station (812–265–2335), at 615 West First Street, is open April through November, 10:00 A.M. to 4:30 P.M., Monday through Saturday, and 1:00 to 4:00 P.M. on Sunday. From December through March the station is open only on weekends.

Across the street is the **J. F. D. Lanier State Historic Site,** a Greek Revival mansion completed in 1844 for a wealthy financier, James Lanier. During the Civil War Lanier's loans to the government of Indiana enabled the state to equip its Union troops and saved the state from bankruptcy. The mansion's south portico offers a particularly fine view of the Ohio River. The site (812–265–3526) is located at 511 West First Street and is open from 9:00 A.M. to 5:00 P.M., Tuesday through Saturday, and from 1:00 to 5:00 P.M. on Sunday.

Near the Lanier House is another Madison landmark, the **Shrewsbury House.** The Regency-style house was built in 1846 by the riverboat entrepreneur Captain Charles L. Shrewsbury and features a beautiful freestanding staircase. Located at 301 West First Street, the Shrewsbury House (812–265–4481) is open daily from 10:00 A.M. to 4:30 P.M., April through December.

Across the street and a block down is a home that is considered to be Madison's first mansion, the 1818 **Jeremiah Sullivan House.** The home is an outstanding example of Federal-period architecture and was owned by Judge Jeremiah Sullivan, a prominent figure in early Indiana history. The Sullivan House (812–265–2967) is at 304 West Second Street and is open mid-April through October, 10:00 A.M. to 4:30 P.M., Monday through Saturday, and 1:00 to 4:30 P.M. on Sunday.

Another landmark in the neighborhood is the 1817 **Masonic Schofield House,** a Federal-style tavern house where the Grand Masonic Lodge of Indiana was organized in 1818. The house (812–265–4759) is located at 217 West Second Street and is open April through November, 9:30 A.M. to 4:30 P.M., Monday through Saturday, and 12:30 to 4:30 P.M. on Sunday.

For insights into the life and work of a nineteenth-century doctor, tour the **Dr. William D. Hutchings Office,** in a Greek Revival building constructed in 1848. Dr. Hutchings used the office until his death in 1903, and its contents have been kept in their original condition. The office (812–265–2967) is located at 120 West Third Street and is open daily from mid-April through October.

A number of Madison's historic mansions operate as bed-and-breakfasts. For information call the Madison Area Convention and Visitors Bureau at (812) 265–2956.

From Madison travel east on Highway 56 for 20 miles to **Vevay,** a river town settled in 1802 by a group of immigrants from Vevey, Switzerland. The new Vevay became a center for trade and river traffic and the county seat of Switzerland County.

The centerpiece of Vevay's downtown is the **Switzerland County Courthouse,** a Greek Revival structure built in 1864. Its grounds include its original six-sided privy and the 1853 old jail. Another landmark is the **Switzerland County Historical Museum,** housed in a former Presbyterian Church constructed in 1860. Inside are displays on local history. The museum (800–435–5688) is located at Market and Main streets and is open Wednesday through Sunday from April through October.

The **Schenck House** is another attraction in Vevay. The 1846 Greek Revival home was built by U. P. Schenck, who was called the Hay King because he made his fortune shipping hay on the Ohio River. The structure includes original antiques and a lovely self-supporting spiral staircase made of cherrywood. The Schenck House (812–427–2894) is located at 209 West Market Street and is open daily from 10:00 A.M. to 5:00 P.M.

Vevay celebrates its Swiss heritage each August during the **Swiss Wine Festival,** an event that includes wine tasting, an Edelweiss Princess contest, grape stomping, a craft fair, and a carnival. Call (800) 435–5688 for information.

For overnight accommodations in the Vevay area, stay at the **Captain's Quarters Bed and Breakfast,** an 1838 home overlooking the Ohio built by the riverboat captain Thomas T. Wright. The B & B (812–427–2900) is located 4 miles west of Vevay on Highway 56.

From Vevay follow the curves of the Ohio by traveling east and north on Highway 156 for 28 miles, then continuing north on Highway 56 for 12 miles to **Aurora,** your last stop on Indiana's portion of the Ohio River. There you'll find **Hillforest,** a mansion built between 1853 and 1855 by Thomas Gaff, a wealthy industrialist, financier, and steamboat owner. Its design was influenced both by Italian Renaissance villas and by the steamboats of the day. Hillforest (812–926–0087), at 215 Fifth Street, is open from 1:00 to 5:00 P.M., Tuesday through Sunday, from April through December.

CINCINNATI, OHIO

The final city on your tour of the Ohio River Valley is Cincinnati. Beginning in the late 1700s, Cincinnati was a key outpost that helped fuel westward expansion, and by the 1820s the settlement had been dubbed the Queen City of the West. Its location on the Ohio River in the middle of a vast expanse of fertile farmland propelled Cincinnati's rapid growth into a major port city and manufacturing center. By the mid-nineteenth century, Cincinnati was a national leader in steamboat building, furniture making, book publishing, distilling, and meatpacking.

Cincinnati today continues to celebrate its close ties to the Ohio River with many parks, restaurants, and other public spaces lining its banks. The **Bicentennial Commons at Sawyer Point** is the centerpiece of the Cincinnati riverfront, a recreational area that follows the river for several miles. A series of overlooks provide great views of the river and along the walking trail is a replica of the Ohio River as it winds from Pittsburgh to Cairo, Illinois.

You can learn more about Cincinnati history at the **Museum Center at Cincinnati Union Terminal.** The center is housed in the city's 1933 Art Deco train station, and includes three major attractions: the Cincinnati Museum of Natural History, an OMNIMAX Theater, and the **Cincinnati Historical Society Museum.** The historical museum is the best place to learn about the development of Cincinnati from a rough frontier river town into a modern city. Costumed interpreters are on hand to answer questions and guide visitors through exhibits that include lifesize flatboat and steamboat models and an entire block of re-created nineteenth-century buildings. The museum (800–733–2077) is located at 1301 Western Avenue and is open from 9:00 A.M. to 5:00 P.M., Monday through Saturday, and from 11:00 A.M. to 6:00 P.M. on Sunday.

The Union Terminal also houses an **African-American Museum** that describes the history of blacks in Cincinnati, a changing exhibits gallery, several museum shops, and the Rookwood Ice Cream Parlor, an old-time shop decorated in beautiful Art Deco style.

Cincinnati's dynamic riverfront area includes many attractions, including the *Showboat Majestic,* a National Historic Landmark that was launched in 1923. Her builder, owner, and impresario was Thomas Jefferson Reynolds, who raised eleven children on board while entertaining at countless rivertowns. The *Majestic* has been a permanent feature of the Cincinnati riverfront since 1968 and is now operated by the city's recreation commission. From April through October the boat offers performances of musicals, comedies, dramas, and revues on Wednesday through Saturday evenings at 8:00 P.M. and on Sunday at 2:00 P.M. Tickets are $10.00. The *Majestic* (513–241–6550) docks at the foot of Broadway on the Public Landing, just east of Riverfront Stadium.

There are a number of cruise options on both the Ohio and Kentucky sides of the river (see page 242 for the Kentucky listings). On the Ohio side, the **Star of Cincinnati** is a 625-passenger, modern cruise ship that offers dining and sightseeing excursions. The *Star* docks at the Cincinnati riverfront just west of the Roebling Suspension Bridge; call (513) 723–0100.

Cincinnati is home to a number of unusual museums. The **Cincinnati Fire Museum** preserves the city's fire-fighting history and tells the story of how the Cincinnati Fire Department pioneered the use of the steam-powered fire engine in 1852 as well as the introduction of paid firemen. The department became the nation's model for urban fire departments for many

Showboat Romance

Jerome Kern's immortal musical *Show Boat* celebrates a part of river history nearly forgotten today. In their heyday during the nineteenth and early twentieth centuries, showboats brought entertainment to nearly every town and city along the Mississippi and its tributaries.

The first vessel built specifically as a showboat, the *Floating Theatre,* was launched in 1831 in Pittsburgh. Its success inspired many other entertainers, who took to the nation's rivers on increasingly elaborate steamboats to present music, drama, humor, and minstrel shows. For the remote and isolated towns they visited, the sound of an approaching showboat's calliope heralded the most anticipated event of the year.

Showboating reached its height in 1910, when nearly thirty of the grand vessels traveled the country's rivers. During the next few decades, however, the advent of cars, radio, and motion pictures led to the showboat's demise, and a colorful and romantic era in American theater history ended.

years. In 1913 motorized fire trucks and pumpers were introduced, many of which were made by the Cincinnati-based Ahrens–Fox Company, which began as a manufacturer of horse-drawn steamers and later helped make the city the center of the fire engine industry. The museum features interactive exhibits on the history of fire fighting as well as displays on fire safety and prevention. The Fire Museum (513–621–5553), at 315 West Court Street, is open from 10:00 A.M. to 4:00 P.M., Monday through Friday, and from noon to 4:00 P.M. on Saturday and Sunday.

The **William Howard Taft National Historic Site** preserves the birthplace and boyhood home of the twenty-seventh president of the United States. Four rooms reflect Taft family life from 1857 to 1877, and the rest of the home contains exhibits on the public careers of President Taft and his family. The Taft birthplace (513–684–3262) is open from 10:00 A.M. to 4:00 P.M. daily.

A home once owned by President Taft's older half-brother now houses the **Taft Museum,** one of the nation's finest small art museums. The 1820 structure is an excellent example of Federal architecture and is furnished in early nineteenth-century style. On display are paintings by Rembrandt, Gainesborough, and Turner as well as Chinese porcelains and French Limoges enamels. The Taft Museum (513–241–0343) is at 316 Pike Street, in downtown Cincinnati, and is open from 10:00 A.M. to 5:00 P.M., Monday through Saturday, and from 1:00 to 5:00 P.M. on Sunday.

The ornate **Hauck House** is an 1880s Italianate townhouse built by the prominent Cincinnati brewer John Hauck. Its interior is restored to its original elegance, and the grounds include a beautiful Victorian garden with a large cast-iron fountain. The Hauck House (513–721–3570) is located at 812 Dayton Street and is open from 10:00 A.M. to 4:00 P.M., Thursday and Friday, and from noon to 4:00 P.M. on Sunday.

On the northern edge of the Cincinnati metropolitan area you'll find **Sharon Woods Village,** a re-creation of a rural Ohio village of the 1800s. Included in the village are nearly a dozen structures ranging from a log home built in 1804 to an 1880 railroad station. The village (513–563–9484) is located in Sharon Woods Park, on Route 42, and is open May through October from 10:00 A.M. to 4:00 P.M., Wednesday through Friday, and from 1:00 to 5:00 P.M. on Saturday and Sunday.

There's no better way to end a guide to the Mississippi, Missouri, and Ohio River Valleys than with a description of the single event that best brings to life the steamboat era. **Tall Stacks** is a celebration of steamboating held

Paddlewheelers line the Ohio River at Tall Stacks, a glorious celebration of the steamboat era.

every three years on the riverbanks in Cincinnati and northern Kentucky. Old and new paddlewheel riverboats from across the nation's inland waterways respond to the Tall Stacks call and form the heart of the five-day event that draws 1½ million people to the Cincinnati area. Riverboat cruises, tours, and races are scheduled, and the riverbanks are filled with roving entertainers, period-costumed actors, food pavilions, historical exhibits, and performance stages featuring Dixieland, jazz, blues, bluegrass, folk, zydeco, country, and gospel music. For anyone with a love of steamboats, the event is the experience of a lifetime. Tall Stacks will be held in mid-October in 1995, 1998, and 2001. Call (513) 744–8825 for information.

FOR MORE INFORMATION ON
THE OHIO RIVER

Illinois

Southern Illinois Tourism Council (800) 342–3100

Metropolis (800) 949–5740

Golconda (618) 683–9702

Kentucky

Kentucky Tourism (800) 225–TRIP, ext. 67

Paducah (502) 443–8783

Henderson (502) 826–3128

Owensboro (800) 489–1131

Louisville (800) 626–5646

Carrollton (800) 325–4290

Northern Kentucky and Covington (800) STAY–NKY

Indiana

Indiana Tourism (800) 289–6646

Evansville (800) 433–3025

Southern Indiana Tourism Bureau (Corydon, New Albany, Clarksville, and Jeffersonville) (800) 552–3842

Madison (800) 559–2956

Vevay (800) 435–5688

Ohio

Cincinnati (800) CINCY–USA

Epilogue

Presently a film of dark smoke appears above one of those remote "points"; instantly a Negro drayman, famous for his quick eye and prodigious voice, lifts up the cry, "S-t-e-a-m-boat a-comin!" and the scene changes! The town drunkard stirs, the clerks wake up, a furious clatter of drays follows, every house and store pours out a human contribution, and all in a twinkling the dead town is alive and moving. Drays, carts, men, boys, all go hurrying from many quarters to a common center, the wharf. Assembled there, the people fasten their eyes upon the coming boat as upon a wonder they are seeing for the first time. And the boat is rather a handsome sight, too. She is long and sharp and trim and pretty; she has two tall, fancy-topped chimneys, with a gilded device of some kind swung between them; a fanciful pilothouse, all glass and "gingerbread," perched on top of the "texas" deck behind them, the paddle-boxes are gorgeous with a picture or with gilded rays above the boat's name, the boiler deck, the hurricane deck, and the texas deck are fenced and ornamented with clean white railings; there is a flag gallantly flying from the jack-staff; the furnace doors are open and the fires glaring bravely; the upper decks are black with passengers; the captain stands by the big bell, calm, imposing, the envy of all; great volumes of the blackest smoke are rolling and tumbling out of the chimneys—a husbanded grandeur created with a bit of pitch pine just before arriving at a town; the crew are grouped on the forecastle; the broad stage is run far out over the port bow, and an envied deck hand stands picturesquely on the end of it with a coil of rope in his hand; the pent steam is screaming *through the gauge cocks, the captain lifts his hand, a bell rings, the wheels stop; then they turn back, churning the water to foam, and the steamer is at rest. Then such a scramble as there is to get aboard, and to get ashore, and to take in freight and to discharge freight, all at one and the same time; and such a yelling and cursing as the mates facilitate it all with! Ten minutes later the steamer is under way again, with no flag on the jack-staff and no black smoke issuing from its chimneys. After ten more minutes the town is dead again, and the town drunkard is asleep by the skids once more.*

Mark Twain
Life on the Mississippi

General Index

Lodgings and restaurants appear only in the special indexes beginning on page 275.

Restaurant Index

275

Lodgings Index

ABOUT THE AUTHOR

LORI ERICKSON is an award-winning travel writer and native Iowan. She holds degrees from Luther College and the University of Iowa, and her articles and essays have appeared in dozens of regional and national publications. She is the author of *Iowa: Off the Beaten Path,* which in 1993 was named the Best Travel Book of the Year by the Midwest Travel Writers Association.

Erickson lives in Iowa City with her husband, Bob Sessions, and sons, Owen and Carl.